# The Latino/a Canon and the Emergence of Post-Sixties Literature

# The Latino/a Canon and the Emergence of Post-Sixties Literature

By Raphael Dalleo and Elena Machado Sáez

Excerpt from "Puerto Rican Obituary" by Pedro Pietri, 1973 is reprinted with permission from Margarita Deida Pietri, executrix of the estate of Pedro Pietri.

Excerpt from *La Bodega Sold Dreams* by Miguel Piñero, 1980 is reprinted with permission from Arte Público Press, University of Houston.

First published in 2007 by
PALGRAVE MACMILLAN™
175 Fifth Avenue, New York, N.Y. 10010 and
Houndmills, Basingstoke, Hampshire, England RG21 6XS.
Companies and representatives throughout the world.

PALGRAVE MACMILLAN is the global academic imprint of the Palgrave Macmillan division of St. Martin's Press, LLC and of Palgrave Macmillan Ltd. Macmillan® is a registered trademark in the United States, United Kingdom and other countries. Palgrave is a registered trademark in the European Union and other countries.

ISBN-13: 978-1-4039-7796-0
ISBN-10: 1-4039-7796-8

Library of Congress Cataloging-in-Publication Data
is available from the Library of Congress.

A catalogue record of the book is available from the British Library.

Design by Scribe, Inc.

First edition: May 2007

10 9 8 7 6 5 4 3 2 1

Printed in the United States of America.

This book is dedicated to the spirits of generosity and hope.

# Contents

# ACKNOWLEDGMENTS

While our intellectual debts will be clear throughout this book, we'd like to begin by emphasizing how inspiring the work of Frances Aparicio, Juan Flores, Lisa Sánchez González, and Silvio Torres-Saillant has been for this project. Román de la Campa has been an important mentor and has shaped our intellectual development in significant ways. We have benefited from the guidance and encouragement of many other people in the process of developing this project, including Maryse Condé, Manthia Diawara, Robert Harvey, and Benigno Trigo. Taína Caragol's knowledge of the contemporary Latino/a art scene helped us find the image that appears on our cover. Our chair, Andrew Furman, has been incredibly supportive. Both the Dorothy F. Schmidt College of Arts and Letters and the Division of Sponsored Research have provided generous funding, course releases, and travel support as well as a nurturing environment for Latino/a studies at Florida Atlantic University. Thanks especially to Luis Duno-Gottberg and Sobeira Latorre, who read this manuscript and whose responses have been invaluable in its revision.

We have been fortunate to have the opportunity to present portions of this book to various audiences. Parts of chapter 1 were presented at the 2005 Society for the Study of the Multi-Ethnic Literature of the United States (MELUS) Conference at the University of Illinois at Chicago, and at the invitation of the departments of English at Drew University, Denison University, and the University of Miami, as well as the American Studies and Latino/a Studies programs at Williams College. Versions of chapter 3 were presented at the 2005 MELUS Conference as well as the 2005 Comparative Studies Colloquium Series at Florida Atlantic University. An earlier draft of chapter 4 was presented at the 2003 West Indian Literature Conference held at the University of Miami. Portions of this chapter are also adapted from the 2005 article, "The Global Baggage of Nostalgia in Cristina Garcia's *Dreaming in*

*Cuban,*" and have been reprinted with the permission of the journal *MELUS*. Chapter 5 was presented at the 2005 Caribbean Studies Association meeting in Santo Domingo and the 2005 Caribbean Migrations Conference at Ryerson University in Toronto as well as at the invitation of the departments of English at Florida Atlantic University, Wesleyan University, The Behrend College of the Pennsylvania State University, and Loyola University Chicago. The project has been affected in substantial ways by discussions stemming from these presentations; we would like to specifically acknowledge Susana Cavallo, Sean McCann, Patricia Saunders, José Torres-Padilla, Alan West-Durán, and Carmen Whalen for their comments. Our teaching also played an important role in the development of our ideas for this book; we therefore extend our thanks to the students, undergraduate and graduate, who have inspired us in class discussions.

We greatly appreciate the generosity of all those who provided us with copyright permissions. Excerpts from "Puerto Rican Obituary" appear by courtesy of the estate of Pedro Pietri and its executrix, Margarita Deida Pietri. Miguel Piñero's "La Bodega Sold Dreams" appears with the permission of Arte Público Press. Miguel Luciano kindly granted us permission to use his work, "¿Cómo se dice boricua en inglés?," for our cover image.

Our gratitude also goes to all our friends who believed in our ability to write this book and to the editors at Palgrave Macmillan who guided us through the publication process. Finally and most importantly, we credit our parents for instilling in us the importance of everyday acts of compassion, the joys derived from intellectual curiosity, and the fruitful work of diligence and detail. Our parents and our sisters continue to inspire us to be better scholars and better people.

# INTRODUCTION

## SELLOUTS? POLITICS AND THE MARKET IN POST-SIXTIES LATINO/A LITERATURE

WHO'S IN? WHO'S OUT? THE CREATION OF A CANON MAY APPEAR to be just another popularity contest, but deciding which writings should serve as the definitive sources for a body of literature is always a tense and high-stakes battle. Canon formation is in effect the academy's euphemism for a turf fight. Due to the constraints of space and time, not everything can be included in an anthology and not everything can be taught in a survey course. As teachers, researchers and readers, we are thus forced to create canons. All of our canons will be slightly different and particular; we justify these with our notions of aesthetics or politics, appeals to universality or our own personal tastes. It is through the struggles over these particular canons that a larger canon emerges. Of course, these negotiations do not take place in a vacuum: writers, reviewers, publishers, and students have a say. The academy is part of what George Yúdice calls a "field of forces," and there are multiple social, economic, and political factors that bear upon the formation of a consensus canon.[1] The struggle is always uneven, with some who hold more cultural capital particularly well situated to argue for their personal canon. Furthermore, certain canons will resonate more broadly because of current events or contemporary structures of feeling. Because of these various forces, the canon remains always in formation.

Latino/a literature stands at a crossroads, a moment of consolidation and institutionalization for a field that has historically thought of itself as marginal and oppositional.[2] In the 1970s and 1980s, anthologies of particular aspects of this tradition began to appear—*Aztlan: An Anthology of Mexican American Literature* (1972), *From the Barrio: A Chicano Anthology* (1973), *Borinquen: An Anthology of Puerto Rican Literature* (1974), or *Inventing a Word: An Anthology of Twentieth-Century Puerto Rican Poetry* (1980); and in the 1990s, anthologies aspiring toward a pan-Latino/a literature began to present their vision of the canon in volumes like *Masterpieces of Latino Literature* (1994), *Latina: Women's Voices from the Borderlands* (1995), *The Latino Reader: An American Literary Tradition from 1542 to the Present* (1997), *Hispanic American Literature: An Anthology* (1997), *The Prentice Hall Anthology of Latino Literature* (2001), *Herencia: The Anthology of Hispanic Literature of the United States* (2001) and *Latino Boom: An Anthology of U.S. Latino Literature* (2005).[3] This multiplicity culminates with the impending publication of what presumably is meant to assert, codify, and institutionalize the ascendancy of the field: the *Norton Anthology of Latino Literature*.[4]

Within this context of canon formation a commonsense periodization has emerged for Latino/a literature, roughly dividing the contemporary literary scene into a Civil Rights generation and what we refer to in our title as the "post-Sixties" writers that have followed. A recent version of the *Norton Anthology* available to reviewers names its final two sections "Upheaval: 1946–1974" and "Into the Mainstream: 1975–2002," opposing these two periods along two vectors, politics and the market. This chronological opposition and its accompanying ideological distinctions appear not only in the *Norton Anthology* but also dominate the framework used by the several different readerships of Latino/a literature that we will discuss. Each of these readerships juxtaposes the marginalized but politically committed writers of the 1960s and 1970s with the market success of the literary professionals from the multicultural post-Sixties era. The earlier writers are depicted as progressive or confrontational because of their rejection of the market and alignment with the ghetto, while the newer writers are seen as apolitical or even conservative, offering tales of upward mobility and becoming darlings of the publishing industry. The shift itself from the Civil Rights to the post-Sixties generation is valued differently according to the political orientation of the readership, although a broad consensus remains about what makes these new writers different.

Such a consensus has been readily accepted and disseminated by nearly all of the professional readers of contemporary Latino/a literature. Despite other ideological differences, three major groups—reviewers, academics with a multiculturalist perspective, and academics with an anticolonial lens—seem to agree that this new relationship to politics and the market defines the post-Sixties generation. Reviewing the ways in which the relationship of literature to these forces is figured by each of these groups reveals how each conceives of a politics of social justice as incompatible with market popularity. To make this case, we will link the varied sites of critical reception by emphasizing the two points on which all groups agree regarding the novelty of contemporary Latino/a literature: first, that this writing has entered the mainstream to an extent that previous works never could; and second, that the politics of this literature has moved away from concerns with social justice. The goal of this book is to distinguish our position from each of these groups by arguing that rather than retreating from politics, or substituting what Nancy Fraser calls a "politics of recognition" for a "politics of redistribution," recent Latino/a literature imagines creative ways to rethink the relationship between a politics of social justice and market popularity—a combination that the critical reception denies by either rejecting one of these elements or articulating them as binary opposites.

This critical consensus rightly calls attention to contemporary Latino/a literature's remarkable market success. Because of this new prominence in the market, reviewers represent the first line of response in the processing of Latino/a texts; they act as crucial gatekeepers, foreshadowing and influencing the way that the broader public sphere will respond to a work. This readership has a specifically market-based analytical lens in evaluating the value of a particular book, shaped by its investment in the production and circulation of fictional texts. The very location of these reviews in major national newspapers and magazines shows how the circulation of Latino/a literature and its canonization are now also negotiated within the mainstream. Questions of legitimacy and authenticity are consequently invoked and reinscribed within such literary circles. Reviewers' responses to Latino/a literature in particular reflect two analytical impulses regarding politics: the reviews either contain an apolitical reading, concentrating instead on the readiness of a text for consumption and mainstreaming, or the appraisals draw upon a multiculturalist analysis that privileges a politics of cultural translation and connection.

The reading of Latino/a literature as apolitical is connected to the formulation of its mainstream value. The link between the absence of politics and the easy processing of Latino/a literature is clear in the packaging of one of the quintessential post-Sixties texts, Junot Díaz's *Drown* (1996). *Hispanic* Magazine breathes an almost audible sigh of relief that "thankfully, Díaz is not a social commentator but an artist," while also attesting to the universality of his work, and by extension the Dominican-American experience, as "fundamentally no different than anybody else's" (Santiago

70). Universality is thus described in terms of the translatability of the Latino/a experience, with claims for social justice rendered as potential obstacles to the reader's identification with the narrative. Reviews of another contemporary Latino/a writer, Julia Alvarez, go so far as to omit the political implications within the texts. For example, in a review of *How the García Girls Lost Their Accents* (1991), the Garcías' presence in the United States is described as a "voluntary exile" that was fueled by a "spiritual and quotidian search" (Stavans, "Daughters" 23) even though the novel clearly depicts the family as fleeing the Trujillo government because of the father's involvement in the Dominican political underground. Implicit in these readings of Latino/a texts is the assumption that their market value lies in their audience's easy consumption of ethnic difference, translated by the Latino/a author into a mainstream product without the messiness of politics to interrupt digestion.

In turn, reviewers reading through the lens of multiculturalism focus on the politics of cultural translation, often speaking of building bridges and of the author as a translator. Multiculturalist readings highlight diversity as an end unto itself, with hybridity serving as a mode of politics that challenges the purity of Americanness by transforming the homogeneity of the mainstream. The flipside, of course, is that this challenge to the mainstream entails the consumption of Latino/a identity as yet another flavor in the multicultural stew. This approach is particularly evident in a *Chicago Tribune* review of Cristina Garcia's *The Agüero Sisters* (1997): "Dropping the Spanish accent from her last name, she announced her arrival as a *traductora*, translating for an American audience the nuances of Cuban women's dreaming" (Behar 1). Through linguistic and cultural translation, Latino/a writers are consequently presented as deconstructing their monolingual U.S. context. For example, Ana Castillo and Achy Obejas are described as "min[ing] the resources" of their cultures in order to spice up the English language, "inflect[ing] and enrich[ing] its syntax, rhythms and vocabulary with the Spanish that was once the language of home" (McLane 6). The multiculturalist reviewer privileges the authenticity of the author as native informant, positioning the Latino/a writer as the ideal representative for bridging the gap between the marginal Latino/a culture and the American mainstream.

Such a politics of representation as the basis for assessment is also evident among multiculturalists in the academy, the second category of critical response to Latino/a literature. It can be difficult to draw a clear line between reviewer and academic, especially if one considers the number of literary critics, including Ruth Behar, Ilan Stavans, and Alan West-Durán, who publish reviews of Latino/a writing in newspapers and magazines.[5] Although the academic multiculturalist lens emphasizes a politics of representation and cultural translation, what defines this approach is its reading of Latino/a texts as embodiments of linguistic hybridity and individual self-construction. Examples of Latino/a literary criticism that reflect this valuation of language and individuality appear in essay titles like "Between Bilingüe and Nilingüe: Language and the Translation of Identity in Esmeralda Santiago's Memoirs" (Sprouse), "Mambo, Merengue, Salsa: The Dynamics of Self-Construction in Latina Autobiographical Narrative" (Gatto), "Travelling Textualities and Phantasmagoric Originals: A Reading of Translation in Three Recent Spanish-Caribbean Narratives" (Irizarry), "If English is Spanish then Spanish is…: Literary Challenges of Representing Bilingual Speech Production and Reception in Esmeralda Santiago's *América's Dream*" (Nance), and "'Cold/Hot, English/Spanish': The Puerto Rican Divide in Judith Ortiz Cofer's *Silent Dancing*" (Derrickson). By isolating Latino/a texts as individualistic narratives significant primarily because of their linguistic challenge to the mainstream, such academic readings do not view this contemporary fiction as community-oriented or concerned with questions of social justice. Rather, the novelty of such artistic production lies in its ability to translate culture, thereby challenging binary understandings of the margin versus the mainstream.

The most influential rendition of this academic multiculturalist reading is likely that of Ilan Stavans. Stavans has emerged as an important figure in shaping the contemporary Latino/a canon. In addition to his importance as a reviewer, he has been at the forefront of anthology projects in Latino/a studies—for example, editing a four-volume *Encyclopedia Latina* as well as the aforementioned *Norton Anthology of Latino Literature*. A celebrated public intellectual who was once described in the *New York Times* as "the czar of Latino literature" (Richardson 13), Stavans emphasizes a politics of representation as well as cultural translation, expressed most forcefully in *The Hispanic Condition* (1995). In that work, Stavans celebrates the process of "mainstreaming" by which "Latinos […] have ceased to be belligerent in the way they typically were during the anti-establishment decade" of the 1960s (Stavans, *Hispanic* 9). Instead, the new generation has learned "to use the mass media, the enemy's tools, to infiltrate the system and to promote a revaluation of things Hispanic" (13). This understanding of politics as infiltration rather than opposition emphasizes "Spanglish [as] an astonishing linguistic force" (xv), part of the "*reconquista*" (5) even now creating "a single hybrid nation of nations, simply called the New World" (xv). In our fourth chapter, we engage both Stavans and Gustavo Pérez Firmat as representatives of this multiculturalist orientation in order to uncover the implications of its emphasis on a primarily individualistic, linguistic politics.

The third group of readers playing a role in the negotiation of the Latino/a literary canon is what we call the anticolonialists. Growing out of such broader Caribbean and even hemispheric movements as the Cuban revolution and the end of the British Empire, the anticolonial vision, inherited from the theorizing of Frantz Fanon, C. L. R. James, Fidel Castro, and others, derives its critical weight from the idea of the intellectual as spokesperson for the pueblo. This strand of Latino/a studies is defined by a concern with a politics of social justice; thus its focus on oppositionality in the service of a fairer distribution of resources leads to a distrust of market success as a form of political betrayal. Unlike the multiculturalists, who tend to emphasize the psychological dimension of identity and self-inscription, the anticolonialists are more likely to read Latino/a experience in relation to broader social and economic forces, as in essays with titles like "Problematic Paradigms: Racial Diversity and Corporate Identity in the Latino Community" (Torres-Saillant) or "Barbie's Hair: Selling Out Puerto Rican Identity in the Global Market" (Negrón-Muntaner). These examples demonstrate the way in which the anticolonialist preference for the subaltern and marginal frequently leads away from literature as high art in the direction of cultural studies more broadly conceived. We maintain throughout this book that the anticolonialists' criticism of post-Sixties literature as apolitical derives from their idealization of such Latino-Caribbean writers of the 1960s as Jesús Colón, Piri Thomas, Pedro Pietri, and the Young Lords.

When the anticolonialists do engage contemporary literature, they are especially critical of the multiculturalist perspective as an assimilationist agenda that surrenders the Civil Rights era's claims to social justice and equality. A central figure of Latino/a anticolonialism, Juan Flores, has established himself as one of the most significant and prolific voices of critique within Latino/a studies, beginning with his vital role in developing the City University of New York (CUNY) Center for Puerto Rican Studies in New York City. His foundational work in Latino/a literary criticism includes writing on Puerto Rican fiction and culture as well as editing such important collections as *Divided Arrival: Narratives of the Puerto Rican Migration 1920–1950* (1987) and *Companion to Latino Studies* (2007).[6] Flores is an influential public intellectual as well, with positions on the advisory boards of the Recovering the U.S. Hispanic Literary Heritage Project of the University of Houston and the Latin Jazz Project of the Smithsonian Institution. Flores specifically positions his work in opposition to Stavans's canon, based on what he identifies as

Stavans's preference for stories of upward mobility or "privileging of privilege" (Flores, *From Bomba* 175). Despite the ideological differences evident between the anticolonialists and the other readers of Latino/a literature, our first chapter's historical overview will show in detail how today's anticolonialists accept not only the concept of a new literary generation originating roughly in 1990 but also agree, as Flores puts it, that "what is new about the recent Latino writing, and goes to inform it as a marketing category, is that it seeks to be apolitical" (174). The earlier writers, in other words, were the poet-warriors and guerilla artists of an anticolonial Civil Rights movement; the post-Sixties writers are sellouts. Anticolonialists such as Flores differ from the other two groups only in the negative value they assign to this apolitical turn. The reviewers welcome the disavowal of any political agenda as necessary for the universality of art, while the multiculturalists see a rejection of oppositional politics as allowing post-Sixties Latino/a literature to perform its political work of crossing over and transforming the mainstream. As a result, all three major readerships agree that the new generation of Latino/a writers has ceased to carry on the legacy of the Civil Rights era's contestational progressive politics.

While we also see the contemporary literary scene as distinct from that of the Sixties, we dispute the assumption that contemporary writing is not living up to the political demands of the Civil Rights generation. We will argue that rather than turning away from politics, contemporary Latino/a writers are renewing that political tradition by engaging with the triumphs and defeats of the past, formulating political projects that will mark our future horizons in substantial and creative ways. Seeing this renewal requires developing new lenses that acknowledge the ways in which the relationship between literature and the public sphere is being redefined in light of post-Sixties realities—the market's centrality in the creation, dissemination, and reception of virtually all contemporary cultural texts.

Intellectuals from the left have encountered this same challenge of adapting their strategies to shifting contexts. Stuart Hall, another diasporic Caribbean, is one of the most important figures in the effort to revitalize progressive thought. His edited volume, *New Times: The Changing Face of Politics in the 1990s* (1989), may have the specific intention of rethinking the role and future of the organized British Left, but it also raises issues relevant to the engagement of Latino/a studies with the post-Sixties world. The introduction to *New Times* begins with the premise that "the world has changed, not just incrementally but qualitatively" (Hall 11), that "the Left's failure to move with the times has been evident for some while" (14), and that as a result, "for a while it looked as if the

Left had not simply lost a campaign, but that its time was up: not defeated by the enemy, but overtaken by history itself" (15). To overcome this fatalism, the contributors to *New Times* seek to theorize the present in ways that both remain true to the historical Left's critique of inequality and exploitation, yet also engage the new world order in creative ways that traditional Left thought may have foreclosed. In one essay from *New Times,* Frank Mort argues that "the twin issues of consumerism and the market lie at the heart of the debate over our vision of the future of socialism" (Mort 160). He notes that "socialism's overidentification with production" (164) has meant that "consuming, as opposed to producing, was at best handled as secondary and trivial, confined to the private, feminised sphere of household duties and personal life," and at worst "cast as a moral evil, buying off working people with an orgy of goodies" (165). Thus the identification of labor with blue-collar factory workers using heavy machinery, combined with a view of consumption as a frivolous or womanly activity, leads to a politics that regards the market as emasculating.

Addressing the contemporary situation as distinct from the past means rethinking culture's relation to the market and reimagining the possibilities of the popular. We have been deeply influenced by both the multiculturalists and the anticolonialists, but our methodology places us much closer to the latter tradition. The anticolonial perspective has developed complex and creative tactics for reading a variety of social and cultural texts; however, labeling post-Sixties Latino/a literature as apolitical is inaccurate and unproductive if we truly want to rethink the political within the contemporary context. One of our goals, then, is a sympathetic critique of the progressive Latino-Caribbean critical tradition. The multiculturalist approach may not be interested in the politics of social justice, and for that reason uncritical about what is seen as a drift away from politics toward the market in the contemporary moment. It is more surprising, however, that critics otherwise especially attentive to brushing culture against the grain so that it might nourish a progressive politics have been willing to cede contemporary writing as lost to conservatism. As the political ideals of the anticolonial project recede ever further into the past, a refusal to lapse into pessimism or nostalgia for that past and a resolve to devise post-Civil Rights and postcolonial ways of thinking about politics and culture are more important than ever for working toward a better future.

Latino/a cultural studies contains an important bibliography for rethinking the complicated political potential of Latino-Caribbean culture in the post-Sixties era and formulating a nuanced approach to music and culture that can inspire new ways of reading literature. In addition to literary critics like Juan Flores, Silvio Torres-Saillant, Román de la Campa, Lisa Sánchez González, and Eliana Rivero, the cultural studies tradition, represented by theorists like George Yúdice, Frances Negrón-Muntaner, Arlene Dávila, Juan Otero Garabís, Frances Aparicio, and Alberto Sandoval Sánchez, has transformed the study of Latino-Caribbean culture since the 1980s and 1990s. Whether considering the contemporary moment neoliberal (*Barrio Dreams*, *The Expediency of Culture*), postcolonial (*Puerto Rican Jam*), postnational (*Latino/a Popular Culture*), or postmodern (*Nación y Ritmo*), these critical interventions treat the present as fundamentally different from the anticolonial Civil Rights era, and thus necessitating different theoretical frameworks. Arlene Dávila's *Latinos, Inc.* in particular argues that Latino/a studies must critically engage the market: "On and on, Latinos' marketing popularity is uncritically treated as a sign of their 'coming of age' in U.S. society or else, equally uncritically, condemned as a sign of their commodification; but seldom have studies looked at marketing as constitutive of U.S. Latinidad" (Dávila, *Latinos* 3). The challenge, then, is to avoid succumbing to reductive ways of reading the relationship of culture, politics, and the market.

The progressive Latino/a cultural studies tradition has been especially attuned to articulating the linkages between politics and culture, and has proven formative to our own thinking about Latino/a literature. The desire that Flores expresses in an interview, to remain "optimistic about popular culture" even while admitting that there is not "any cultural space outside of and untouched by the workings of the 'culture industry'" (Flores, "Puerto Rican Studies" 144), frames the challenge of dialectical thought about Latino/a culture today. Flores's forays into popular culture, his ability to look past the "fact of co-optation and duping [that] is obvious and transparent," have enabled him to tease out the "persistence of unmediated or countermediated cultural production in the midst of generalized commodification [that] goes mainly ignored or denied" (144). He admits that "it's a stretch from these democratic cultural practices to an explicitly political agenda, but my sense is that a political project which is heedless of these expressions, what I refer to as 'moments of freedom,' has no chance of engaging people in a substantial and gripping way" (144). These strategies—of bracketing but never ignoring the contaminated and mediated nature of contemporary cultural forms in order to read their sometimes heavily coded or contingent political content— inform our reading of what has become an increasingly popular Latino/a literature via the mass market.

To that end, instead of conceiving of the relationship between Latino/as and the mainstream as the purely binary model underlying both anticolonialist resistance and multiculturalist synthesis, we want to emphasize the process of negotiation described by the influential cultural studies thinker, Néstor García Canclini. Negotiation means that "identity is a coproduction" between the author as producer and the market (Yúdice, "From Hybridity to Policy" xxv). García Canclini explains: "Identities are constituted not only in the bipolar conflict between classes but also in contexts of institutional action—in a factory, a hospital, a school—that operate insofar as all of their participants, whether hegemonic or subaltern, consider themselves part of a 'negotiated order'" (García Canclini, *Consumers* 143). In other words, any cultural form that enters the market—and today, it is that entry that allows a text to become popular—becomes subject to negotiation between the cultural producer and the culture industry. As García Canclini puts it: "Popular cultures are the product of *unequal appropriations* of cultural capital, the *people's own reflections* about their living conditions, and *conflict-ridden interaction* with hegemonic sectors" (García Canclini, *Transforming* 22). For literature, this statement means that every writer becomes part of the literary field and operates within the rules of that order. Writers enter the field in distinct ways and are processed by it differently, and the critic must be attuned to these particularities. In order to elucidate the ways in which differences of positioning affect both enunciation and reception, the first half of this book will examine writers whose work deploys and interrogates the conventions of the marketing category of "ghetto fiction"— Pedro Pietri, Piri Thomas, Miguel Piñero, Abraham Rodriguez, and Ernesto Quiñonez—while the second half will turn to writers who have been more readily labeled as "mainstream"—Junot Díaz, Angie Cruz, Cristina Garcia, and Julia Alvarez.

In this book, we bring the double vision that has been developed for the exploration of mass culture to our assessment of post-Sixties Latino/a "mass literature," in order to give the literary field the thorough reconsideration that Latino/a cultural studies has had. In her study of salsa, Frances Aparicio articulates this dialectical cultural studies perspective—of looking at the interaction of cultural producers and market forces as a negotiation and not purely an exercise in appropriation and domination:

> To reify salsa music as merely a victim or object of hegemony is virtually to preempt its powers for creativity, cultural resistance and reaffirmation, and possibly social change. And to sort salsa music as either "commercial" or "sociopolitical" is, again, another reifying practice that takes into account only the moment of initial production or the isolated text and that fails to consider listening practices and the larger sociopolitical context within which a musical performance is embedded [...] The production of

> meaning, the process of signification in cultural acts, cannot be traced uniquely to a fixed text but will vary according to an array of extra- and intratextual factors. (Aparicio, *Listening* 93)

Aparicio points to the inadequacy of analyses that identify such forms of popular culture as salsa music as either purely resistant or accommodating. Our reading of Latino/a literary production echoes Aparicio's call for the development of a cultural studies perspective that navigates between these binary readings of cultural production. By extending the frame of Aparicio's argument, we approach literature through a cultural studies lens open to the complexity involved in its production, circulation, and reception.

In seeking to revitalize progressive politics by thinking *through* the market, the post-Sixties authors we will examine here run up against a number of contradictions. We do not argue for an uncritical celebration of this literature. None of these writers offers a fully articulated and easily implemented political project; in fact, their visions of politics are frequently idealistic. Nevertheless, their value lies in offering something crucial to our postcolonial, post-Civil Rights era: serious engagement with the legacy of the past in the context of a present that Arnaldo Cruz-Malavé defines as haunted by the "collapse [...] of the future" ("Colonial Figures" 8). Anticolonialism, embodied by Pedro Albizu Campos, Fidel Castro, or the Mirabal sisters, provided a theoretical critique of modern colonial regimes and became an ideological springboard for political praxis. Contemporary writers offer new ways of understanding postcoloniality, and in so doing can move us past a potentially pessimistic or backward-looking politics that can only lament the end of an era of possibility, toward hope for a renewed political Latino/a literature able to speak confidently in the public sphere.

We will look at a set of Latino-Caribbean novelists from New York, writing in the 1990s and early twenty-first century with a distinctive post-Sixties sensibility.[7] While this group of writers is only one manifestation of contemporary Latino/a literature as a panethnic category, this localization will also allow us to examine New York as a crossroads for the three major groups from the Spanish-speaking Caribbean: Puerto Ricans, Dominicans, and Cubans. On the one hand, the cultural or physical location of these writers in New York means a proximity to the city's publishing industry, a close relationship that is both blessing and curse. Chicano/a writing, with its imagined and institutional centers far from New York City, has a much different historical relationship to the city's publishers, as José David Saldívar shows with regard to Arturo Islas's novel *The Rain God* (Saldívar 106–11). For that reason it requires separate discussion that would do justice to the particularities of Chicano/a writing and publishing.

At the same time, focusing on New York will underscore the ways in which recent Latino-Caribbean writers connect to and build on the radical Civil Rights tradition of that city. These Latino-Caribbean groups have distinct anticolonial histories but have enough in common to allow us to discuss them together. Furthermore, looking at all three groups brings an international perspective to Latino/a experience and highlights the historical parallels central to building interethnic identities and solidarities. Since the nineteenth century, intellectuals and organizers from those islands have worked together for independence and social justice. For Nuyoricans, Dominican Americans, and Cuban Americans in New York, the mid-twentieth century represents a high point in both social struggles against international imperialism and in the intellectual articulation of those struggles. While these groups may have different memories of that history, and different relationships to those movements, all of us today are still working through the successes and failures of this anticolonial watershed; it is a history that still haunts us. The goal of this book will be to examine the ways that Latino-Caribbean critics and writers continue to rehearse and begin to rethink the common inheritance of the anticolonial Civil Rights Sixties.

In chapter 1 we trace the emergence of a post-Sixties Latino/a literature through the work of Pedro Pietri. Pietri became known during the late 1960s as a major figure in the Nuyorican poetry movement closely associated with the Young Lords and the social struggles of that period. Although we do not focus on that period, it nonetheless forms a backdrop for everything that follows. We will therefore outline the anticolonial Civil Rights project through Pietri's "Puerto Rican Obituary"(1973), the title poem of his first collection, in order to explore the ways in which that poem figures politics, the market, and the role of the intellectual. This anticolonial vision of literature becomes a dominant model for the development of Latino/a literary criticism even as a post-Sixties literature emerges. By comparing a poem first performed in the 1960s to one of Pietri's more recent works, "El Spanglish National Anthem" (1993), we will show a shift in concerns and interests in the work of one writer—one whose own aspirations are strongly infused with the anticolonial worldview but who has sought to reconcile himself to the emergence of a post-Sixties order.

Chapters 2 and 3 show how writers from the post-Sixties generation deconstruct the equation of ghetto fiction as the proper discourse for a critical and resistant political project. The second chapter begins with an exploration of how in privileging the works of Nicholasa Mohr, the Nuyorican poets, and above all Piri Thomas, the politically committed criticism of anticolonialists like Juan Flores and Lisa Sánchez González identifies what we call ghetto fiction as the genre that most successfully rejects the market and cultural assimilation. While these critics lament the disappearance or commercialization of this kind of ghetto fiction in the post-Sixties era, blaming a sanitizing and homogenizing culture industry that publishes only works which reinforce the system, chapter 2 will show that, while ghetto fiction has not disappeared since the Civil Rights era, its practitioners have had to rethink its meaning. The chapter begins by looking at the way in which Abraham Rodriguez's *Spidertown* (1993) deploys the conventions of ghetto fiction to launch a critique of American capitalism resembling what we see in the writers of the 1960s and 1970s, although this deconstructive vision eventually turns on the genre of ghetto fiction itself as another form of false consciousness. From this point, the second half of the chapter moves to Ernesto Quiñonez's *Bodega Dreams* (2000) as an even more direct engagement with the inheritance of the Civil Rights generation, pointing to the pleasures of the market as that variable which anticolonial opposition appears unable to reconcile.

The third chapter focuses on the categorization of Dominican-American literature as immigrant writing and the ways in which the work of Junot Díaz and Angie Cruz presses the boundaries of that definition. In comparing the critical with the popular reception of these writers, we will show how Díaz and Cruz challenge the notion that immigrant Latino/a literature is apolitical and assimilationist in form and subject. Introducing Flores's formulation of a lowercase Latino/a literature allows us to also engage these writers in conversation regarding the centrality of the ghetto in post-Sixties Latino/a fiction and theory. Junot Díaz's collection of short stories, *Drown* (1996), reveals the limits of a theory that regards the ghetto as the only site of authentic cultural production. More specifically, the stories set in New Jersey call into question the potential for progressive politics by depicting a ghetto in which bonds of solidarity are impossible, especially when upward mobility can be narrated only as betrayal. Ultimately, the text does not imagine an alternative space, representing instead the ever-present drowning of the collective. Angie Cruz's novel *Soledad* (2001) embodies an alternate mode of Latino/a representation by supplementing ghetto realism with elements of magical realism. This shift in genre redefines the binaries of ghetto versus assimilation and resident versus immigrant by constructing a narrative of upward mobility that points to its own political content, highlighting what Flores calls the "lite colonial" context that spans and connects the urban space to the Caribbean islands.

Our discussion of Díaz and Cruz thus serves as a bridge to the second half of the book, in which we move from revisiting the "mean streets" of the Bronx, El Barrio, and Washington Heights to the upward and outward mobility reflected in works by Cristina Garcia and Julia Alvarez. While the first half of *The Latino/a Canon* rereads ghetto fiction to unsettle its reification as oppositional or resistant, these final chapters reexamine two of the most celebrated contributors to the post-Sixties canon in order to map their relationship to the market and tease out the political implications of their work. Chapter 4 makes a more in-depth critique of the multiculturalist approach by highlighting the role that consumption plays in the formulation of the Latino/a subject. First, the chapter will focus on the representative figures of multiculturalist theory, Ilan Stavans and Gustavo Pérez Firmat, and show how their reliance on food imagery for the formulation of Latino/a identity implies the erasure of that very subjectivity. We will turn to the work of Néstor García Canclini and Arlene Dávila as a way of calling attention to how Latino/a cultural studies offers alternate understandings of the relationship between identity and consumption practices. Within this context of multiculturalist and cultural studies approaches, we reread Cristina Garcia's canonical novel *Dreaming in Cuban* (1992) in order to contest the ways in which critics have glossed over the representation of consumption and commodities in the novel. By addressing the novel's depiction of consumer citizenship, we complicate readings of the main character, Pilar, as utopically recuperating a hybrid Cuban-American subjectivity. We emphasize that this hybrid identity is dependent upon the formulation of a market-based Latino/a public sphere that requires the demise of an alternative worldview that invests possibility in revolutionary projects.

The fifth chapter examines Julia Alvarez as the contemporary Latino-Caribbean writer who most explicitly positions Latino/a literature at the crossroads of the legacies of the Civil Rights movement in the United States and international anticolonial struggles. Taken as a whole, her body of work theorizes the limits and possibilities of authorship in a post-colonial, post-Civil Rights moment. Her novels of personal experience—*How the García Girls Lost Their Accents* (1991) and *¡Yo!* (1997)—depict the author as exhausting her own story as a source of material, eventually becoming unable to speak with authority. At the same time, through her historical novels—*In the Time of the Butterflies* (1994) and *In the Name of Salomé* (2000)—Alvarez draws upon a transnational history of social struggle and committed literature in the figures of the Butterflies and

Salomé Ureña. By telling these stories from the present, her novels thus become a meditation on the place of that history in our contemporary imaginary. The storytellers reflect on the ways in which they can adequately mourn these pasts in order to move beyond their failures while taking their successes with them. We thus end our discussion of the New York-based post-Sixties literature with this literary appraisal that points to "minor" and everyday struggles as inspiration for a renewed left political project.

Finally, our conclusion points to new directions in recent literature from the Miami Cuban-American community, traditionally the most insular and politically conservative Latino-Caribbean group. In particular, we will address the way in which the accusation of selling out in this alternate geographic and cultural context produces a double bind for Cuban-American writers attempting to reassess the relationship of the Cuban-American community to the Sixties. By looking at the ways in which work by Nilo Cruz, Chantel Acevedo, and Ana Menéndez questions some of the most basic political assumptions of and about this community, we demonstrate the range of the post-Sixties literary reconsideration of Latino/a politics.

# PERIODIZING LATINO/A LITERATURE THROUGH PEDRO PIETRI'S NUYORICAN CITYSCAPES

WE REFERRED IN OUR INTRODUCTION TO A CHRONOLOGICAL DIVIDE in contemporary Latino/a literature between a Civil Rights and a post-Sixties generation. Yet many of the writers closely associated with the Civil Rights movement have continued to write well into the post-Sixties era. To trace the contours of these two periods in Latino/a literary history, we will look at two texts by a seminal Nuyorican figure whose work straddles these generations. Through reading one of Pedro Pietri's major works from each period, "Puerto Rican Obituary" (1973) and "El Spanglish National Anthem" (1993), we will argue for placing these poems within the context of broader historical movements in the poet's work specifically and Latino/a literature more generally.[1] This chapter thus serves as an overture, introducing the central themes that later chapters will develop.

To make this argument, we will spend the first part of this chapter showing how the earlier poem expresses an anticolonial political project based on the rejection of the market and alignment with the oppressed. Pietri embodies the concept of the poet as part of the struggle; he favored performance over publication, famously performing "Puerto Rican Obituary" at the takeover of the First Spanish Methodist Church by the Young Lords in 1969. He was also an early and eager participant in the Nuyorican Poets Café. After defining the anticolonial elements of Pietri's early work, we will move to an exploration of how critics periodize Latino/a literature and form canons that emphasize this anticolonial

ideal. Their preference for this form of anticolonialism leads to judg-
ments of subsequent literary periods as pale imitations corrupted by the
market that fail to measure up to the literature of the Sixties. As we will
show, these critics turn away from literature towards music as the only
post-Sixties Latino/a cultural expression that continues the traditions of
the Civil Rights writers. But as Pietri's "El Spanglish National Anthem"
suggests, contemporary music and literature have more in common in
terms of their relationship to the market than this academic flight from
literature admits. As the last section of the essay will reveal, reading
Pietri's more recent poem allows for new ways of deploying a postcolonial
or post-Civil Rights lens in order to analyze the relationship of commodity culture to Latino/a identity and artistic practices. This lens enables the
readings we will present throughout this book, reconsidering literature as
an ongoing space for such conversations.

### THE ANTICOLONIAL VISION

From the first lines of "Puerto Rican Obituary," Pedro Pietri describes
the condition of Puerto Rican immigrants in the United States as excru-
ciatingly atomized oppression. The protagonists of Pietri's poem—Juan,
Miguel, Milagros, Olga, and Manuel—find themselves living in decaying
neighborhoods working in dead-end jobs. The poem establishes a rhythm
that expresses the repetitive drone of inevitability—fourteen of the first
twenty-two lines begin with the word "they," and the phrases "they
worked," "they never," and "they died" appear a number of times (Pietri,
*Puerto Rican* 1)—as the characters march inexorably through life toward
death. Although the protagonists accept the social contract promising
upward mobility in return for hard work, they remain unable to break
out of this cycle of poverty and exploitation. Their failure comes from an
inability to develop a consciousness about their plight; throughout the
poem, they never speak, remaining silenced and inarticulate. Unable to
imagine alternatives to buying into the system, unwilling to voice their
complaints, they can only be hollow, silenced, and defeated.

Juan, Miguel, Milagros, Olga, and Manuel are the literal victims of
the American dream, "Dreaming about queens," (4) but at the same time
"Never knowing / that they are beautiful people / Never knowing / the
geography of their complexion" (9–10). The promise that hard work will
yield success is a false dream for this immigrant proletariat. The poem
makes quite clear that the source of these dreams is an American culture
industry, "the after-effects / of television programs" (4) that show "the
ideal / white american family / with black maids / and latino janitors"

(4–5). Juan's American dream leaves him dead, "dreaming about a new car"; Olga dies "dreaming about real jewelry" (5). The poet laments:

> If only they
> had turned off the television
> and tune into their own imaginations
> [...]
> If only they
> had kept their eyes open (10)

The poet can see that these people are beautiful, because within their souls and imaginations they have the secret of a better world, but the culture industry has compromised their Puerto Rican essence and turned a potentially redemptive and revolutionary proletariat into consumerist zombies.

This blind adherence to materialism at the expense of "their latino souls" prevents Juan, Miguel, Milagros, Olga, and Manuel from ever developing a sense of solidarity (10). Along with a failure of imagination, this is the other side of the tragedy of their colonized consciousness— their failure to organize themselves politically to improve their condition. Instead, they fight among themselves for the scraps thrown to them: at one point the poem lists each character's grievance against one of his or her neighbors, describing how they all die "hating" someone who they perceive to have more than they do (8). This competition among the oppressed for status defined by the ability to acquire money and commodities is made even more pathetic by the fact that these status symbols—the used car, "five dollars more on the same job" (8)—will always be seen as flawed by the mainstream. In the characters' quest for upward mobility, they choose between playing the lottery or "Hating fighting and stealing / broken windows from each other" (7); their highest aspirations, the "broken windows" as much as the "broken english," are imperfect imitations of true success (8). The mutual hatred among the subjects of "Puerto Rican Obituary" means that the one place in which the poem can imagine solidarity lies in the "groovy hereafter" (9) described in the poem's final stanza—the only part of the poem in which the word "together" (11) appears. The "groovy hereafter" is a place where there is a community, "where beautiful people sing / and dance and work together," and "where you do not need a dictionary / to communicate with your people" (10–11). It is also a utopia devoid of commercialism: "Aqui there are no dial soap commercials" (11). Both sides of Pietri's "aqui," the presence of a community and the absence of commodity culture, appear to be necessary parts of this paradise.

The way in which "Puerto Rican Obituary" frames the problem and offers solutions is not without contradictions. Most obviously, while the poem does appear in the end to overcome its pessimistic litany of suffering by offering an alternative way to organize society around uncontaminated folk knowledge, the utopia that ends the poem is the "aqui" of both an impossible return to a mythical Puerto Rico and the reality of an anonymous funeral in Long Island Cemetery. Only in death do Juan, Miguel, Milagros, Olga, and Manuel find paradise. Furthermore, it is the poem's rhythm and tone themselves that arguably participate in the silencing of its characters, none of whom speak in the poem. It is precisely the inability of the "Dead Puerto Ricans / Who never knew they were Puerto Ricans" (2) to articulate their suffering that makes it necessary for the poet to show them the way. Their deaths matter only insofar as the poet can invest them with meaning, making them necessary sacrifices for breaking the cycle of poverty and suffering. The characters suffer because of their lack of imagination and political consciousness, which are not coincidentally the very strengths possessed by the poet. In this way the poet establishes his importance by positing that his articulateness and the characters' revolutionary essence—"their latino souls"—must be joined if society is to be reshaped.

By framing the tragedy of Puerto Rican immigrants in New York during the 1960s in this way, "Puerto Rican Obituary" contains an imperative: reject the trappings of U.S. commercial culture, stop deluding yourselves about your situation, and organize yourselves to fight against exploitation. This command also implies a certain argument about the poet's role: the poet is the one who understands the problem, having lived among the people and listened to them, but he has also attained a level of consciousness that the people lack. Because of this higher knowledge, only the poet can lead them to freedom. We might characterize this stance as typical of the anticolonial literature of the Caribbean in the 1950s and 1960s, and of U.S. Latino/as in the 1960s and 1970s. In the wake of the Cuban revolution and the withdrawal of Great Britain from the Caribbean, this generation of writers and intellectuals—from Fidel Castro and Che Guevara to Franz Fanon and Malcolm X to the Young Lords and Black Panthers—expressed considerable faith in the peasantry and working class as agents of redemption for the Caribbean and its diaspora. Refusing to accept the modern division between writing and political action, these leaders saw themselves as spokesmen for the "folk" or "pueblo," positioning themselves as authors of revolutions and their writings as weapons in the struggle for decolonization.[2]

The anticolonial orientation of "Puerto Rican Obituary" becomes even clearer when read alongside an explicitly political text from this period, such as the Young Lords Party's "13 Point Program and Platform." The party's platform, announced in 1969 in concert with its sanitation strike in Upper Manhattan and the takeover of the First Spanish Methodist Church where Pietri performed "Puerto Rican Obituary," demands liberation, equality, and control of land and institutions.[3] The Young Lords' demands begin with liberation for Puerto Rico but also move outward to "self-determination for all Latinos" and eventually "liberation of all third world people" (point 3). In asserting solidarity with other hemispheric and global struggles against imperialism, the Young Lords declare themselves socialist, appropriating such slogans from the Cuban revolution as "¡Hasta La Victoria Siempre!" (point 13) and "¡Viva Che!" (point 11) They warn that even though "our people are brainwashed by television, radio, newspapers, schools and books to oppose people in other countries fighting for their freedom," now "no longer will our people believe attacks and slanders, because they have learned who the real enemy is" (point 11). Assuming that they possess a higher consciousness is a necessary part of their mission to wake up the people. In calling the people "they," and even with their rallying cry "¡Despierta Boricua!" the group clearly expresses its mission as vanguardist by positioning itself as the agent of change separate from the pueblo. At the same time, vacillation between this distancing and the ownership implied in the formulation of "our people" points to the ambivalence of the anticolonial stance.

Perhaps no author better captures the relationship of the artist and intellectual to this anticolonial ideology than Jesús Colón in *A Puerto Rican in New York and Other Sketches* (1961), one of the first literary endeavors by a Puerto Rican written in English. In the book's preface, Colón frames his project as an intervention into the public sphere by outlining his objective to correct the misperceptions and stereotypes about Puerto Ricans encountered in "the New York press": "Invariably, this treatment harps on what is superficial and sentimental, transient and ephemeral, or bizarre and grotesque in Puerto Rican life—and always out of context with the real history, culture and traditions of my people" (Colón 9). Colón suggests that he will counter those misrepresentations by describing "our international outlook, our solidarity with the struggles of other peoples [...] the deep traditions of striving for freedom and progress that pervade our daily life" (10). As a corrective of stereotypes, writing thus takes on a heroic mission, allowing the anticolonial writer to serve his people and participate in broader social movements.

The first three sketches are especially instructive illustrations of the aspects of Latino/a experience that Colón wants to emphasize, and of what he sees as his relationship to that material. The opening sketch, "A Voice Through the Window," describes young Jesús growing up near a cigar factory in Cayey. The sketch focuses not only on the proletarian existence of the factory workers but also on the role of the lector, who reads to them as they roll cigars. Colón marvels at the "cigarmakers who hardly knew how to read and write, discussing books like Zola's *Germinal*, Balzac's *Pere Goriot*, or Kropotkin's *Fields, Factories and Workshops* during the mild Puerto Rican evenings in the public square" (11). In this sketch, Colón thus lays out an idealized vision of a democratized culture, a public sphere open to all thanks to the lector's mediation. The lector's position is admittedly privileged and centralized—as young Jesús "looked for the source of the voice to which they were listening," he first sees the lector "sitting on a chair on a platform" (11). But it is the lector who introduces Jesús to Cervantes, Zola, Balzac, and Hugo as well as to Marx. Indeed, the sketch ends with Colón identifying the lector's real message as one of a solidarity that reaches across classes but that must necessarily position the intellectual as separate from, even if sympathetic to, the proletariat: "The confusions, misunderstandings, disillusions, defections and momentary defeats will be overcome. In the end, if we keep on struggling and learning from struggle, the workers and their allies will win all over the world" (13). Colón draws a clear distinction here between the workers and their intellectual "allies."

The next sketch moves from the figure of the lector to briefly recount what it titles "My First Literary Venture." Jesús's classmate Mercedes loses her mother, and the principal of the school announces that "we must write a letter to Mercedes and her family in which the whole feeling of this class is reflected" (14). The project becomes a contest: "All of you, individually, are going to write a letter to Mercedes in the name of myself, your teacher, and this class. The one letter that in the opinion of your teacher and myself best conveys the sympathy and emotions of all of us will be the one we will send to Mercedes' family" (14). Of course, Jesús's letter is chosen. If the story of the lector emphasizes a more didactic shaping of people's consciousness, this second sketch is meant to affirm Colón's suitability not only to instruct the people but also to understand and distill their "sympathies" and "emotions." The anticolonial writer instructs the people, but only because he is sensitive to their dreams and aspirations.

The third sketch, "My First Strike," brings together the notion of Jesús as a representative of the other students with his sense of solidarity with the rest of his classmates. The story takes place in the classroom, calling attention to the teacher as the traditional intellectual with whom Jesús as an organic intellectual must compete. Whereas the teacher, Mr. Whole, draws authority completely from himself and his position, Jesús finds another more powerful source. When Mr. Whole, a North American, finds out that one of the students has lost her history book, he accuses the class of having stolen it and tells them that they will have to pay to have it replaced. The incident thus pits the teacher and his authority against the whole class. Reacting to this injustice, the students elect Jesús to present their grievances to the principal. His meeting with the principal, in which he "presented the case very concisely in the name of the committee and of our school class" (16), coupled with the students' threat to boycott the class, convinces the principal to capitulate to their demands. Once again, the lesson drawn from the incident is the power of joining together Jesús's intellectual articulateness with the physical presence of the whole class. This solidarity can then overcome the teacher's authority, which proves to be false and lacking—a hole rather than a whole. By the fourth sketch, "The Way to Learn," which recounts Jesús's election to the board of his school's magazine, *Adelante*, the coordinates of the role of the anticolonial intellectual have been definitively established. Such an intellectual must be simultaneously a reader, writer, leader, and visionary; however, to be able to speak with authority, he needs to harness the power of the people. To achieve these goals, he must be able to understand and express the consciousness of the people, speaking in their best interests even when they do not recognize those interests themselves.

Colón thus delineates his project in *A Puerto Rico in New York* just as Pietri does in "Puerto Rican Obituary." The task of the writer is to represent the hopes and desires of the people. At the same time, however, the people lack the consciousness to properly understand their situation—in Pietri's poem they "never know" that "they are beautiful people" (*Puerto Rican Obituary* 9–10). They must be awakened and educated, their "eyes open" (10) to the realities that capitalist ideology has obscured from them. As in "Puerto Rican Obituary," *A Puerto Rican in New York* identifies formal education (for example in "The Way to Learn") or the culture industry (in "Hollywood Rewrites History") as purveyors of this false consciousness. Colón and Pietri thus construct a role for the poet or writer that we see mirrored in this same period in such publications of the Frankfurt School as Horkheimer and Adorno's *Dialectic of Enlightenment* (1944) or Marcuse's *One-Dimensional Man* (1964). According to these texts, the anticolonial intellectual must reject the seductions of this corrupt mass culture in order to see the unequal and exploitative relationships that this culture is meant to obscure, thus awakening the people to true consciousness and leading them forward into revolution.[4]

## CRITICAL NOSTALGIA FOR THE ANTICOLONIAL

Originally published in 1961, *A Puerto Rican in New York* reappeared in the 1980s thanks to the efforts of Juan Flores, who edited and reissued the collection. It is no coincidence that Colón's crucial work of Latino/a anticolonialism was one of the first texts to be championed by Flores in his effort to translate or republish important works of Puerto Rican and Nuyorican literary history. Flores, who has been instrumental in bringing works like Edgardo Rodríguez Juliá's *Cortijo's Wake* (2004) and Manuel Zeno Gandía's *The Pond* (1999) to a wider English-speaking audience, focuses in his introduction on the anticolonial aspects of Colón's text: the author's career as a worker himself ("as a dishwasher, dockworker, postal clerk, and at dozens of other menial posts" [Flores, "Foreword" xii]), and his experience in the "new battleground of the North American cities" where Colón "was a man of action" who organized and committed himself to social movements (xiii). Flores frames the reissuing of *A Puerto Rican in New York* as part of his larger project of configuring a Latino/a canon: "Colon's [sic] stories foreshadow the vibrant literature of the 'Nuyoricans' that has emerged since the late 1960s" (xvi). In order to construct a genealogy of Latino/a literature as oppositional and resistant, Flores seeks to establish Colón's work as a founding text, noting how "Piri Thomas, Nicholasa Mohr, Tato Laviera and Sandra Maria Esteves, to name a few, are carrying forward traditions introduced by Jesus Colon [sic]" (xvii).

In his critical essays, Flores further demonstrates this interest in recovering and constructing literary tradition. For example, in the essay "Puerto Rican Literature in the United States: Stages and Perspectives" (1988), Flores follows Colón in lamenting a situation in which "Puerto Rican literature still draws a blank among American readers and students of literature"; indeed, "even the writing of Puerto Ricans writing in the United States, mostly in English and all expressive of life in this country, has remained marginal to any literary canon, mainstream or otherwise" (Flores, *Divided* 142). As a remedy for this lack of critical engagement, Flores offers an overview of what he identifies as the three phases of this literary history: the autobiographical writings of the political exiles of the nineteenth and early twentieth centuries; the gritty fiction of immigrant authors like José Luis González and Pedro Juan Soto; and finally "the third, Nuyorican stage" (150). While a true continuity between these phases may not exist—Flores admits that the third stage "arose with no direct reference to or evident knowledge of the writings of either earlier period" (150)—nonetheless, he argues for a clear trajectory in which the "Nuyorican creative expression effectively draws together the firsthand testimonial stance of the 'pioneer' stage and the fictional, imaginative approach of writers" of the second stage (150). Flores identifies "this combining of autobiographical and imaginative modes of community portrayal" as best exemplified in Piri Thomas's *Down These Mean Streets* (1967). Flores thus positions Thomas's text as a synthesis of the first and second stages, with *Down These Mean Streets* becoming the apogee of Flores's literary history.

Flores's literary history of Puerto Rican writing in English is in many ways his own, but on certain major points it coincides with Lisa Sánchez González's *Boricua Literature: A Literary History of the Puerto Rican Diaspora* (2001). As Colón sought to tell the "real" story of Puerto Ricans in the United States (the group Sánchez González refers to as "Boricuas"), Sánchez González gives herself the same mission to "render visible" (Sánchez González 3) and "uncover" (5) the submerged and marginalized Boricua literary production. Like Flores, she contributes mightily to Latino/a literary history in her archival research, which allows her to trace a "Boricua cultural intellectual history" that she positions in explicit opposition to previous canons. She focuses in particular on the narrative Flores constructs in "Puerto Rican Literature in the United States," which she criticizes because "the bulk of his article concerns [...] outsider perspectives" (19). While Flores identifies canonical figures from the island like Ramón Emeterio Betances and Eugenio María de Hostos as part of his first wave, Sánchez González calls them "bourgeois revolutionaries" (21). She chooses instead to begin with Luisa Capetillo and Arturo Schomburg, whose writings "have been all but completely ignored" (21) because, she suggests, "Black and women writers from the diaspora's working class" (20) are not so easily assimilated by the concept of "Puerto Rican literature in the United States" as an extension of the island's "insular disciplinary canons" (17). Instead of this canon, Sánchez González uses archival research to assemble her own contestatory literary history. Her first chapter begins by looking at the writings of Capetillo, a little-known anarchist; the second provides a rereading of two canonical mainstream modernist figures, Schomburg and William Carlos Williams, from the perspective of their Boricua backgrounds; and the third recognizes the librarian and social organizer Pura Belpré as an important writer in her own right.

Although Sánchez González frames her project in opposition to other canons, after this point her narrative converges with Flores's story: chapter 4 of *Boricua Literature,* titled "The Boricua Novel: Civil Rights and 'New School' Nuyorican Narratives," focuses on "the Nuyorican Renaissance" (103), the generation of the Sixties. Just as Flores sees *Down These Mean Streets* as consolidating the tradition of Thomas's literary forebears, Sánchez González argues that "the ethical and aesthetic motives of the earliest extant Boricua narratives—Arturo Schomburg's African diasporan research, Luisa Capetillo's anarcho-feminist fiction, William Carlos Williams's historical deconstrutive poetics, Pura Belpré's allegorical pedagogy—set the epistemic founda-tions" (102) for what she sees as "the most extensive articulation of this new Boricua literary sensibility […] Piri Thomas's autobiographical novel *Down These Mean Streets* [1967] and Nicholasa Mohr's novel *Nilda* [1973]" (103). These texts become part of a "larger enunciation of dissent," allowing them to "constitute a paperback challenge to the fan-tastic fictions of American democracy and racial equality" (105). Thomas and Mohr thus become once again the heroes of Nuyorican or Boricua literary history, the cultural arm of anticolonialism, their texts "interven-tions" (133) and "resistance literature" that "subvert[s] the very language and literary forms of the colonial metropole from within the proverbial 'belly of the beast'" (132).

Unlike Flores's 1988 essay, *Boricua Literature* doesn't end with the Civil Rights generation but with two chapters that bring this genealogy up to its date of publication in 2001. The first of these is subtitled "Three Women's Texts," and discusses works by Judith Ortiz Cofer, Esmeralda Santiago, and Carmen de Monteflores. The second, titled "¡*Ya Deja Eso!* Toward an Epi-*fenomenal* Approach to Boricua Cultural Studies," looks at "three albums that became huge hits on the Latin Afro-Caribbean circuit around 1992" (170). This turn to music for the last chapter of a "literary history" is a curious development to which we will return later. But more pertinent to our current discussion is the way in which Sánchez González positions the chapter on post-Sixties literature. After Sánchez González has shown how Thomas and Mohr build on the groundwork laid by Capetillo, Schomburg, Williams, and Belpré, her chapter on Ortiz Cofer, Santiago, and Monteflores appears as an anticlimax. Sánchez González's attitude toward these writers is betrayed in a passage from the introduc-tion in which she outlines her trajectory:

Capetillo's insurgent anarchism, Williams's reinvention of the Americas' history as a living legacy, Schomburg's call for African diaspora collaboration, Belpré's preoccupation with allegory and orature, Thomas's Afro-Rican quandaries, and Mohr's crosshatching of different art forms—all of which mutually inform the lyrical inventions and rhythmic signification of *the* twentieth-century Boricua social text par excellence—salsa. (13)

In this passage, Sánchez González lists each author from her study and their significance to show the underlying continuity of the tradition. Strikingly, she fails to mention any of the authors from the post-Sixties chapter, the only chapter of *Boricua Literature* that does not include the word Boricua in its title. Skipping over contemporary writers and ending this passage by identifying salsa, the topic of her final chapter, as the inheritor of all of these different strands clearly implies that the literature of the 1980s and 1990s is nothing more than a digression from her Boricua genealogy. We suggest that this refusal to read these writers in relation to that tradition, to see them as anything other than betrayers of it, marks a gap in the theoretical imagination that a postcolonial, post-Civil Rights approach to literature must overcome.

The post-Sixties generation of writers thus becomes a detour in Sánchez González's lineage. It cannot be understood in relation to the Civil Rights tradition, and as such its members are not authentic inheritors of that literary legacy. The reasons for excluding these writers from the lineage become clear in the opening pages of the chapter on Ortiz Cofer, Santiago, and Monteflores. Sánchez González accuses post-Sixties Latino/a literature of abandoning politics and colluding with domination, producing books "dictated by market analysts in corporate headquarters" (136). True Boricua cultural expression embodies resistance, while this literature has become "reactionary and self-aggrandizing" (135). She clearly identifies the problem as one of capitalist co-optation: "Given this growing market and the industry's profit motives, certain priorities that respond to industry readings of market potential determine which titles get published and promoted" (136). In response to the market, then, Santiago, Ortiz Cofer, and Monteflores produce narratives of uncomplicated upward mobility in which Puerto Rico "represents outgrown, retrograde communal and family values, while in the final instance 'America' (that is, any area of the mainland United States unpopulated by Boricuas) is celebrated as the utopia of the mature female protagonist's liberatory exile" (141). Thus these "mainstreamed Latina feminist texts" are part of a "literary trend in the 1990s" that "marks a clean break with the progressive and radical narrative politics characteristic of the Boricua feminist literary enterprise throughout the twentieth century" (140).

Sánchez González identifies the intrusion of the market as the primary cause of this deterioration of a resistant Boricua literature. When Flores returns to writing about what he now calls "Latino" (rather than Puerto Rican or Nuyorican) literature in the essay "Life Off the Hyphen" (2000), he echoes Sánchez González, lamenting "the demise of the idea of Latino culture as resistance" (Flores, *From Bomba* 173). Beginning with the award of the 1990 Pulitzer Prize to Oscar Hijuelos's *The Mambo Kings Play Songs of Love,* Flores sees "the ascendancy of a Latino literature which, however nostalgic for the old culture and resentful of the new, is markedly assimilationist toward American society and its culture, thus departing from the contestatory and oppositional stance characteristic of much writing by Latino authors in the past" (170). Rather than regarding the Pulitzer as recognizing the quality of Latino/a literature, Flores argues that it really rewards the literature's readiness to affirm "wholesome" American "manners and values" (168). Thus, "what is new about the recent Latino writing, and goes to inform it as a marketing category, is that it seeks to be apolitical" (174).

These critics thus dismiss nostalgia as politically suspect, even while displaying a longing of their own for a lost time when politics were purer and Latino/a literature oppositional. At the same time, each shows an awareness that the terrain has shifted to such an extent that these anti-colonial positions are no longer feasible. Sánchez González admits with some regret that "gone are the days when Latina writers were clearly outside the realm of commodification, when their significance, by virtue of this literature's historical moment and modes of production, automat-ically sidestepped and outmaneuvered the distortion of mainstream marketing" (Sánchez González 137). Although the question remains open whether an inherently resistant Latino/a literature able to "auto-matically sidestep" the market ever existed, Flores emphasizes the same opposition by juxtaposing the 1960s and the 1990s even more explicitly:

> Social consciousness and cultural expression of this new geopolitical real-ity burst out in the late 1960s. Inspired by the Civil Rights movement and the Cuban Revolution, countless movements, causes and organizations rallied thousands of Mexicans and Puerto Ricans to the cries of "¡Viva la Raza!" and "¡Despierta Boricua!" The political momentum of the Latino imaginary was set in those spirited movements, and found vibrant artistic expression [...] By our time, in the 1990s, that heyday is long past, no longer even a living memory for young Latinos. (Flores, *From Bomba* 191)

Flores comes up with the concept of the "lite colonial" in order to think through the newness of this historical moment (36). His definition of what makes contemporary colonialism "lite" coincides with what we are calling the post-Sixties, postcolonial, and post-Civil Rights condition: "The idea is that colonialism has been taking on a new face as its economic and political legitimations become so thoroughly veiled by cultural and commercial ones, and the colonial subject is mostly visibly so as a consumer" (12). In light of these new forms of domination, any understanding or critique of the present must move beyond the categories of modern colonialism. The desire to retain the anticolonial critique of capitalism, coupled with a realization that changing times require rethinking some assumptions, leads the critics into contradictory positions. As we will see, they celebrate music as more accessible, less elitist, and therefore better able to offer a mode of resistance to a wider community; yet post-Civil Rights Latino/a literature, when it makes this same move to become a commodity, sells out its oppositionality by becoming popular.

### THE MUSICAL TURN

In light of this argument, namely that the literature of the post-Sixties era abandons politics and colludes with domination and imperialism, what is a committed literary critic to do? Flores, Sánchez González, Juan Otero Garabís, and others have turned to music in this context. As Sánchez González puts it, "If we are looking for more poetically or politically engaged forms of Boricua self-representation, what is left to read?" (Sánchez González 160). To answer this question, Sánchez González concludes with a sixth and final chapter that "suggests the limitations of analyzing only published and archival documents as artifacts of Boricua cultural production, and ultimately proposes salsa as the Boricua cultural text par excellence at the turn of the twenty-first century" (160). She points to literature as "inescapably affianced to brutal institutional partners" (188) in order to declare it a "handmaiden to the bourgeois project of cultural nationalism" (166). Literature, as a "kind of knowledge" aspiring to "philosophical truths, populist mantras, or any other positivist theorems," is a hopelessly modernist knowledge that forecloses "quintessential human experiences that formal literacies and the fetishes they imply cannot ever hope to arrest and detain" (188).

On the other hand, Sánchez González's "epi-*fenomenal*" approach "attends to provocative new sounds *and* bodies in the scripting of cultural studies" (166) by putting music at its center. Listening to the noises and bodies silenced by literature, the cultural critic hears the alternative "subaltern" forms of knowledge they convey (167). The critic thus assumes the position that Colón carves out for himself in "My First Literary

Venture" and "My First Strike," listening to the subaltern and translating that experience into a usable resource for opposing inequality and domination. For this project to work, the music must represent the whole, literally embodying the Latino/a community: "Perhaps more than any other Boricua expressive art, salsa *is* this community in motion and in metaphor, abstracted by lyric and made flesh by rhythm" (168). The anticolonial relationship of writer and pueblo is thus recreated. According to Sánchez González, because of the salsero's position as one with the community, this "subaltern aesthetic collaboration [...] renders the corporate appropriation of 'salsa' (a convenient misnomer at best) irrelevant" (169).[5] Inseparable from the community, salsa's subalternity is inherently resistant, as even entry into the market cannot contaminate it.

Other Latino-Caribbean critics make a similar move away from literature and into music, echoing Sánchez González's argument for music as the privileged form of expression for contemporary Latino/a identity and politics. The Puerto Rican critic Juan Otero Garabís, for example, makes the case that technological and political developments now mean that literature no longer articulates the nation. Otero Garabís begins from Benedict Anderson's concept of the nation as an imagined community; he summarizes Anderson's argument that "the appearance of newspapers was fundamental to the creation of the 'horizontal comradeship' that we call nations" (Otero Garabís 15).[6] If print-capitalism, in particular the newspaper and the novel, was during the eighteenth and nineteenth centuries the most important vehicle for transmitting the idea of the nation, Otero Garabís wonders whether "the growth of what Walter Benjamin calls the 'age of mechanical reproduction'—what would later become an age of mass communication—implies a reconfiguration of the groups who participate in nation building" (15). He continues to reflect on the new forms that dominate our contemporary imaginary, and what kinds of communities they might be imagining: "In this sense, the appearance of the film industry, the music industry, radio and television provoked and promoted new forms of social representation which affected the ways in which national communities conceived (of) themselves" (15). Finally, Otero Garabís links these reflections to the concept Doris Sommer develops in *Foundational Fictions* (1991) of the centrality of the novel to nation-building in Latin America: "These means of communication will be the new producers of 'foundational fictions' [...] they will construct new national imaginaries which reflect changing relations between social groups" (16).

Meditating on the historical place of various cultural forms and modes of production in their respective societies and historical moments, Otero

Garabís posits popular music as the form that has taken the place of novels and newspapers. Otero Garabís locates popular music, in contrast to the cultural elitism of the experimental novel, as an art form created by and for the "pueblo" (155–56). Music, because of its wide dissemination by the culture industry, travels more effectively across national, linguistic, and class boundaries, and is more effective in producing transnational and sometimes translinguistic communities. As his argument proceeds, Otero Garabís parallels Sánchez González by moving away from a reading of a Puerto Rican novel in his first chapter to subsequent chapters that analyze the salsa of Willie Colón, the nueva trova of Silvio Rodríguez, and the hybrid rhythms of Juan Luis Guerra as the forms in which Puerto Rican, Cuban, and Dominican transnationalism are simultaneously imagined and challenged in a contemporary context.

Flores's work makes a move from literature to music similar to Sánchez González's and Otero Garabís's trajectories, as is evident in the transition from his first collection of essays, *Divided Borders: Essays on Puerto Rican Identity* (1993), to his second, *From Bomba to Hip-Hop: Puerto Rican Culture and Latino Identity* (2000). Flores's first set of essays, written between 1979 and 1991, engage in an against-the-grain literary criticism of the Puerto Rican canon. Flores develops the strategy in this volume of deploying literary texts in order to draw conclusions about Puerto Rican culture and society as a whole. One essay, first published in 1981, begins with the question, "Are Puerto Ricans becoming Americanized?" (Flores, *Divided* 157), and moves toward an answer through an extended reading of Tato Laviera's poetry collection, *La Carreta Made a U-Turn*. Another essay, published in 1980, argues that "detailed critical treatment of *Insularismo* [an essay by Antonio Pedreira] is crucial to an assessment of the cultural life of Puerto Rican people, whether in Puerto Rico or in the United States" (15).

This technique of using literary texts to draw conclusions about society predominates in *Divided Borders,* though not all of the essays adhere homogeneously to such a methodology. The essays written during the latter half of the 1980s begin to privilege music as the object of study. *Divided Borders* features an essay recounting the history of plena and another celebrating the composer Rafael Cortijo, published in 1988 and 1991 respectively. The essay "Living Borders/*Buscando América:* Languages of Latino Self-Formation," first published in 1990, most explicitly articulates Flores's transition from studying literature to music. In this post-Sixties context, he finds that "salsa, perhaps better than any other cultural form, expresses the Latino ethos of multiculturalism and crossing borders" (215). For Flores, salsa has the perfect attitude towards

"crossing over," in that "crossover does not mean that Latinos seek willy
nilly to 'make it' in the political and commercial spheres of the general
culture" (215). Flores celebrates salsa because of its ability to both circulate and resist selling out: "Originating in the barrios, it made its way to
'down-town' clubs and across borders to the diverse audience of the
Latin American subcontinent [...] despite its popularity and certain
minor breakthroughs, salsa has not (yet?) 'made it' in mainstream U.S.
culture" (215–16).

The progression that takes place within the essays of *Divided Borders*
foretells the transition that will be evident in the title of Flores's second
collection of essays. In *From Bomba to Hip-Hop,* music supplants literature as the hermeneutical tool of choice for understanding Latino-
Caribbean cultures. Flores explains his emphasis on popular culture as
"not only because of my own personal tastes and predilections, but
because it retains the dimensions of class and cultural capital which are so
easily lost sight of in considerations of group identities and interactions
along ethnic cultural lines" (Flores, *From Bomba* 14–15). When literature
is discussed, as in the essay "Life Off the Hyphen," it is decentered and
approached from a cultural studies perspective. Flores calls the novels that
most interest him a "lowercase literature [...] illustrative of oral tradition"
instead of "an institutionalized, canon-forming literature" (184).

Taken together, the cultural turn in Flores, Otero Garabís, and Sánchez
González suggests some of the reasons that Latino/a critics have begun to
deprivilege literature, in particular by inverting its relationship with such
popular cultural forms as music. These critics reveal their own postcolonial
impulse toward suspicion of literature as part of the desire for indigenous
cultural forms. For each, literature is aligned with the high culture of the
ruling classes and the cultural imperialism of the mainstream. The novel,
with its "assimilationist proclivities" (Flores, *From Bomba* 183), has abandoned its stake in the political and can no longer represent a Latino/a
form of knowledge to be used against U.S. capitalism. Focusing on music
allows the critics to animate their intellectual endeavors with political
significance, a way to create a public role for an increasingly privatized
academic field. These critics choose salseros who present themselves as
resistant figures—think of the album cover for *La Gran Fuga/The Big
Break,* in which Willie Colón is pictured on a Federal Bureau of
Investigation (FBI) "Most Wanted" poster, with text that reads:

> Armed with trombone and considered dangerous [...] They have been
> known to kill people with little provocation and without a moment's
> notice, by their exciting *rhythm*. [...] these men are highly dangerous in a
> crowd and are capable of *starting riots*: people immediately start to dance.[7]

This imagery is clearly meant to tap into the tradition of the artist as revolutionary. Coming from the ghetto, the artist is the anticolonial leader whose cultural productions simultaneously capture the people's unspoken or even unconscious desires, and act as a catalyst for setting the inert but dangerous masses into motion.

Rubén Blades is the salsero who emerges as a main protagonist in both Flores's and Sánchez González's account of progressive music, and as the hero of numerous other academic efforts to establish salsa's political significance.[8] This academic celebration of Blades comes from his ability to clearly position himself as the successor to the anticolonial writers of the 1960s, even more than other politically conscious salseros of the 1970s like Willie Colón and Héctor Lavoe. In a song like "Plástico" (1978), Blades deploys the language of the Cuban revolution ("p'alante," "seguiremos unidos y al final venceremos") to call honest hard-working people ("se ven las caras de trabajo y de sudor / de gente de carne y hueso que no se vendió / de gente trabajando buscando el nuevo camino") to join together to fight against the foreign threat of the U.S. culture industry, which turns the Latino/a middle classes into mimic men and women, "plastic" people who worship the dollar.[9] Yet while Flores and Sánchez González would like to read music as the true expression of the subaltern, Blades, as a bilingual Panamanian educated at Harvard and possessing a law degree, is not all that different from the post-Sixties Latino/a writers whom Flores describes as "middle-class exiles, bearing with them and reproducing the cultural capital inherent in their family lines" (Flores, *From Bomba* 176).

In taking contemporary literature to task for becoming commodified, critics adopt a perspective already seen in "Puerto Rican Obituary," envisioning the market as corrupting, co-opting, or depoliticizing. Progressive politics in this formulation is incompatible with the market. Yet as Blades's ability to reach a broad international audience with a political message demonstrates, perhaps it is not simply the market that is the problem here. Just as anticolonial movements opportunistically took advantage of precisely the levers of domination that were being used against them—nationalism, high art, and physical force—perhaps we can imagine different kinds of markets and different kinds of commodities. Blades's message is affected by its entry into capitalist circuits; however, for a critic interested in popular culture, the route to popularity goes through the market. While critics like Flores and Sánchez González remain steadfast in their anticolonial framework when they are dealing with literature, we can see in Pietri's work a move towards rethinking that view. "El Spanglish National Anthem" offers us a different, more affirmative vision in which commodities can be constitutive of identity and community, a vision that points to the progressive possibilities of a popular literature.

In this way, Pietri's more recent work rethinks literature's political potential in the postcolonial, post-Civil Rights world. What we are here proposing as the politics of post-Sixties Latino/a literature is not unlike the commercially circulated politics that Brittmarie Janson Perez notices in salsa:

> Politics has rarely been absent from Latin American music. Mexico's politicised *corridos* are well known. Puerto Rican composers voiced their independentist concerns in a few boleros, also a Latin American dance genre. The highly committed *nueva canción latinoamericana* has been amply documented. Salsa differs from these, however, in that it is a large-scale capitalist commercial production, a commercial product aimed at all of Latin America and Hispanics residing in the United States but which, nevertheless, contains critiques of capitalism from various points of view. The *salsa* of socio-political themes is not the type of protest song sung in demonstrations, rallies, or overtly political contexts. It is protest embedded in everyday life: songs heard over the radio or record-player, and music danced to at parties and in nightclubs or discos. (Janson Perez 150)

Janson Perez distinguishes salsa from traditional forms of protest music precisely because of its "large-scale capitalist commercial production" (150). Unlike examples of the "overtly political" protest music that Janson Perez identifies with the generation of the 1960s—she points to "U.S. blacks of the civil rights movement who sang 'We Shall Overcome'" (150)—salsa, as a distinctly post-Sixties phenomenon, articulates what might be called a politics of the everyday. This politics comes in its subject matter as much as its stance. Combining humor and satire with catchy and memorable descargas and rhythms yields an interstitial critique—not the confrontational didactic message of anti-colonialism but rather an invitation to join a heterogeneous community making meaning. As a reading of "El Spanglish National Anthem" indicates, other cultural forms of music and literature share this vision of a quotidian politics as the mode suited for a postcolonial, post-Civil Rights world in which issues of national sovereignty and the seizure of power may no longer be the only way to conceive of politics.

## "EL SPANGLISH NATIONAL ANTHEM"
### AND POST-SIXTIES IMAGINARIES

The critics may remain nostalgic for the golden literary age of the 1960s and view the mainstreaming of Latino/a literature via the market with suspicion, but as the rest of this book will show, Latino/a writers of the 1990s are equally nostalgic for that period, when literature seemed to have a clear political role and privileged voice in the public sphere. At the same time, the writers couple this nostalgia with a critique of the elitist and antipopular notion that writers can speak for or lead the people. It may at first appear ironic that it is the poets and novelists who suggest a more dialectical approach to literature and the market in the post-Sixties context. Sometimes, however, literary practitioners are better at holding together apparently conflicting and contradictory ideas. Even in Pedro Pietri, we can see a move away from the didactic anticolonialism that permeates the "Puerto Rican Obituary" to a postcolonial reassessment in the "El Spanglish National Anthem." We suggest that works like "El Spanglish National Anthem" point to the ways in which both music *and* literature are commodities, and as such may function in similar ways.

As its name suggests, "El Spanglish National Anthem" is performed as a song, in this case to the tune of the nostalgic bolero, "En Mi Viejo San Juan." Explicitly adopting a musical form is only the most obvious way in which "El Spanglish National Anthem" demonstrates that cultural products circulate by becoming commodities—in this case, how the song "En Mi Viejo San Juan" is available to consumers in both Puerto Rico and its diaspora—and thus form linkages necessary for building a transnational community. The poem's musical mimicry belongs to a lineage of post-Civil Rights Latino/a literature that extends from Oscar Hijuelos's *The Mambo Kings Play Songs of Love* (1989) and Achy Obejas's *Memory Mambo* (1996) to Black Artemis's *Explicit Content* (2004) and Angie Cruz's *Let It Rain Coffee* (2005). These works use music metaphorically or literally as a model cultural form able to reach a broad market. Literature and music are both commodities, although they do circulate in different ways, produced and consumed by different populations. As Pietri's career demonstrates, however, these populations overlap and blend. Emphasizing performance has allowed the Nuyorican poets to go beyond the usual audience for high art; as the performance of "Puerto Rican Obituary" outside the People's Church makes clear, the goal is to speak directly to the community. Still, the historical advantage of written text has been its ability to circulate more widely, beyond the group of people with whom the poet has face-to-face contact. Pietri long resisted publishing with major presses, one reason his poetry collections can be difficult to find.[10] In fact, "El Spanglish National Anthem" appears as part of *El Puerto Rican Embassy* project, an Internet site whose founders describe themselves as "a new generation of experimental Puerto Rican artists working at the margins of established art movements."[11] Just as Frances Aparicio describes dancing as an alternative way of consuming music (Aparicio 95), publication of a poem via the Internet is a new way to reach a wide audience while sidestepping major publishing institutions, neither a wholesale acceptance nor a rejection of the notion of entering the market.

First performed in the early 1990s, "El Spanglish National Anthem" serves as an update and counterpoint to the bleak world of "Puerto Rican Obituary." Its tone is the first and most obvious contrast: if "Puerto Rican Obituary" tells tragic tales of immigrant woe, Pietri's performance of the "National Anthem" is clearly comic. The poem is no less serious, but is hopeful and funny rather than dark and pessimistic. This new tone depends from its first stanza to its last on the creation of a Latino/a community in the United States that is unimaginable in "Puerto Rican Obituary." The first two stanzas of "El Spanglish National Anthem" name a subject who is not an atomized individual like Juan, Miguel, Milagros, Olga, or Manuel, but rather an "I" who is part of "everyone."[12] There is a community of "Puerto Ricans" like the "I," all living together and all "Dressed in tropical garments" (Pietri, "Spanglish"). In direct contrast to "Puerto Rican Obituary," the setting of "El Spanglish National Anthem" is no longer the alienating city whose monotonous industrial rhythm threatens to drown out the voices of beautiful people singing and dancing in their own language; the poem claims "El Barrio" as its "Latin Community." Rather than the tone of a disciplined and inevitable march towards death found in "Puerto Rican Obituary," this poem is a song whose voice and rhythm are distinctively Latino/a.

Toward the end, the anthem returns to the theme of whether U.S. Latino/a identity is being diluted or preserved in the context of this expanding market presence, referencing two populations: those who assimilated and "got rid of de accent" as well as a "majority" who "kept their identity." In "Puerto Rican Obituary," Juan, Miguel, Milagros, Olga, and Manuel aspire to get out, to pass, to move to Queens. They hate one another and they hate themselves. In "El Spanglish National Anthem," the majority are willing to identify with this Latino/a community. Before, solidarity was only a dream, the opiates of religion and television standing in the way of the creation of a community. A national anthem, on the other hand, supposes a nation, a group of like-minded people who imagine themselves as belonging. "El Spanglish National Anthem" thus celebrates the existence of both Latino/a identity and community—what could be called a U.S. Latinidad—once thought impossible.[13] How, then, has the context changed so dramatically that the "Dead Puerto Ricans / Who never knew they were Puerto Ricans" (Pietri,

*Puerto Rican* 2) can become "proud not ashamed / Of their Boricua names" (Pietri, "Spanglish")?

The poem itself alludes to two factors that enabled the historical development and sustenance of this community, both of which came out of the 1960s. Most obviously, Pietri himself is an emblem of the social, political, and cultural awakening of the 1960s and 1970s that was crucial to the establishment of both Latino/a identity and community. In Suzanne Oboler's book on the development of Latino/a as a panethnic category, she notes how "participation [in Sixties social struggles] served to unify Puerto Ricans and Mexican Americans/Chicanos and Chicanas within their respective movements and served to establish their respective collective and individual identities within the nation" (Oboler 44). In a chapter titled "'Establishing an Identity' in the Sixties," Oboler describes a dual process set in motion by these social currents. On the one hand, these nationalist affirmations promoted ethnic identification; at the same time, these movements created new spaces in the public sphere unavailable to previous generations by forcing their way into a broader mainstream consciousness.

This radical anticolonial tradition is widely accepted as giving energy to and shaping the emergence of the Latino/a community in the U.S. public sphere. In the book *Latinos, Inc.*, Arlene Dávila argues for another more controversial factor in this historical narrative. She points to the rise of a Hispanic advertising market in the 1960s, as the Civil Rights movement made corporate America aware of the existence of "Hispanics" as a group of potential consumers, as crucial in the formation of contemporary U.S. Latinidad. As she puts it, "In a context where nothing escapes commodification, commercial culture cannot be easily reduced to sheer pleasure or commercial manipulation, but must be considered as constitutive of contemporary identities and notions of belonging and entitlement" (Dávila, *Latinos* 10). For that reason, Spanish-language media, along with Hispanic-oriented programs, consumer products, and advertising, have become one of the most important vehicles through which Latino/a identity is imagined. For example, Dávila points to the move from locally autonomous affiliate Spanish-language television to the beginning in 1976 of Univisión's ability to broadcast one format to all its markets via satellite as one of the preconditions for the emergence of a pan-Latino/a ethnicity (25–26).

This Spanish-language advertising industry, according to Dávila, "has played a central role in raising Hispanics' visibility in public life" (86). When academic critics have acknowledged Spanish-language media and advertising as a factor in public awakening and world-building, however, they have positioned it as secondary in both importance and chronology, a less pure cause than the social movements. This is the narrative that Frances Aparicio outlines in explaining the birth of Latino/a studies in the academy: "Latino Studies developed as an academic field in the late 1960s and early 1970s and was triggered by the battles fought by minorities in the United States who sought to defend their civil rights" (Aparicio, "Latino" 4). Pedro Cabán similarly points to student takeovers of buildings in New York and California as the point of origin for academic units devoted to ethnic studies (Cabán 7). While we do not dispute the accuracy of this history, its repeated deployment is meant to reemphasize the field's anticolonial essence, recalling its roots as more purely resistant and oppositional than its current state. Cabán marks off the "formative stages of the field" as "late-1960s to mid-1980s" (14), while Aparicio argues that "in literature, as well as in the visual arts, popular music, and movies, the mainstreaming of Latinos within the dominant Anglo society has been clearly visible since the 1980s" (Aparicio, "Latino" 24). This narrative once again references the 1960s as the moment of authenticity, as opposed to the post-Sixties period as contaminated by commercialism.

Dávila's research shows that the market has not been of secondary importance for an emerging Latino/a consciousness, and that commercialization is as closely aligned to the Sixties social movements as the academy is: "Advertisers had been lobbying for the acknowledgement of a common Hispanic culture or identity since the 1960s, and this category became the legitimization of their claims and the springboard for the industry's rapid growth after the mid-1970s" (Dávila, Latinos 40). Her interviews show the self-image of many of these advertising executives as "playing a key role in challenging stereotypes and promoting a more sophisticated view of Hispanics, and with contributing to [Hispanics'] representation" (42). This is the same role that Pablo Gúzman, the Young Lords' Minister of Information, assumes in pointing specifically to gains in visibility and presence in the public sphere as the greatest accomplishments of his organization: "In 1969, when the Lords were coming up [...] there were no 'Kiss me, I'm Puerto Rican' buttons. Salsa concerts did not sell out Madison Square Garden [...] WCBS's Gloria Rojas and J. J. González were the only Latinos reporting local news on TV" (Gúzman 159). The executives of this "first generation of Hispanic [advertising] agencies in the mid 1960s and early 1970s" explicitly describe themselves as part of "larger social and political contexts of the times" (Dávila, Latinos 44), positioning themselves as yet another cultural wing of the Civil Rights movement. Furthermore, these executives credit their successes with being "proud not ashamed" of their heritage: Dávila notes that she heard "members of the first Hispanic marketing generation assert that they had created the market because they were not *acomplejados* (shamed and embarrassed by their identity)" (32).

The successes of the Sixties social movements, academic institutional change, and the growth of the advertising industry combined to create the category of Latino/a. Within the context of this complex history, "El Spanglish National Anthem" references these factors in positing a culturalist notion of U.S. Latinidad typical of post-Sixties Latino/a literature. This culturalist construction of identity and community is identified by Néstor García Canclini as characteristic of the postcolonial, postmodern condition:

> We live in a time of fractures and heterogeneity, of segmentations within each nation, and of fluid communication with transnational orders of information, fashion and knowledge. In the midst of this heterogeneity, we find codes that unite us, or at least permit us to understand each other. But those shared codes refer ever less to the ethnicity, class and nation into which we were born. Those old units, insofar as they endure, seem to be reformulated as *mobile pacts for the interpretation of* commodities and messages. The definition of a nation, for example, is given less at this stage by its territorial limits or its political history. It survives, rather, as an *interpretive community of consumers,* whose traditional—alimentary, linguistic— habits induce them to relate in a peculiar way with the objects and information that circulate in international networks. (García Canclini, *Consumers* 43)

In some moments, "El Spanglish National Anthem" still emphasizes what García Canclini sees as the essentialist modernist codes of race, class, and nation. As in "Puerto Rican Obituary," in the first stanzas of "El Spanglish National Anthem" there are objective economic conditions that form this community, not only as a motivation for emigration—the change in the price of bread—but also as one of the members' primary bonds. The subject finds community by looking for a neighborhood with "low rent," and the "everyone" of the poem is defined by the common condition of receiving welfare. Racial or national character, too, remains central in defining the community of "El Spanglish National Anthem," with the poem mentioning the concept of a "soul" that "nunca died" and a "spirit" that makes blood "thicker than Coca-Cola." But this emphasis on what García Canclini sees as the modernist biological notion of race or ethnicity is balanced by a notion of community based on a shared experience of racism, a "we" accustomed to being called "spicks," white trash, and "niggers" (Pietri, "Spanglish").

Overall, the poem maintains that a common culture is created as much as by a common experience as by heredity or economic circumstance. As the title suggests, language is the most obvious of these commonalities. This is a community built around Spanglish, distinguishing it from either Spanish-speaking puertorriqueños or the English-speaking U.S. mainstream. Formulations of national belonging, from Johann Gottfried von Herder's to Benedict Anderson's, always speak of language as primary to defining an imagined community. Language is a cultural sign that can be easily naturalized to indicate such absolute differences in character as to become almost biological markers of belonging. The failures that Carmen Whalen describes of the Young Lords' attempts to "return" to Puerto Rico to set up branches on the island in the 1970s are part of this history of Spanish- and Spanglish-speaking communities finding themselves unable to communicate across language differences (Whalen 118–19). At the same time, the emphasis on language is not necessarily exclusionary or chauvinistic. Spanglish is an interstitial language, clearly meant to evoke a transnational rather than national community intimately connected to both Puerto Rico and the United States. In contrast to the Young Lords' ventures of the 1970s, Pietri's triumphant return to the newly opened Nuyorican Café in San Juan during the winter of 2002 and his performance of "El Spanglish National Anthem" in this space, suggests that the poem offers the possibilities of new relationships between island and diaspora. Furthermore, this poem is *not* the Nuyorican National Anthem; a Spanglish anthem clearly extends beyond any one ethnic group to speak to Latino/as as a panethnicity.

If a community based on language nonetheless evokes modernist master narratives, "El Spanglish National Anthem" refers to a variety of even more spectral cultural practices. At these moments, the poem acknowledges that cultural practices, rather than appeals to blood or soul, make the subject part of a community. What the subject eats (rice and beans, cuchifrito), the games he plays (dominoes), the music he listens to (plena and mambo): all these practices of everyday life—what García Canclini refers to as cultural codes—mark him as part of El Barrio's "Latin Community." Furthermore, this is not some vague or traditionalist notion of "culture" as a static and inherited commonality. In a significant move away from the critique of commercialism in "Puerto Rican Obituary," the community in "El Spanglish National Anthem" depends on commodities. It is the places where the subject spends his money (botánicas and bodegas) and what he buys (Bustelo coffee) and doesn't buy (aspirin, Coca-Cola) that assert his identity and belonging. The availability of these Latino/a businesses and products reassure the poem's subject of his own presence and the presence of others like him. At the same time, these examples also may be proof of the penetration of the culture industry into all parts of everyday life and consciousness. The poem's construction of the originary homeland, for example, appears to be the Puerto Rico of tourist advertising, characterized in the song's moments of nostalgia as "Island blessed by the sun" and "Land of de palm trees."

"El Spanglish National Anthem" thus serves a double purpose as a postcolonial, post-Civil Rights Latino/a text. On the one hand, the poem celebrates the status of Latino/as in the United States and the gains that they have made; at the same time, it engages with and critiques the avenues through which those advances have been achieved and measured. These conflicting attitudes towards the past converge in the final stanzas, in which the poetic subject both embraces and rejects nostalgia. The vertiginous experience of transnational existence comes to an apex in this passage, in which home, return, and roots become impossible to untangle. This section invites at least two possible readings. First, there is the inevitable return that ends both "Puerto Rican Obituary" and the original version of the song, "En Mi Viejo San Juan." In this reading, when the aircraft is leaving New York City, the poem's subject is on it, headed back to his Viejo San Juan and knowing he will stay: "No return trips for me / Back to New York City." At the same time—if those two verses are read as distinct sentences—it is just as possible that the plane is taking off without him, and that it is the return to Puerto Rico that he realizes is impossible. In the second reading, he leaves the airport to head back to El Barrio, Manhattan becoming the "Island blessed by the sun" where his "roots are from." Either reading taken alone resolves the issue of nostalgia. In the first reading, the return home fulfills nostalgic desire; in the second reading, the demands of nostalgia are ultimately denied and refused. But the ambiguity between the two readings keeps this tension alive, making nostalgia something to be overcome even while it remains the source of the creativity that might allow such an overcoming.

The goal of anticolonialism is to let the dead bury the dead, to write an obituary for the colonized consciousness, and to move into a new stage of human existence. The lesson of postcoloniality is the impossibility of this total rupture; radically new men and women will always be embedded in and burdened by history. The romance of anticolonialism that David Scott describes in *Conscripts of Modernity* is its promise that a history of oppression will be overcome and redeemed through struggle. Even when that redemption seems to defy the logic of the text itself, as in "Puerto Rican Obituary," the poem ends by describing the utopia that can be achieved. "El Spanglish National Anthem" concludes by reaffirming commitment to the struggle, by refusing to give up struggling along with the belief that "One day we'll be free." But there are no guarantees. There is no sense that the struggle will end or that this goal will be achieved. This realism is a much less attractive offer than anticolonialism's promise that a better world is inevitable; it is hard to organize a politics around the idea that we may never reach a point where we can stop and look around and declare that our vision of utopia has been made a reality. But this is what "El Spanglish National Anthem" asks of us: continued belief, hope, and faith, no matter how impossible the dream of freedom may now appear.

In this chapter, we have outlined the anticolonial vision that characterizes Latino/a literature of the 1960s and 1970s. The post-Sixties writers that we examine in this book present a challenge to that vision, insisting on looking at the world through different lenses. The categories and concepts of anticolonialism are therefore ill-suited for engaging these new writers. As with music, entry into the market makes literature both more widely available and more beholden to corporate and mainstream interests. These forces certainly change the ways in which literature is produced, processed, and consumed. The desire to keep alive the goals of the anticolonial project should not lead us to refuse the challenge posed by the post-Sixties writers and to label them sellouts; if progressive readers give up on literature altogether, we will also miss the "moments of freedom" it can suggest. Comparing Pedro Pietri's "El Spanglish National Anthem" with works from the Civil Rights generation makes clear how the more recent poem both renews the anticolonial project and breaks away from it to suggest new alliances and possibilities. Each of these moves is important to keep in mind, as these contradictory impulses energize contemporary Latino/a writing.

In the next two chapters, we will look at the genre of ghetto fiction, the way in which it becomes positioned as the privileged bearer of the anticolonial worldview, and how post-Sixties Latino/a writers call into question the genre's political orientation. Chapter 2 examines how novels by Abraham Rodriguez and Ernesto Quiñonez deploy the conventions and discourse of ghetto fiction in order to explore the efficacy of the genre in a post-Sixties context. In the process, both novels directly and indirectly invoke the legacy of the anticolonial Civil Rights struggles. Rodriguez's *Spidertown* (1993) and Quiñonez's *Bodega Dreams* (2000) thus move the discussion into the post-Sixties ghetto in order to interrogate the continued purchase of anticolonialism for confronting contemporary struggles. At the same time, by writing ghetto fiction from an explicitly post-Civil Rights point of view, these novels call into question the identification of the genre as the privileged locus of an anticolonial politics, setting the stage for the work of Junot Díaz and Angie Cruz that will be the subject of chapter 3.

## CHAPTER 2

# MERCADO DREAMS
## THE END(S) OF SIXTIES NOSTALGIA
## IN CONTEMPORARY GHETTO FICTION

THE COMMITTED LITERARY CRITICISM DISCUSSED IN CHAPTER 1 laments
the apolitical turn in post-Sixties Latino/a fiction, as contemporary writers
move away from the Civil Rights narratives of Piri Thomas and Nicholasa
Mohr. These critics identify Thomas and Mohr, along with Nuyorican
poets like Pedro Pietri and Miguel Piñero, as the models for a politically
progressive literary field because of the anticolonial ideology those writers
embody. These writers have in common a particular sensibility—what we
will call a ghetto aesthetic—that enables them to protest the Nuyorican
condition and critique the hypocrisy associated with the American dream
from a political position with a particularly revolutionary ideology.
Chapters 2 and 3 will discuss the political contours of how contemporary
writers deploy ghetto fiction. According to critics like Lisa Sánchez
González in *Boricua Literature* (2001) and Juan Flores in *From Bomba to
Hip-Hop* (2000), Latino/a literature beginning in the 1990s—the most
frequent targets are the works of Esmeralda Santiago, Judith Ortiz Cofer,
Cristina Garcia, and Julia Alvarez—simply cannot live up to the anticolonial ideals of the Civil Rights generation. The post-Sixties writers
Sánchez González discusses are uniformly inadequate politically, for rea-
sons we will explore. For Flores, the one exception to this impoverish-
ment of the political imaginary among post-Sixties fiction is the work of
Abraham Rodriguez.

The first section of this chapter analyzes Rodriguez's first novel,
*Spidertown* (1993), in order to demonstrate how the author uses the genre
of ghetto fiction to highlight and debunk various levels of false consciousness in the New York Latino/a community. While Flores rightly

places Rodriguez within the genealogy of the ghetto aesthetic of the Sixties, our reading will argue that although aspects of *Spidertown* can be interpreted as reaffirming that tradition, its version of "realism" presents itself as a critique of the romantic basis for the progressive political project found in anticolonial writers. *Spidertown*'s deconstructive vision is relentless; we will show in this chapter's second section that the novel ultimately refuses all bonds of community and solidarity, rendering suspect even the ideology of anticolonialism or the generic possibilities of a politically committed ghetto fiction. Without a positive or constructive alternative, *Spidertown* threatens to leave us in a post-Civil Rights and postcolonial abyss.

To find a way through this impasse, the second half of the chapter turns to another post-Sixties rendition of ghetto fiction, Ernesto Quiñonez's *Bodega Dreams* (2000), which ruminates on a positive vision that might be attached to Rodriguez's negative, deconstructive one. As the chapter's third section will explain, the novel offers a renewal of the dreams of the 1960s as one possibility through the resurrection of the Young Lords in the figure of Willie Bodega. Yet the novel eventually judges that sort of backward-looking political project too romantic for our tragic times. In the final section of the chapter, we look at the ways in which *Bodega Dreams* questions the relationship of the market to a ghetto-centric artistic and political project through characters with such suggestive names as Willie Bodega and Julio Mercado, as an alternative to a complete withdrawal from or rejection of market values. *Spidertown* and *Bodega Dreams,* in their renditions of a post-Sixties ghetto fiction, open up new perspectives for looking back on the Latino-Caribbean literary tradition in New York, as well as new vantage points for imagining the political horizons of the future.

### GHETTO FICTION AND THE AMERICAN DREAM

Both Sánchez González and Flores praise the writers of the Sixties for their refusal to frame their stories as narratives of upward mobility and their insistence on chronicling the realities of ghetto life. The critics identify this sort of ghetto fiction as the truly politically committed genre for a variety of reasons: it takes as its subject the popular subaltern masses; it represents the struggles of these everyday people; and it depicts the system against which they struggle as a cruel and unjust form of domination. The genre's main political value, then, comes from its effective deconstruction of the American dream as a form of false consciousness, the promise of a happy ending through hard work and obedience. Sánchez González locates the political possibility of this literature in its identification of the structural inequalities built into capitalism and its intense descriptions of the plight of those cast off or left behind by this system. She points to the historical context of the Cold War, with the United States promoting an image of itself as a beacon of democratic ideals and opportunity for all, as the reason that protests from internally colonized populations resonated so loudly during the 1950s and 1960s. She labels "Boricua civil rights-era novels" as "a paperback challenge to the fantastic fictions of American democracy and racial equality" because of how effectively they portray a Nuyorican experience of poverty, struggle, racism, and constricted horizons of hope (Sánchez González 105).

According to Sánchez González, the protagonists of both *Down These Mean Streets* and *Nilda* give "realist renditions of situations they experience," while "visible around and underneath these situations is a palimpsest of larger antagonistic forces, including racism, colonialism, poverty, sexism, and other problems that arise as Puerto Rican youths attempt to make sense of themselves in a society and in institutions that actively refuse to accommodate them" (107). This interplay between strictly realist descriptions of conditions and reference to broader social, economic, and political causes is what defines political ghetto fiction. At the same time, these novels provide more than simple naturalistic descriptions of exploitation— they show the growth of Piri and Nilda within and in spite of these circumstances, "less the 'coming of age' often associated with the *bildungsroman* than particular ways of coming to consciousness" (105).

To make this argument, Sánchez González must insist that these narratives are not the story of an individual—instead, she argues for reading these texts as "the diaspora's coming to consciousness as a distinct community of color" (132). It is equally important to her argument that these narratives show the world as mutable and subject to human intervention. The genre "portrays social context not as a given, static set of conditions, but rather as a contradictory and flexible situation in which characters not only can but must create new models of social agency" (106). These two characteristics distinguish Thomas and Mohr from the corrupted post-Sixties form of ghetto fiction, "unimaginative reiterations of the popular 'gang-banger' novel" that Sánchez González blames on "the U.S. publishing industry learn[ing] to profit from civil rights-era texts that could be advertised as 'ghetto' testimonials" (134). According to this point of view, Rodriguez's *Spidertown* and Quiñonez's *Bodega Dreams*, as contemporary examples of ghetto fiction, are mere renditions of this "gang-banger" subtype. We suggest, however, that far from being formulaic and unoriginal, these two novels deploy that generic model self-reflexively in order to critique its limits.

In "Life Off the Hyphen," Flores shares many of Sánchez González's concerns, revealing his preference for ghetto fiction by heavily criticizing what he considers its opposite—a recently emerging "Pulitzer-eligible Latino literature" that he defines as "a literature by U.S. Latinos that is compatible with the prescribed 'wholesomeness' of American life, a literature that, with all its play on cultural differences, matches up convincingly to the 'standards of American manners and manhood'" (Flores, *From Bomba* 169–70). In focusing on the experience of suburban middle- and upper-class Latino/as, these stories of upward mobility court a wider, whiter readership by providing a palatable and unthreatening Latino/a experience, and thereby contribute to the possible "demise of the idea of Latino culture as resistance" (173). To be resistant and oppositional, true ghetto fiction must offend mainstream sensibilities, and in so doing make what this formulation assumes to be its affluent outside readers a bit uncomfortable by confronting them with the overwhelming violence and claustrophobia of the inner-city streets.

Although Flores sees this sanitized literature overtaking ghetto fiction in terms of visibility and becoming a new canon, he identifies as the exception Abraham Rodriguez, the post-Sixties Latino writer whose work most explicitly "return[s] in the 1990s to the 'mean streets' of inner-city Puerto Rican life first fictionalized by Piri Thomas in his 1967 autobiographical novel *Down These Mean Streets*" (180). Rodriguez's first novel, *Spidertown*, occupies "social turf staked out by Piri Thomas," deploying a "style reminiscent of the familiar cadences of poets like Pedro Pietri and Victor Hernández Cruz" to present "the sense of entrapment and alienation of the social experience" typical of earlier Nuyorican literature (181–82). In these comments, Flores indicates that both in genre and in spirit, Rodriguez is carrying forward the anticolonial tradition of the Civil Rights generation into the post-Sixties period. We will argue, on the other hand, that while Rodriguez certainly connects with this tradition, his relationship to it is deeply conflicted as he offers a seriously critical vision of ghetto fiction's political potential.

In Flores's reading, what allows *Spidertown* to avoid the "assimilationist proclivities" of Rodriguez's peers and revive the spirit of *Down These Mean Streets* is its recognition of upward mobility as an illusion and its refusal to buy into that script: "Time and again we are reminded that [*Spidertown*] is a world modeled after the American Dream, that it follows the rules of capitalist society. But at the same time, it is a bitter abortion of that dream, a 'business' lacking in any real social power or recognition" (180). *Spidertown* certainly makes clear how the logic of capitalism has penetrated every aspect of these characters' lives and presents a serious challenge to their humanity. One character defines a friendship by saying "sometimes you can say our business functions interact" (Rodriguez, *Spidertown* 14); romantic entanglements, meanwhile, are so commodified that the narrator states that "sex was just another deal, another transaction, something that was available as long as your pocket bulged with money" (16). Within this commodified context, the novel's opening scene takes on symbolic weight as an assault on the logic of the capitalist market and its institutions of social reproduction: *Spidertown*'s first story describes the protagonist's best friend, Firebug, setting fire to his classmate, the provocatively named Anna Mercado, in the middle of science class, capturing the careless sexist violence in these boys' senseless and misplaced rebellion against what they cannot have. But just as this early incident encapsulates the violence that *Spidertown* harbors against mainstream American institutions and values, Sánchez González's and Flores's readings of ghetto fiction's political commitment downplay the genre's ambivalence toward the seductions of capitalism and these novels' conflicted relationship with anticolonial solutions.

Through its protagonist, Miguel, *Spidertown* repeatedly identifies the American dream as a form of false consciousness, promising material fulfillment in return for docile obedience: "Miguel was the one with the American dream, of making it to the top honestly and cleanly. It was a stupid dream and he had no reason to even hope for it. Inside he felt like the American dream was a lie. No spick kid was going to make it that way" (185). More than Firebug or his boss, Spider, Miguel wants to believe that he can succeed within the system. The experience of the postindustrial ghetto's disappearing opportunities, though, has taught him that the rules of the game make it not worth playing. He therefore chooses to opt out of that ideology, dropping out of school, moving away from his family, and following Firebug and Spider into life as a hustler.

Miguel sees Spider as offering an alternative, an avenue to a kind of success that going to school or getting a legitimate job cannot provide. Spider encourages Miguel and others to reject participation in the mainstream in order to join him in his fight against that unjust social order. His rhetoric explicitly figures his project as a better way of fulfilling the seemingly impossible promise of achievement and material comfort:

> It was a negation of THE AMERICAN DREAM or maybe a twisting around of
> it, like Spider was always "speechifying." "This is an American Dream idea
> I bet they didn't think about," he would drawl with his eyebrows flying up
> and down. Miguel learned he didn't need THEM. They could shove their
> schools and the 9-to-5 life, the work-hard-it-pays-off life, the read-a-book-
> and-get-ahead universe. (275)

In these instances, Spider articulates his own rags-to-riches success as the
perverse realization of Horatio Alger's promise; Spider suggests that
young Latino/as can pull themselves up out of poverty and get what they
want, but only through joining his drug-dealing empire.

More frequently, Spider sees himself not just as an ironic fulfillment
of the American dream but also as a direct attack upon the capitalist system: "He saw it as a kind of revolution. Pretty soon, he'd suit up like
Che and head for other cities, to spread his operation out, to use the
same principles that have worked so well here" (67). In adopting anticolonial language and the imagery of revolution, Spider suggests that an
ideology lies behind his actions. Like the critics who see in ghetto fiction an anticapitalist proletarian energy directed against inequality and
oppression, Spider implies that he is not only offering employment to
young men from the ghetto but also channeling their violence toward a
reorganization of society: "Are poor people wrong to get money any way
they can? THE WORLD IS A LOCKED DOOR. Ain't this a war? It's a god-
damn people's revolution!" (68).

Despite this utopian impulse, though, Spider proves to be all talk, his
project circumscribed by its adherence to precisely the same aspirations as
the system he sees himself confronting. Far from offering an alternative,
he can envision achievement and articulate his desires only along the
same lines as the social order he wants to challenge: "The idea [...] is to
inculcate in the youth the idea that they too can have big cars and guns
[...] It's my job to open the world to them, to introduce them to the concept of business, free enterprise" (67). Unable to imagine any measure of
success other than material excess, Spider can promise gold chains and a
pimped-out car, but as Miguel realizes, Spider can't promise a way out of
a dead-end life. As our second section will discuss, *Spidertown*, as an
example of post-Sixties ghetto fiction, comes to the conclusion that rather
than representing a negation of the American dream or a revolutionary
assault upon it, Spider's romantic idea of rebellion proves to be seduced
and conditioned by it.

## GHETTO FICTION AND FALSE CONSCIOUSNESS

One of *Spidertown*'s major concerns, then, is with the ways in which economic desires undermine the possibility of a progressive ghetto-centric political project. In *Boricua Literature*, Sánchez González is equally suspicious of commercialism's effect on the potential for oppositionality, locating the entry of economic considerations into Latino/a literature in the post-Sixties period. She mounts her attack on the corrosive effects of commodification on Latino/a literature by lamenting that "the important literature of protest from the late 1960s and early 1970s has disappeared from the shelves, as classic texts such as Pedro Pietri's *Puerto Rican Obituary* (1973) and Piri Thomas's *Savior, Savior, Hold My Hand* (1972) have gone out of print" (Sánchez González 135). This observation opens a chapter about "three women's texts," by Judith Ortiz Cofer, Esmeralda Santiago, and Carmen de Monteflores. The implication is clear: the publishing industry and its multinational corporate masters who have gotten involved in Latino/a literature reward writers whose easily digestible fiction promotes a capitalist, assimilationist, and pro-United States agenda, while tacitly censoring truly resistant work with the excuse that it is less viable commercially. In Sánchez González's words, "It is as if [Boricua] literature's narrative politics have migrated toward the conservative epistemological center in tandem with its academic and industrial institutionalization [...] Some of the texts enjoying the widest audience are outright reactionary and self-aggrandizing" (135).

The choice of Thomas's *Savior, Savior, Hold My Hand* as an example of the marginalization of politically oppositional literature raises an obvious question: why has the other half of Thomas's ghetto memoir, *Down These Mean Streets*, become in Thomas's own words "a classic of its kind" that has been "in print since [1967]" and was recently republished in a special thirtieth anniversary edition (Thomas, *Down* 333)?[1] Sánchez González indicates that Thomas's ghetto fiction is too "raw" for the market to easily digest; however, the continued acceptance and canonization of *Down These Mean Streets* seems to show that even the "enunciation of dissent" (Sánchez González 105) can be welcomed by the market and turned into a commodity. We suggest that reading Thomas's two works together from a post-Sixties perspective informed by works like *Spidertown* makes clear that it is precisely the radical alterity of *Down These Mean Streets* that accounts for its enduring popularity over *Savior, Savior, Hold My Hand*'s less confrontational political orientation. The stable marriage, the religious awakening, and the short-lived house in Long Island which form the plot of the latter work are less dangerous, more familiar, and apparently less compelling to readers than the "rage, confusion and vio-lence" of *Down These Mean Streets* (Sánchez González 107).

The rethinking of Latino/a urban politics in *Savior, Savior, Hold My Hand* has its aesthetic parallel in its different relationship towards lan-guage. Sánchez González identifies Thomas's use of nonstandard English and Spanish without translation as part of his most radical challenge to literary standards. Unlike the writers of the 1990s, she argues, *Down These Mean Streets* does nothing to make outsiders feel at home in the ghetto. This observation may be true, but extending this logic to *Savior, Savior, Hold My Hand* suggests that its linguistic politics are much less confrontational. In contrast to *Down These Mean Streets*, *Savior, Savior, Hold My Hand* makes liberal use of translation, often quite obtrusively providing an English gloss in parentheses after words or phrases whose meanings are frequently obvious or completely unnecessary to under-standing the sentence: for example, "I could smell the rice and beans and frying chuletas (pork chops)" (Thomas, *Savior* 16). Furthermore, the pro-fanity which so dramatically assaults the reader in *Down These Mean Streets* as part of the project of "disregard[ing] the standardization of English [...] to create narrators and characters who speak and signify completely in Boricua and other urban vernaculars" (Sánchez González 107), has been cleaned up and replaced in many instances with euphemistic self-censorship. Such usages as, "Yeah but it beats a *blank*, better than being locked up" (Thomas, *Savior* 9, emphasis added) or, "This one couldn't be a *blank*—it hadda be for real" (75, emphasis added), show a general tendency in *Savior, Savior, Hold My Hand* away from the rawness that gave *Down These Mean Streets* so much force.

In fact, as these linguistic politics suggest, the move from *Down These Mean Streets* to *Savior, Savior, Hold My Hand* is premised on a disavowal of the former work's glamorization of ghetto life as an assault on main-stream values. The last scene of *Down These Mean Streets* finds young Carlito shooting up with heroin while Piri wistfully looks on; the work ends with Piri declaring that he is clean even as he nostalgically remem-bers this earlier strung-out version of himself. Unlike *Savior, Savior, Hold My Hand*, the primary authorial energy in *Down These Mean Streets* is invested in accounts of heroin addiction, armed robbery, gang violence, and ultimately prison, making the author and his readers appear to be equally fascinated by this descent into the hell of the ghetto. Although the author's vision of political consciousness forces him to renounce his previous life, the writing of *Down These Mean Streets* fea-tures above all else a recreation and glorification of his bad boy persona. The young Piri is depicted as cool and dangerous, an outsider whose very

way of being—clothes, speech, and actions—marks a protest against
poverty and injustice. The trajectory of the text plots Piri's overcoming of
this earlier self, but the weight of the narrative leans more toward
recounting young Piri's exploits than exploring his saved self.[2]

*Savior, Savior, Hold My Hand* completes the story of salvation, narrating the way in which Piri escapes the dead end of drugs, crime, and
violence that defined his youth. As such, the story begins by leaving
Carlito and his heroin abuse behind, literally opening as Piri exits the
apartment where *Down These Mean Streets* ended. As he leaves, he is
struck by the thought that perhaps Carlito's emulation of Piri has led to
his drug addiction. The novel opens: "I cut down Lexington Avenue. I
couldn't help bouncing Carlito inside my head. [...] *had he copied using
drugs from me? My God, I hoped to hell it wasn't from me*" (Thomas, *Savior*
1, emphasis in original). Piri knows that it is not only his drug abuse but
also his entire bad boy persona that Carlito is imitating. *Savior, Savior,
Hold My Hand* thus begins by rethinking his depiction of street life in
*Down These Mean Streets*. That work's desire to create a resistant and
oppositional subjectivity, whose drug abuse and criminal activity are part
of a larger political consciousness premised on the rejection of mainstream laws and mores, feeds into the glamorization and selling of that life
not only to an insider like Carlito, but also to a wider reading public.
Despite Sánchez González's assertion that the publishing industry has
ignored Thomas because he is too revolutionary, the fact that *Down
These Mean Streets* has stayed in print for almost four decades must be
closely linked to the continuing appeal of its confrontational anticolonial
stance. The everyday politics Thomas relates in *Savior, Savior, Hold My
Hand,* of neighborhood outreach programs aimed at keeping kids out of
gangs, meanwhile, has proven less compelling to the publishing industry
and academic critics alike.[3]

On one level, the protagonists of Rodriguez's *Spidertown* and Quiñonez's
*Bodega Dreams* are present-day Carlitos, the next generation following in
Piri's footsteps and retracing the path of *Down These Mean Streets*. At the
same time, Rodriguez finds himself in an authorial position much like
Thomas's: each author is excited and energized by the counterculture he
chronicles, even though each ultimately adopts a critical view of what
he eventually decides is false consciousness. Part of ghetto fiction's political appeal comes from the way in which the gang-banger refuses to
conform to an unjust rule of law or accept a social ladder that admits him
only to its lowest rung. But for Miguel, refusal to conform is finally not
enough. He comes to see his life and his rebellions as too easily turned into
performances for an outside world. He sees himself, his environment, and

his experience all over the mass media, a drama consumed by an audience of outsiders: "The crime shows on TV bored him. Watching people get drilled like that just didn't excite him anymore. He was living it. Only fools in the suburbs dug that" (Rodriguez, *Spidertown* 198).

This is the audience that Spider ultimately seeks in insisting that Miguel write his life story. He tells Miguel, "You should write about somebody real amazin', a real amazin' kinda life [...] mines is a million-dolla' story" (62). Although Flores complains that Puerto Ricans in the United States are "bereft [...] of cultural capital" (Flores, *From Bomba* 184), meaning cultural institutions and structures of support, Spider recognizes that ghetto fiction is a form of symbolic capital, and that by deploying stereotypes of ghetto life, the writer can quickly turn this symbolic capital into mainstream success. But Miguel refuses to play along, replying "I don't write, man. It was just some dream" (Rodriguez, *Spidertown* 62). By dismissing writing as a "dead dream," Miguel suggests that romanticizing ghetto fiction turns it into another fantasy. Ghetto fiction, like the voyeuristic television programs Miguel criticizes, allows "fools in the suburbs" to look at neighborhoods that both scare and fascinate them from a comfortable distance. As the canonization of *Down These Mean Streets* suggests, rather than overturning mainstream sensibilities, ghetto fiction may reinforce power structures depending on how it is read and processed—once again emphasizing that neither author nor market has complete control over interpretive practices or the meaning of a work.

While *Spidertown* unveils the American dream as a form of deception, the novel ultimately is unwilling to accept the glorification of Spider's rebellion against it as anything but another level of false consciousness. Spider may have physical strength and the ability to organize the young men of the ghetto into an army ready to die for him, but he cannot offer them any positive ideology other than an overtly capitalist materialism. Amelia literally names his attitude as "self-deception": "We get some money an' it buys us VCRs an' stereos an' gold chains an' we drive through the streets shooting at each other like we're big bad successful men. But it's a trap. White people couldn't a' come up with a better way to screw up blacks an' Latinos" (81). Amelia sees that Spider is not so much the negation of the American dream as its flip side, his illicit economy and uncivil society created by the same aspirations as their legitimate counterparts and circumscribed by the same horizons.

This insight is a second stage of awakening for Miguel, from the unveiling of the hollowness of the American dream to the recognition of the ideological poverty of Spider's "revolution." In this awareness Miguel eventually perceives the futility of this form of revolt. Rather than a larger-than-life hero, he finally comes to regard Spider as a small and powerless insect:

> Spider had made him feel like he was a master of his own universe. Too bad that Miguel had come to realize that in a sense they were all roaches, ruling their little kingdom under the kitchen sink, content to devour crumbs until the fucken bastids came in and turned on the lights—then it was mad scurry time. Roaches. Ruling their under-sink world. Happy to feed on crumbs. Until that huge slipper comes down. (275)

Although Miguel may have a sense of power driving around in his "Baby," and think that he has found a way of circumventing the system to get what he wants, he ultimately realizes that this sense is illusory, his power contingent, and his rebellion always already contained: "You can be a big man on Fox Street, but once you head downtown you're just another ugly spick kid" (80).

The last section of the novel repeatedly returns to the themes of consciousness and self-deception, of Miguel's ghetto life as fantasy and of his gradual acceptance of reality. His stepfather, Melo, makes precisely this distinction, telling Miguel that if he chooses to move home, "Your old life will effectively be over, almost as if you had woken up from some fantasy. Now comes reality" (237). The reality, according to Melo, is that Miguel is a sixteen-year-old who should live with his mother and return to high school. At this point in the novel, this life sounds to Miguel too much like the "work-hard-it-pays-off life, the read-a-book-and-get-ahead universe" (275). By the end, however, Amelia finally convinces him that choosing such a life doesn't make him a sellout. As a drug runner, "you didn't have no life," she tells him, "That shit you were in…that WE were in, that wasn't life. THIS is life, Miguel, look around'ju. People strugglin' to make it without havin'na deal rocks [...] I think you'll have to be realistic" (305). Despite the contention that social realism keeps it real—in contrast to magical realism, which we will discuss in the next chapter—Amelia suggests that ghetto fiction is simply not realistic. To be realistic is to resist romanticizing outlaws rising up against the system and to focus instead on the everyday struggles of everyone else to find ways to cope with or change the system from within.

Finally, however, *Spidertown* appears to deny the possibility of progressive politics in the context of the ghetto, adopting a vision that has frequently been called nihilistic by commentators on African American culture.[4] The powers that be are simply too large and too remote to be challenged directly—"It was all bigger than any of them [...] They were tiny pins on a map" (288)—and people like Miguel seem to be left with the choice of either futile acting out or resigned accommodation. The novel ends with Miguel choosing to give up the first option, the gangster life he has lived to that point. Joined by his two love interests, Amelia and Cristalena, he sets fire to his car; this destruction of a marker of material success becomes a purification ritual signaling the end of his affiliation with Spider's gang and adherence to Spider's dream. The final lines of the novel stress the extreme atomization of this moment: "There were no more posses in his world. There was only the three of them, walking away from it" (323). Unlike Piri's move from an isolating street life to a more satisfying life as a neighborhood activist, Miguel's community in these final lines is virtually nuclear; only the bonds of heterosexual love are possible in the quasi-nuclear family that Miguel, Cristalena, and Amelia will form. Solidarity, revolution, or anything else that might offer hope within this novel appears only as various levels of false consciousness.

### GHETTO FICTION AND SIXTIES DREAMS

*Bodega Dreams* bears much in common with *Spidertown,* beginning with its interest in dreams as true or false consciousness. Strictly in terms of plot structure, the two novels are virtually parallel. In both cases, the sensitive and somewhat artistic protagonists (Chino and Miguel respectively) find themselves seduced by the dangers and pleasures of street life, represented by their small-time thug best friends (Sapo and Firebug) as well as the larger-than-life drug dealers who run their neighborhoods (Bodega and Spider). At the same time, the women in their lives (Blanca and Cristalena), too pure for street life and upwardly mobile in their aspirations, are primary forces in inspiring the leading men to get away from their homosocial life and "go straight." The pull of these contradictory forces generates each novel's dramatic conflict, as the protagonists try to find ways to either battle against or accommodate to an overwhelmingly powerful system. As avid readers, both Chino and Miguel run across possible philosophical frameworks for understanding their plight: in one parallel example, Amelia is constantly recommending that Miguel read Jean-Paul Sartre (Rodriguez, *Spidertown* 28) and describes herself as an "existentialist exercising her right to self-destruct, to plan an exit" (20), while Chino turns in one of his darkest moments to reading Albert Camus's *The Stranger* (Quiñonez 183). But ultimately, it is outside their books, and in the streets, that each young man must come to terms with his world.

As we have seen in *Spidertown, Bodega Dreams* makes an obvious critique of the hypocrisy and seedy underside of the American dream. Chino never turns to drug dealing, choosing instead to marry and stay in school. He contrasts his choices with the lure of the fast life that Sapo leads: "I had enrolled at school thinking about other ways to come out on top, ways that didn't hurt anybody and weren't as dangerous. Graduate, get a good job, save, buy a house" (160). While these are the choices Chino makes, he admits that the avenues he has chosen "held no guarantees of success just because they were legal" (160). Indeed, Chino regards both of these choices, his and Sapo's, as "gambles, rolls of the dice" (160); the American dream is ultimately less a matter of investment than a lottery, the numbers game Pedro Pietri describes in both of the poems discussed in our first chapter.

While Chino narrates the novel, Willie Bodega emerges as the central focus, a compelling spokesman for extralegal options. He has chosen to be a hustler and take whatever he can get, and he too explains his choices in terms of the American dream: "Joe Kennedy was no different from me. He already had enough money in the twenties but he still became a rum-runner. Alcohol is a drug, right? Kennedy sold enough booze to kill a herd of rhinos. Made enough money from that to launch other, legal schemes. Years later he fucken bought his kids the White House" (25–26). As Spider does in his speeches, Bodega justifies his illegal activities as different from legitimate businesses only because a racist legal system has labeled them differently.[5] Bodega insists on getting his share of "the spoils of the father," stating that "this country is ours as much as it is theirs" (26). In equating himself with Joe Kennedy, Bodega identifies himself as a true and patriotic American, like the Puerto Ricans he mentions who died in World War II. As he sees it, the American dream owes him because, as the title of the first section puts it, "men who built this country were men from the streets."

Despite Spider's best efforts to find an ideological justification for his activities, he never succeeds in convincing Miguel that he is anything more than a drug dealer out to make a buck. Bodega, by contrast, finds a much more compelling discursive justification for his actions. Although the characters in *Bodega Dreams* find themselves confronting the same dead ends that *Spidertown* so effectively outlines, the novel tries to move past the point of despair that Miguel has reached. Quiñonez's novel offers Bodega as an alternative, a source of hope because of the way that he manages to link the ghetto's violence, rage, and frustration to an ideological project, suggesting how everyday resistance might translate into political practice. Chino sees him as an incarnation of hope: "Now I realize that's what attracted me to Willie Bodega. Willie Bodega didn't just change me and Blanca's life, but the entire landscape of the neighborhood.

Bodega would go down as a representation of all the ugliness in Spanish Harlem and also all the good it was capable of being" (14).

Bodega's difference from Spider comes in part from the fact that the Spanish Harlem of the 1990s is a fundamentally different ghetto from the South Bronx of the 1980s. The problem in *Bodega Dreams* is less urban blight than incipient gentrification; as one character puts it, "This neighborhood will be lost unless we make it ours. Look at Loisaida, that's gone" (106). The solution can thus be proposed that "if we build a strong professional class and accumulate property, we can counter that effect [...] It'll take some time. But one day we might be strong enough, with enough political clout [...] to knock those projects down [...] And we'll free our island, without bloodshed" (106). With this project in mind, it is possible for Chino to identify Bodega as the "spirit of the age" for a neighborhood and a community that the characters believe can still be saved:

> Unlike Blanca, I believed it was dishonest people that brought change. It was paradoxical people like Bodega who started revolutions [...] Spanish Harlem needed a change and fast [...] The neighborhood was ready to boil. You couldn't see the bubbles yet, but they were there, simmering below the surface, just waiting for someone to turn up the heat and all hell would break loose. The fire next time would be the fire this time. (38)

Yet what this revolution entails is specific to the postindustrial New York of *Bodega Dreams*. In a city from which industry has fled, acquiring the means of production is not imagined as seizing factories as a vehicle for redistribution, but instead acquiring the most valuable contemporary resource for the production of wealth: Manhattan real estate.

In this way, *Bodega Dreams* takes the unharnessed energy against the system depicted in *Spidertown*, whose characters can aspire only to individual material excess, and gives form to a positive social project that could provide a progressive goal for this oppositional sentiment.[6] From the beginning, both novels identify the primary obstacle as a lack of imagination, an inability of the protagonists to see how things could be different or how social and political transformation is possible. Because Bodega refuses to succumb to this lack of vision, he labels himself "a throwback"; Chino calls him a "lost relic from a time when all things seemed possible" (31), a time explicitly identified with Bodega's history as a former Young Lord named William Irizarry. Although Chino thus locates that moment of possibility in the past, he is inspired by Bodega's ability to have "somehow brought that hope to my time" (31). Bodega preaches and practices the Sixties ideology of community uplift by any means necessary—in this case participating in the illicit economy of the drug trade in order to buy and renovate buildings from the city to house his neighbors: "Bodega didn't just believe it, he was actually practicing it. He had learned from the past and knew change couldn't just come from free love, peace, and brotherhood. Extreme measures would have to be taken, and all you could hope for was that the good would outweigh the bad" (31). While Spider ironically appropriates the imagery of revolution to describe his criminality, Willie Bodega's past gives his project an ideological content, allowing him to talk the talk and convince Chino that he may actually have an answer.

While *Bodega Dreams* constantly refers back to a past of lost possibilities, *Spidertown* remains entirely tied to the present. Miguel dismisses the dreams of the Sixties as another panacea, a fantasy having nothing to do with his current life. While this evaluation of the Sixties is made only obliquely in *Spidertown,* Rodriguez engages the theme quite explicitly in one of his first short stories, "The Boy Without a Flag" (1992). In that story, the unnamed first-person narrator tries to come to terms with an older anticolonial generation represented by his father, a "frustrated poet" who reminds his son that "all this country does is abuse Hispanic nations" (Rodriguez, *Boy* 14), and his teacher, Miss Colon, who brings her dashiki-clad husband to class to talk "about protest marches, the sixties, the importance of an education" (12). The narrator finds only discouragement when he tries to inhabit this legacy. First, when he gives his father the plays, novels and biographies he has been writing, the "frustrated poet" generally ignores his efforts and finally tells him that "you have to find something serious to do with your life" (16). Later, when the narrator takes the small step of civil disobedience in refusing to say the Pledge of Allegiance at school, neither his teacher nor his father side with him. Their rhetoric appears completely out of touch with his actions: the father constantly lectures his son about "Juan Bosch and Allende" (14) and forces him to read Albizu Campos, while Miss Colon tells the narrator toward the end of the story to "go home and listen to the Beatles" (29). The adults' vision of the meaning of the Sixties has become completely ossified, fixing social protest and political commitment around symbols that have been emptied of all content, and preventing parent and teacher from seeing and supporting the narrator's own creative interpretations of that tradition.

From "The Boy Without a Flag" to *Spidertown,* the figure of the father is transformed into the stepfather who suggests that Miguel read Pablo Neruda and encourages a vague sort of Latin pride even while appearing to be somewhat prudish and conservative about his stepson's behavior. This distancing from the filial relationship and the demands that blood entails reflects the novel's move away from the tentative allegiances and inheritances set up in the short story. *Spidertown* consistently identifies the social breakdown in the South Bronx of the 1980s as the fault of that older generation and their inability to provide stable families and economic opportunities for their children.[7] Rejection of the Sixties appears most overtly in Amelia's complaint about what she sees as the hypocrisy and sexism of that brand of radical nationalism. Rodriguez focuses his attack on Amelia's former boyfriend, who "was big on Latin culture [...] always talking about Betances, Albizu Campos," but who, she later finds, "wanted a woman who could devote herself to a man, kids, family" (Rodriguez, *Spidertown* 140).[8]

While the critique articulated in *Spidertown* contains little of the nuance or sympathy we see in "The Boy Without a Flag," *Bodega Dreams* has a much more conflicted relationship with the legacy of the 1960s, refusing to reject it entirely but insisting on interrogating its relevance today. Quiñonez explicitly invokes three major Nuyorican literary works of the Civil Rights generation that engage the legacies of the American dream and its anticolonial critique: first, *Down These Mean Streets*, through its cover photograph of a New York street scene and the chapter titled "My Growing Up and All That Piri Thomas Kinda Crap"; second, Pedro Pietri's "Puerto Rican Obituary" (1973), which provides epigraphs for the first two sections; and third, Miguel Piñero's "La Bodega Sold Dreams" (1980), which serves as the inspiration for the novel's title as well as the epigraph of the final section.[9]

Of these intertexts, Piñero's self-conflicted poem bears the most important and most complicated relationship to *Bodega Dreams*. As a meditation on the poet's position in relation to the public and the market, "La Bodega Sold Dreams" contains two apparently paradoxical sentiments. The poem begins by expressing the anticolonial ideal of the poet as a cultural combatant, awakening "those asleep" and leading them forward by creating "strong and powerful" poems that can serve as weapons to deconstruct and destroy the edifices of the "minds weak" from colonized consciousnesses:

> dreamt i was a poet
> &
> writin' silver sailin' songs
> words
> strong & powerful crashin' thru
> walls of steel & concrete

erected in minds weak
&
those asleep
replacin' a hobby of paper candy
wrappin', collectin'
potent to pregnate sterile young
thoughts (Piñero 5)

In this opening stanza, Piñero, like Pietri in "Puerto Rican Obituary," identifies empty commodities—"paper candy wrappin'"—as those things that stand in the way of consciousness and must be impregnated by the poet's "potent" words. Instead of selling false goods—the "make-believe steak / and bullet-proof rice and beans" (Pietri, *Puerto Rican* 2) that Quiñonez borrows from Pietri for his first epigraph—Piñero dreams of bodegas that sell something more real and necessary for the people, the "silver sailin' songs" (Piñero 5) that could provide them with sustenance and implant in their "sterile" minds some positive vision of the future.

Yet the second stanza, which makes up the bulk of the poem, turns quickly from the optimism of this first stanza to a darker pessimism. Piñero continues:

i dreamt i was this poeta
words glitterin' brite & bold
strikin' a new rush for gold
in las bodegas
where our poets' words & songs
are sung
but
sunlite stealin' thru venetian
blinds
eyes hatin', workin' off time
clock sweatin'
&
swearin'
&
slavin'
for the final dime
runnin' a maze
a token ride
perspiration insultin' poets'
pride
words stoppin' on red
goin' on green

> poets' dreams
> endin' in a factoria as one in a million
> unseen
> buyin' bodega sold dreams (5–6)

In the first stanza, the poet's entry into the marketplace of the bodega allows him to reach out to the public with cultural commodities that offer people hope: he can use the market to disseminate dreams. In the latter half of the poem, the poetic subject, the "i" of the first half, disappears; the ideal of a proletarian poet whose labor makes him one of the "unseen" people may appear as a casting off of the artistic aura, just as in the essay "The Author as Producer," Walter Benjamin talks about replacing the romantic conception of the author as creative genius with the idea of writing as labor. At the same time, though, by entering the market the poet is subjected to the laws of instrumentality, his words now "stoppin' on red / goin' on green." The poem as commodity goes from being the beautiful "silver sailin' song" to the false "glitterin' [...] new rush for gold" that the bodega will sell—not to benefit the people but to turn a profit for itself.

Quiñonez chooses this transitional passage of "La Bodega Sold Dreams" as an epigraph for the third section of *Bodega Dreams*, focusing on the lines balanced between the anticolonial optimism of the first stanza and the postcolonial cynicism of the second. The epigraph reads:

> i dreamt i was this poeta
> words glitterin' brite & bold
> strikin' a new rush for gold
> in las bodegas
> where our poets' words & songs
> are sung (Quiñonez 202)

By cutting off the poem before Piñero's next line—"but," the point where the poem turns truly cynical—Quiñonez allows us to remain suspended in a moment of uncertainty and flux. These lines embody all the ambivalence of Piñero's positioning. The passage begins by reiterating the dream of this idealized poet (now called "this poeta" instead of "a poet," the demonstrative adjective emphasizing the coercive nature of the role that anticolonial ideology dictates he perform) before immediately undercutting that utopian vision by accusing it of offering the same empty American dream as a gold rush. The dreams sold in the bodega are bound to be corrupt and contaminated because of their complicity with the circuits of economic exchange. Yet even here Piñero expresses ambivalence: while the rhymes *bold* and *gold* almost demand that the last half of this section read "in las bodegas / where our poets' words & songs / are sold," of course it doesn't. Instead, the bodega is where the "poets' words & songs / are sung." This difference suggests that Piñero hangs on to some hope that even a poem distributed through the market can create and sustain community. At the same time, the obviousness of this alternative rhyme also indicates the precariousness of Piñero's utopian dream. The reader knows that although he says the songs are "sung," that may be just wishful thinking; the poem's rhyme scheme dictates that we also hear it as "sold."

By invoking Piri Thomas and Pedro Pietri, *Bodega Dreams* makes a move toward a dialogue with the anticolonial tradition of ghetto fiction and its critique of American materialism and exploitation; but by making "La Bodega Sold Dreams" its central intertext, Quiñonez moves away from the wholesale rejection of the marketplace that we see in our reading of "Puerto Rican Obituary" in the first chapter. Quiñonez's novel, like Piñero's poem, wonders how we might imagine a progressive political project that doesn't dismiss people's desires for material comfort, or even material excess, as self-deception, and that takes seriously the potential of the market as a way to organize community and effect change, a bodega that nourishes its people spiritually as well as physically.

Willie Bodega is a throwback to 1960s ideology, waxing nostalgic about his youth when "the Young Lords were beautiful [and] El Barrio was full of hope and revolution was in the air" (32). At the same time, he talks about supplementing the idealism of the Sixties with realism about people's needs and desires. He has not given up the project of redistributing wealth, but he does not trust the government to be the agent of social justice. "The government isn't pouring money in here anymore" (107), so Bodega takes on the responsibility himself, purchasing unwanted property as a way of taking control of his community away from a hostile city. This real estate empire leads Chino to initially see Bodega as a sellout: he complains to Sapo that "Bodega might talk all this shit about helping the community and shit like that but what it all comes down to is making money" (40). But Sapo's rejoinder suggests that the two goals, of taking on the community's marginalization from capitalist circuits and of participating in that very capitalism, may not be mutually exclusive: "Shit, I was there. He didn't lie to you. He said things about money. He said he had to give some away in order to keep some. Money is important. I don't deny that. But there are othah things involved here" (40). Indeed, what Bodega provides for the neighborhood is first and foremost some fulfillment of their material desires, helping people with rent or paying for them to go to college. But as Sapo reminds Chino, there are "othah things" that Bodega offers his community—an optimism that they can succeed together and a concrete plan for doing so:

> Bodega placed a mirror in front of the neighborhood and in front of himself. He was street nobility incarnated in someone who still believed in dreams [...] During that time Bodega would create a green light of hope. And when that short-lived light went supernova, it would leave a blueprint of achievement and desire for anyone in the neighborhood searching for new possibilities. (14)

In addition to this "green light of hope," Bodega's "blueprint" for redistribution through real estate acquisition sketches out a real model for how community desire can be advanced, merging the political and economic realities of postindustrial New York with the material desires of his community.

As the novel proceeds, Bodega's dreams for the community become inextricably tied to the search for and eventual return of Veronica, the lover from the 1960s who abandoned Bodega, moved to Miami, married a rich Cuban exile, and changed her name to Vera.[10] Vera/Veronica becomes the embodiment of the community's aspirations for upward mobility, the side of El Barrio that Bodega's rethought project endeavors to win back. Veronica was originally fascinated by the Young Lords, attending meetings with Bodega and falling "madly in love with him" because of his "passion" for social struggle (82). In those days, Chino imagines that Veronica pictured Bodega as "her liberator who was first going to free her from her mother, free Puerto Rico, and later they would both sail back to America like conquistadors in reverse" (125). Veronica's dreams of getting out and enacting the liberation of Puerto Rico from above (like a conquistador) contrast with Bodega's commitment to uplifting El Barrio from within. Her triumphal vision of personal liberation is not enough to keep her patience with Bodega's total commitment to the movement from wearing thin. Bodega explains to Chino that "back then, politics was all I knew [...] She said she loved me. She said that she didn't care if I didn't have any money. The problem was, she said, I didn't have any vision of how to get it. She said she wouldn't mind being poor for a few years, but since I only had a vision for political stuff, I was going to be poor for the rest of my life" (79). Bodega repeatedly refers to his "vision" from the 1960s as incomplete, not enough to satisfy Vera's materialist aspirations; it is this limitation that the 1990s version of his project seeks to correct.

## GHETTO FICTION AND THE ROMANCE OF THE SIXTIES

In the end, Bodega's dreams collapse. The novel points to his contradictory nature as the reason for his failure: he is at once visionary and blinded, too ambitious in his hopes for the future and too embedded in his dreams of the past. He is able to draw energy and inspiration from his nostalgia for the Young Lords and for Vera (which become indistinguishable; as Sapo puts it, "he's also in love with some bitch from his past. Or he's still in love with the past" [50]), and yet his inability to see the past through any lens other than nostalgia is precisely what destroys him. Refusing to give up the great social projects of the 1960s or the role of the heroic individual in bringing them forth, Bodega proves himself to be "still the idealist," as Vera at one point calls him (123). He is, in the language of David Scott's *Conscripts of Modernity*, a romantic living in a tragic time.

According to Scott, romantic versions of history are "narratives of overcoming, often narratives of vindication [...] to tell stories of salvation and redemption" (Scott 8). For that reason, anticolonialism has preferred the narrative structure of the romance as a way of plotting a history of oppression as prelude to a future of revolutionary justice. While Scott focuses primarily on C. L. R. James's *The Black Jacobins* as an exemplary rendition of the anticolonial romance, our reading of "Puerto Rican Obituary" in chapter 1 makes clear how this poem also depends on a construction of colonialism as a negative power that must be overcome for the true realization of Latino/a identity. The romanticism of anticolonialism, as Scott makes clear, need not be a limitation; virtually all the great social movements of the twentieth century found their inspiration in the narrative of redemption through suffering that the romance constructs. Bodega's own history demonstrates how thoroughly he believes in what Scott identifies as romance's primary lesson, that "we are masters and mistresses of our destiny, that our pasts can be left behind and new futures leaped into" (135). Since the Sixties, Bodega has invented a new name and persona for himself as part of a plan for taking hold of his and his community's future. Chino puts it precisely in terms of genre when he observes that "from his younger days as a Young Lord to his later days as Bodega, his life had been triggered by a romantic ideal found only in those poor bastards who really wanted to be poets but got drafted and sent to the front lines" (Quiñonez 14).

Yet despite this early observation by Chino, the story of Bodega turns out to follow the conventions not of romance, but of tragedy. We find out that he does not have total control of the outcome, that contingency and the unexpected can derail even the best-laid plans; thus Bodega's is not a story of fulfillment and overcoming but of failure and thwarted desire. The reason for this painful outcome appears to be the unsuitability and exhaustion of the romantic narrative in our time. Chino initially sees Bodega as perfectly matched to his moment, saying that "I came to believe I was living in a rare moment when a personality becomes so interlocked with the era that it can't be spoken in different sentences" (31). In identifying Bodega as what Scott would call the "World-Historical-Individual" (Scott 75), Chino envisions him in the role of a revolutionary agent of social change. Becoming so closely attached to this historical moment, Bodega opens up its epochal possibilities, making Chino feel that "for a small while, those dreams seemed as palpable as that dagger Macbeth tried to grab" (Quiñonez 14).

As this allusion to the tragic Shakespearian side of Bodega's story suggests, what Chino finds is that the time is out of joint—that not only does Bodega not embody the spirit of the age, but that he understands the moment much less than others, in particular his second-in-command, Edwin Nazario. If Bodega is the dreamer, Nazario emerges as his shadow, the practical lawyer who understands the nuts and bolts of enacting or stifling those dreams. Nazario is the one who can icily state that, "This is not the sixties" (107); his dispassionate vision and relentless realism allow him to work behind the scenes, manipulating everyone else without their awareness. The distance between Bodega's romantic vision and Nazario's cynical perspective, not surprisingly, can be measured in their eyes: "Unlike Bodega's eyes, which were pools of ghosts and sadness, Nazario's eyes were black holes, nothing could escape them, not even light, as if he could read your mind" (98).

For a novel that places hope for community uplift in the professional class, Bodega is finally just too small-time and lower-class. He is set up by Nazario, whose education gives him the trappings of true class and intelligence recognized by everyone: "Even Bodega with his street smarts and cunning lacked what Nazario had. The presence that tells the people this man can lead. He was what we all wanted to be like, the Latin professional whom the Anglos feared because he was just as treacherous, just as devious, and he understood power" (108). Like Veronica's dream of being a conquistador, Nazario measures his success by his ability to become just like an Anglo. Bodega never overcomes the street that formed him; his tragic contradiction is that it is this street sensibility that both gives him his successes and leads to his failure: "Bodega had an unforgettable blend of nobility and street, as if God never made up his mind whether to have Bodega be born a leader or a hood" (85). Nazario may be even more complicated—we are given repeated hints, eventually confirmed, that he is not what he seems—but he manages to submerge those contradictions, "by blending his education with politeness" (98), to present a more coherent persona: "Unlike Bodega, Nazario spoke cleanly and used his slang only when it suited him. Nazario's and Bodega's speeches were as different as a glass of tap water and a glass of wine. And unlike Bodega, who said exactly what was on his mind, Nazario would tell you only what he felt was necessary" (99). Whereas Bodega's romantic vision finally proves unable to see what is going on around him, Nazario turns out to be much closer to the spirit of the age.

By killing off Bodega in the end, *Bodega Dreams* suggests the death of a way of seeing the world as well as the end of an historical moment. The novel's final chapter calls itself a eulogy—its title, "P'alante, siempre p'alante," invokes the past in borrowing the slogan of the Young Lords even as it points forward towards the future. The chapter alternates between desires to praise and bury Bodega and everything he has come to represent. This eulogy begins with Chino expressing disillusionment with his neighbors, that "when [Bodega] was killed, no cars were overturned. No fires were set. No cops were conked. Nothing. The people of Spanish Harlem had to go to work. They had families to feed, night schools to attend, businesses to run, and other things to do to improve their lives and themselves. No, no one took to the streets" (203–4). Bodega's dream has failed, not only because he could not see it through but also because it appears that he has left no legacy—people are too busy with everyday concerns to take it upon themselves to fulfill or renew his romantic vision. With his death, the hope he provided dies with him: "Bodega was gone and his dreams had dissolved like a wafer in water" (205).

Chino's initial judgment of Bodega's legacy proves too absolute; what he comes to realize is that the neighborhood honors Bodega in how they choose to mourn him. The sites for his death rites are carefully chosen to evoke Bodega's symbolic legacy: the First Spanish Methodist Church that the Young Lords once took over and renamed the People's Church, and the funeral home where the wake was held for one of the Young Lords' original martyrs. Finally, there is Bodega's funeral procession, which most of El Barrio attends: "Those who didn't come out to the street would stare out of their windows. Young women would holler and scream. Older women would bring out pots and pans, and bang on them with wooden spoons. This was to let the world know this wasn't just any empty body inside that hearse. It once held the soul of Willie Bodega. So the people *had* taken to the streets, but in honor, not anger" (208). Banging pots and pans and telling stories about how Bodega helped them, these Spanish Harlemites acknowledge both the intellectual inspiration that Chino's romantic version tends to emphasize—Bodega's vision and dreams—as well as the quotidian economic support he often provided— "he once helped me with my rent," "he helped put my daughter through school," "he helped me and my sister get jobs," or even "he once bought me a case of Miller beer" (207). While minor, these acts become as important an aspect of his legacy as his prophetic leadership. Bodega's wake and funeral become rituals for members of the community, not only to lay the past to rest but also to demonstrate their interpretation of his legacy's demands; it is not, after all, the dead who bury the dead.

With Bodega's funeral, the novel positions itself as a eulogy for the political and artistic aspirations of the generation of the 1960s. Chino gives testimony to those who attend Bodega's funeral in order to locate his symbolic significance:

> Bodega's pallbearers were ex-Young Lords: Pablo Guzman, Juan Gonzalez, Felipe Luciano, Denise Oliver, Iris Morales. Standing near them were some artists from Taller Boricua: Fernando Salicrup, Marcos Dimas, Irma Ayala, Jorge Soto, Gilbert Hernandez and Sandra Maria Esteves, along with some ex-cons and poets. Miguel Algarin, Reverend Pedro Pietri, Martin Espada, Lucky Cienfuegos, and even Miguel Piñero cried their eyes out next to Piri Thomas, Edward Rivera and Jack Agueros. (208)

In creating this imagined roll call of the "Spanish Harlem aristocracy" (208), Quiñonez depicts the scene not only as Bodega's funeral but also as a moment for reflection on an entire intellectual and artistic project. When Chino sees the neighborhood graffiti including Bodega alongside "Zapata, Albizu Campos, Sandino, Martí and Malcolm" (213), it is clear that this project goes beyond just the Nuyorican movement of the 1960s to connect with the most famous anticolonial struggles of the hemisphere.

Bodega's literal and symbolic death leaves in its wake the kind of vacuum of political imagination typical of what we are calling post-Sixties Latino/a literature. Nazario's cynical materialism, devoid of any regard for community or ideology, appears as one possible future. But the novel finally refuses to privilege his cold and calculated vision; in this last section, Nazario is outwitted by Chino and arrested for Bodega's murder. Just as Miguel does in *Spidertown*, Chino turns to the authorities in the resolution of *Bodega Dreams*. Instead of the self-destructive descent of traditional gang-banger fiction like *Carlito's Way* (1975), both Miguel and Chino go to the cops, giving up Spider and Nazario to save themselves. Despite their initial fascination with oppositional attitudes and outlaw sensibilities, they choose law and order over the posses. While the police are treated as the enemy and distrusted by both protagonists—the most intensely threatening scene in *Spidertown* occurs in the back seat of a police car—both novels include a desire for cooperation between the forces of power and the community. In fact, the cops who help Miguel and Chino are both Latinos who understand the rules of the street.

With Bodega dead and Nazario defeated, Chino is thus left to carry forward Bodega's legacy. The novel ends with Chino meeting "an old man and a young boy carrying suitcases" on the street (210). The old man tells Chino that they have just arrived from Puerto Rico and are looking for Willie Bodega to help them out. After breaking the news to the old man—"They had missed the party. 'Willie Bodega doesn't exist,' I said to him" (210–11)—Chino sees that no one else will help the new arrivals. Overcome by compassion, he agrees to let them stay with him. The man comes to believe that Chino is really Willie Bodega, and there appears to be some truth in this mistake—namely that Chino is taking up where Bodega left off, reaching out to those in need, albeit in an individual way perhaps resembling the "minor key" that we explore in our final chapter. Community is still a work in progress, under construction by these individuals when the novel ends, expressed in the metaphor of Spanglish as "a new language being born" (212).

The death of Bodega and the inheritance of his legacy by Chino suggest a narrative movement from Willie Bodega to Julio (Chino) Mercado. June Dwyer interprets this resolution as a move towards assimilation, as "*bodega* (the Spanish word for those little grocery stores, often associated in the *barrio* with the selling of drugs) becomes *mercado* (a larger, more legitimate American market)" (Dwyer 171). Still, the differences between bodega and mercado are hard to reduce to this formula; to begin with, to say that a mercado is an "American market" obscures the fact of linguistic difference. Furthermore, the final scene in which Chino becomes confused with Bodega in the minds of the newcomers to the neighborhood suggests that the mercado has become "bodega-fied," as the novel's protagonist has gone from an atomized individual looking to make it on his own to a politically conscious representative of the community.

However we read this progression, the surnames of each of these characters remind us once again that the novel places economic considerations in the foreground of its vision of the political dimension of life. While the precise ways in which progressive politics might be reconfigured through the market remain to be sketched out, the broader challenge emerges. In its reassessment of the Young Lords and the anticolonial generation, *Bodega Dreams* interrogates the possibility of a radically democratic politics that eschews the market. It offers no definitive judgment; the question of whether we can work through the market to create a new left political project remains open. The answer may very well be no, but refusing to entertain the question comes at the peril of ignoring one of the novel's insights—that a political project that aspires to be truly representative and popular must engage people's often impure and "vulgar" economic desires. Bodega offers one possible rendition of a political project that engages market desires, although its future remains uncertain. But where Nazario earlier criticized Chino for lacking vision— "You, Julio, think small! You live small and you'll die small! Always paying rent because you never thought big. Like most of the people in this neighborhood you think that things are impossible!" (Quiñonez 103)—ultimately, neither Bodega nor Nazario can see the whole picture as well as Chino, who both narrates the story and solves the mysteries at its center. Nazario's cynicism makes him incapable of dreaming, while Bodega's dreams prove compelling but incomplete. The novel points to a future that Chino will attempt to fulfill with his Mercado dreams.

Is Chino's path not the very definition of selling out: his abandonment of opposition by cooperating with authority, his turn towards individualism, his acceptance of the dictates of the market? From an anticolonial perspective, *Bodega Dreams* as well as *Spidertown* prove politically inadequate, their vision decidedly post-Marxist and their efforts to formulate effective political projects finally incomplete. It is a measure of the continued purchase of the anticolonial point of view that both novels end with deep ambivalence about their political bearing, wishing to reaffirm anticolonial opposition but doubtful of the future it promises. *Spidertown* combines longing for dramatic social transformation with a deep cynicism about any political project that promises change. As a result, because the novel cannot endorse allegiance to any overarching movement, it must turn to personal romance to give the reader some kind of resolution and a happy ending, tying up the plot by bringing together Miguel, Cristalena, and Amelia. In the context of the commodified attitude towards sex displayed earlier in the novel, this ending appears to be a successful escape from those circuits of exchange on the part of these characters. This escape, however, happens only as part of a larger withdrawal from the broader forces of history and politics.

As much as the ending of *Spidertown* offers closure, *Bodega Dreams* strictly refuses any form of romance, most obviously in its refusal to have Chino and his wife, Blanca, reconcile in the novel's final pages. Thwarting our desire for resolution—for a final answer to what a successful Latino/a progressive politics should look like—is part of the novel's important critique of the temptations of romance, choosing a view of history as tragedy over Bodega's romantic vision. Unlike the

romantic redemption that Miguel and Chino so fervently desire, a philosophy of history as tragedy insists that there are no guarantees; that historical actors are not always aware even of their own motives; and that
history does not necessarily have a happy ending.[11] As the tragedy of
Willie Bodega, *Bodega Dreams* suggests that all of that is true, but that
even with this knowledge, we must keep struggling to make a better
future. In the last chapter's eulogy, Bodega's dreams may be dead, but
they will continue to provide inspiration for other projects. When the
novel ends with Chino mistaken for Bodega as the helper of the down-
trodden, he knows that he cannot take on the part of larger-than-life savior
of his people. His is a personal and everyday act of generosity, but at the
same time, this ending is not strictly individualistic. Chino may be suggesting that each person must make their own choices and take whatever
small steps they can to helping their neighbors, but he makes this overture
in the name of community.

The tension between individual and community can be felt most
palpably in the ambivalence toward upward and outward mobility that
our next chapter will investigate. *Spidertown* is relentlessly ghetto-centric,
refusing virtually any acknowledgment of a world beyond the South
Bronx. *Bodega Dreams'* protagonists consider moving up and out, but the
novel ultimately stays in the ghetto, refusing to allow them to choose outward mobility as the goal. Although Chino initially sees in Sapo's flying
kite his own dream to "get out of here" (11), the novel returns in the final
chapter to a scene recalling the end of *Down These Mean Streets:* Chino is
back on the rooftop where he began, watching Sapo's kite and knowing
that he will stay. As in *Spidertown*, "Not once does the scene shift from
the run-down streets and abandoned buildings" (Flores, *From Bomba*
180). Chino has moved up in the world—from a one-bedroom apartment to a two-bedroom in a nicer building—but he never leaves El
Barrio. Unlike a standard version of the American dream that depends on
an individual's succeeding by overcoming his background and moving
beyond his community, *Bodega Dreams* imagines a form of upward
mobility that raises the economic potential of the entire community.

Our third chapter takes as its point of departure the anxiety produced by
the equation of getting out with both succeeding and selling out. It looks
more closely at the relationship between individual and community in two
works by Dominican-American writers, Junot Díaz's *Drown* (1996) and
Angie Cruz's *Soledad* (2001). We return to Flores's articulation of lowercase literature as *the* authentic political and cultural form produced by
internally colonial and non-migrant Latino/as. Post-Sixties Dominican-
American fiction questions the distinction between Chicano/as and Puerto

Ricans as residents and other Latino/a groups as immigrants as well as the labeling of immigrant Latino/a literature as apolitical and assimilationist. We will reflect on the ways in which Díaz's stories reveal the limits of a ghetto fiction imaginary and how Cruz also references the ghetto setting while incorporating elements of magical realism to broaden the location of Latino/a identity. The chapter ultimately argues that these immigrant Latino/a authors do provide a political vision—one that reconsiders the boundaries of Latino/a cultural production and community.

## CHAPTER 3

# MOVIN' ON UP AND OUT

## LOWERCASE LATINO/A REALISM
## IN THE WORKS OF JUNOT DÍAZ
## AND ANGIE CRUZ

THIS CHAPTER WILL REASSESS THE POSITIONING OF Dominican-American writing as immigrant literature within Latino/a criticism by turning to the fiction of Junot Díaz and Angie Cruz. By citing the critical and popular reception of these two writers, we foreground how their categorization as immigrant writers requires their differentiation from resident Latino/as in terms of their relationship to politics and the market. Anticolonial criticism in particular equates the terms *ghetto*, *real*, and *resident*, suggesting that resident Latino/a writing embodies an urban realism and resistant politics while immigrant Latino/a fiction appears upwardly mobile and destined for market assimilation. Our reading of Díaz and Cruz will focus on how their work challenges the logic behind this binary on several levels. First, the writings of these Dominican-American authors clearly situate an immigrant Latino/a identity within the ghetto. Second, the urban ghetto is shown to be a restrictive setting for the Latino/a imaginary. Finally, their work outlines the limits of realism, questioning whether the genre is the only politically committed mode by which to represent Latino/a experience. We will argue that Junot Díaz's *Drown* (1996) points to the limitations involved in idealizing the inner city as the primary locus of progressive politics, while Angie Cruz's *Soledad* (2001) reframes the metaphor of drowning to imagine the possibilities for moving up and out of the ghetto in politically redemptive terms. Before delving into the broader reception of Díaz's and Cruz's fiction, however, we will first map the anticolonial discussion within Latino/a studies that the writers are entering by analyzing Juan Flores's work in greater depth.

## THE POLITICS OF GENRE

We have already noted that anticolonialist intellectuals view immigrant Latino/a writing as politically suspect in terms of its relationship to the Sixties tradition. Juan Flores, in the chapter "Life Off the Hyphen" from his theoretical study, *From Bomba to Hip-Hop* (2000), provides the most detailed articulation of the anticolonial critic's discomfort with what is perceived to be a trend in immigrant writing. Flores argues that immigrant Latino/a authors have a different relationship to "infrastructures of production and consumption" as opposed to their resident Latino/a brethren (177). More specifically, their position as immigrants and therefore "overseas representatives" provides them with access to a social framework of consulates and government-sponsored events that nurtures and in effect guarantees their literary success (177). This type of cultural capital gives them an advantage that the resident Latino/as—Chicano/as and Puerto Ricans—do not have, resulting in the immigrant writers' easy "accommodation" into the book market (177). Flores specifically mentions "English-language authors like Dominicans Julia Alvarez and Junot Díaz, [who] in addition to their access to major U.S. publishing opportunities, gained rapid recognition in the Dominican Republic and among Dominican writers, which included the translation and publication of their work" (177). While apparently enviable, the cultural capital that Flores sees the Dominican-American authors as enjoying also seems to dilute their capacity to be oppositional, enabling the creation of a Latino/a "literary community in New York and nationally, an umbrella of legitimation" for the market category of Latino/a literature as a whole (177–78). The translation of their works is also regarded as evidence of a crossover that substantiates the foreignness or immigrant nature of the texts themselves, which in their market circulation ultimately leave behind the urban spaces that Flores sees as the original and authentic sites of Latino/a culture and resistance. The immigrant, who is mobile by definition, must travel into the United States and be transformed by that crossing, while the resident Latino/a ironically has a more secure oppositional stance because s/he is always already within the borders of the United States.

This juxtaposition of the immigrant versus the resident Latino/a is developed in Flores's detailed discussion of two threads of Latino/a literature in "Life Off the Hyphen." In a move typical of what we have been calling anticolonial criticism, Flores locates the emergence of the literary tradition during the Sixties as infused with the vibrant political movements of its time, and therefore oppositional in form and subject matter. This literature of "the lowercase people" is defined not only by its urban setting but also by the experience of the "resident Latino/a presence" (183–84). The "resident Latino/a" community is a population whose presence within the United States has been established via a history of colonial relations, as in the case of Chicano/as and Puerto Ricans. The imperial movement westward of the United States during the Mexican-American War in the 1840s and into the Caribbean basin during the Spanish-American War at the end of the nineteenth century transformed members of these populations into U.S. citizens and at the same time colonized subjects. The literature produced by resident and lowercase Latino/as is consequently located within a space of marginality, containing stories of "the Latino bordering on destitution" that are "mercilessly, programmatically antinostalgic," with "the unabating presentness of the action contributing directly to a sense of entrapment and alienation of the social experience" (181). The specific examples Flores cites of such ghetto realist writing, which we discuss in detail in chapters 1 and 2, are Piri Thomas's *Down These Mean Streets,* the Nuyorican Poets movement, and Abraham Rodriguez's *Spidertown.*

While Flores longs for the continuation of this lowercase tradition, he situates the emergence of immigrant Latino/a writing as a threat to that tradition. This difference in political positioning between the resident lowercase and the new immigrant literature is based on U.S. residency and implicitly on a relationship to U.S. colonialism. Flores refers most explicitly to this difference by stating that the "newly arrived Latino writers [are] immigrating from countries relatively free of direct colonial subordination" (177). Within anticolonial criticism then, the question of genre is inexorably linked to issues of authentic Latino/a subjectivity in terms of politics and U.S. colonialism. The generation of immigrant writers is specifically ushered in by the 1990 Pulitzer Prize awarded to Oscar Hijuelos's *The Mambo Kings Play Songs of Love.* Flores sees this moment of public recognition as significant in the development of Latino/a literary tradition for two reasons. First, it marks the arrival of culturally assimilationist writing; second, it signifies the consolidation of Latino/a literature as a market category approved by the literary establishment. This literary establishment is represented not only by the Pulitzer review board but also, and more significantly for Flores, in the migrant figure of Ilan Stavans, who Flores describes as "arriv[ing] in the United States from his native Mexico as late as 1985" (172), ready to import a foreign literary movement. Rather than being lowercase, this literature is defined by mainstream desires and a "newcomer" immigrant Latino/a experience (183). In addition to its assimilationist tendencies, Flores critiques the literary movement as "apolitical" (174), written "from the vantage point of those who need not worry about being taken for Blacks or ghetto-dwellers" (183). While Flores admits that this "newcomer" literature does approach "controversial themes of gender and sexuality," he regards it as nevertheless consumed by "fits of nostalgia" that thematize the logic of upward mobility, providing only "glimpses of middle class Latino/a life" (176).

The perspective that Juan Flores articulates in equating economic success with assimilation is not foreign to the writers we discuss in this chapter. Junot Díaz, for example, echoes Flores's concern regarding an assimilationist tendency in U.S. Latino/a writing. In an interview with Diogenes Céspedes and Silvio Torres-Saillant, Díaz criticizes successful assimilationist minority writers for failing in their responsibilities to their community:

> I had so many negative models, so many Latinos and black writers who are writing to white audiences, who are not writing to their own people. If you are not writing to your own people, I'm disturbed because of what that says about your relationship to the community you are in one way or another indebted to. You are only there to loot them of ideas, and words, and images so that you can coon them to the dominant group. That disturbs me tremendously. (Céspedes and Torres-Saillant 900)

The relationship between the writer and the audience is of immense importance to Díaz. Indeed, Díaz formulates his writing philosophy in opposition to these negative models of Latino/a authorship by rejecting the role of "native informant" and refusing to "explain cultural things, with italics or with exclamation or with side bars or asides" (900). This opacity is accomplished most obviously on the linguistic level, through the insertion of Spanish into a primarily English-language text. Díaz explains that "allowing Spanish to exist in my text without the benefit of italics or quotation marks was a very important political move" and that "by keeping Spanish normative in a predominantly English text, I wanted to remind readers of the fluidity of languages, the mutability of languages" (904). Díaz's explanation of how Spanish works to disrupt the narrative links him to anticolonial and multiculturalist critics who similarly view Spanish or Spanglish insertions as moments of writerly resistance. This is one of the qualities to which Lisa Sánchez González attaches great importance in her formulation of the Civil Rights Boricua novels as texts that "disregard the standardization of English in the novel" to subvert "the very language and literary forms of the colonial metropole" (Sánchez González 132). Céspedes describes this as a "linguistic violence" within Díaz's writing that "makes readers read that which they may not want to read" (Céspedes and Torres-Saillant 904). Here, Céspedes implicitly acknowledges an audience that will regard the Spanish insertions as intrusions in the text. In other words, while perhaps not writing *for* a non-Spanish language reader, Díaz is certainly writing *against* a specific readership that his text will encounter. Rather than disengaging the non-Spanish-speaking reader, Díaz sees this linguistic strategy as a means of representing the Latino/a experience without "looting" that experience by maintaining a certain cultural and textual opacity (900). The result is a writing style that seeks to create a disjuncture between reading and understanding, to separate the act of reading from the production of meaning.

The opening epigraph of *Drown* further emphasizes the reader's inability to read or discern meaning in the text. Citing Gustavo Pérez Firmat, the narrative opens with the statement that "the fact that I am writing to you in English already falsifies what I wanted to tell you." But is *this* "you" an insider or outsider to the Latino/a community? The epigraph refers to an inability to fulfill the narrative project, to relay what the writer "wanted to tell you." This "you" implies a second reading audience—the community the author *does* want to communicate with, possibly the Latino/a population. Interestingly, in his interviews Díaz also formulates his relationship with his Latino/a audience in both pluralistic and antagonistic terms, explaining that, "I'm just a lot more passionate about having a critical dialogue with my communities. Exposing white racism and white arrogance is important, but, if I don't criticize myself and my peoples, how are we ever going to get better?" (Céspedes and Torres-Saillant 901). In this case, opacity as a writing strategy also comes into play, but this time by veiling the political project itself: "I have an agenda to write politics without letting the reader think it is political" (901). Thus, the relationship Díaz constructs with the Latino/a reader is also one that aims to prevent easy surface readings. The submerging of politics within the text creates another layer of opacity that disrupts any interpretation's claim to a truth-full reading.[1]

Having a writerly project that is oppositional in form and set in the ghetto, Junot Díaz would appear to be a model lowercase Latino/a author. For Flores, however, Díaz's primary disqualification would be his status as an immigrant Dominican American, born in the Dominican Republic and arriving in the United States at the age of seven. Rather than disputing the terms of Díaz's exclusion or that of Dominican

Americans as a whole, however, we will argue that the strategy of writerly opacity in *Drown* and its veiled critique of the barrio as a space for political projects of solidarity and resistance expose the limits of a lowercase realism. The text critiques the association of upward mobility with betrayal while also revealing how the oppositional strategy of opacity restricts the formulation of Latino/a subjectivity and sexuality. *Drown* indicates that such an articulation of Latino/a identity entails a self-censorship that ultimately stifles the development of alternative modes of meaningful cultural production. That is to say, the narrative itself seeks to embody the imaginative limits that opacity places on Latino/a writing and identity.

*Drown*, Junot Díaz's collection of short stories, was published in 1996 to much critical acclaim. Critics took particular note of the absence of nostalgia in the narrative alongside its representation of "the bleak, barren, and decayed margins of New Jersey's inner cities" (Paravisini-Gebert 164). The lens of grim realism produces an aesthetic of negation that is further developed by "the absence of a clear political intention" (165). This lack of an overt political message is interpreted as a deviation from the earlier tradition of what we have been calling Sixties Latino/a literature. Specifically, politics is seen as absent because the narrative evinces no "faith in concerted community action" and there is "little semblance of a community" (165). This reading of *Drown*, however, implies that political conviction can be expressed only through the positive valorization of community. As Díaz himself points out, the politics that interests him is a politics of oblique critique, one that pushes the community toward a potentially painful recognition of its limits and potential. We will consequently focus on two stories within the collection, "Edison, New Jersey," and "Drown," both set in the United States, which specifically address the issues of ghetto solidarity, upward mobility, and sexuality.

### POLITICAL OPACITY AND THE DEAD END OF GHETTO FICTION

The narrative of "Edison, New Jersey" represents a failed attempt at solidarity between two characters sharing similar socioeconomic backgrounds. The text's depiction of these characters, the nameless narrator and nameless woman, is a cynical rendition of community-based movements locating shared suffering as motivation for a progressive political project. Similarly to the anticolonial Civil Rights literary tradition, materialism hinders the development of collective attachments; however, Díaz's work departs from this trajectory by refusing to specify any alternative locus of belonging, shattering the idealization of the barrio as a potential space for reconnection. This particular story follows an unnamed narrator obsessed with material goods as he delivers and assembles game tables in numerous neighborhoods with varying living standards. The narrator appraises the value of these communities accordingly. For example, he interprets deliveries of cheap card tables to less affluent customers as signifying that "they aren't going to give you too much of a hassle but they also aren't going to tip" (Díaz 122). Meanwhile, the pool tables that "go north to the rich suburbs" (122) mean that the tips will presumably be better but also that he will encounter "an asshole customer" (132). The logic of profit deems that the narrator must endure the quirks of the wealthy, which are derived from their fear of poverty's contamination, whether it be "laying down a path of yesterday's *Washington Post*" to prevent the soiling of their floors or nervously leaving the workers alone in the house to "jet to the store," all the while "agoniz[ing] over leaving" and "trying to memorize everything they own" because they assume that the working-class poor cannot be trusted (122–3). The narrator's response to this classism and racism is to carry out his own rebellion by stealing "cookies from the kitchen, razors from the bathroom cabinets," and if the customer is extremely rude, "tak[ing] a dump" in their toilet and "leav[ing] that for them" (123). Despite the spirit of revolt underlying these modes of resistance, they appear ineffectual and desperate. Within this system of employment and monetary exchange, the loss incurred by stealing such small household items is quite negligible. Rather, it is the symbolic nature of the "dump" that seeks to ultimately frustrate the clients' desires for purity by contaminating the intimate spaces of their homes.

The narrator does gain real pleasure from his small acts of defiance within the system of labor exploitation, but he does not describe himself as a proto-revolutionary. The narrative resists following the logic of anticolonial politics by presenting an ambivalent lowercase character, ultimately remaining skeptical about the possibility of a pure resistant subject. Indeed, the narrator appears to covet the wealth and leisure embodied by his suburban clients, revealing the coercive nature of the American dream of upward mobility. The narrator recognizes his own commercial value, aware that the boss needs a bilingual worker: "Only when he needs my Spanish will he let me help on a sell" (125). The narrator responds to the exploitation of his abilities by stealing from the register, yet this act of resistance feeds back into the matrices of consumerist desire. The narrator remarks that "a hundred-buck haul's not unusual for me and back in the day, when the girlfriend used to pick me up, I'd buy her anything she wanted [...] Sometimes I blew it all on her" (125). The pleasure gained by this materialist shopping frenzy, which could be seen as a selfless act of generosity, is accomplished via a performance of affluence, the illusion of upward mobility: "This is the closest I've come to feeling rich" (125). Like Miguel's consumption practices described in chapter 2, excessive acquisition of material goods emerges as empty resistance. The narrator's petty thefts attempt to disrupt the exploitation of labor by enacting a renegade redistribution of wealth, but remain complicit with this system by accepting the hierarchy of power relations and leaving them undisturbed. Consumption remains the ultimate form of social, economic, and political power; it appears that the logic behind the capitalist system is unchallenged by the narrator's robberies.

With this context of economic despair and consumerist desire, the story explores the limits of community bonding via the narrator's abortive attempt to "save" the Dominican woman he encounters on one of his deliveries. The woman shares the narrator's nameless status in the text as well as an even more ambiguous job position. The narrator notes that the woman "didn't look like she owned" the house; rather "she looked more like the help" (126). The narrator's own racial lens seems to be rationalizing the woman's position as a service worker, for the description of this "look" of servitude is substantiated only by the fact that "she's black" and wearing a "t-shirt that said *No Problem*" (126). Following the narrator's initial totalizing gaze, the story proceeds to deconstruct his reading of her as "the help." Although she is in the house when the narrator and his partner Wayne try to deliver the pool table the first two times, the woman never opens the door. One could argue that her rejection of their appeals for access to the building implies a claim upon the house as property for which she has some responsibility, albeit limited. Additionally, when asked why she did not open the door, the woman explains that she wanted to "piss him off" (133). Although she does not answer the narrator's question, "Piss who off?", it is evident that patrolling the home's borders is a mode of resistance, implicitly against Pruitt, the actual owner of the house (133). And yet something else underlies this act of resistance apart from its marked similarity to the impotent gestures of revolt staged by the narrator. The woman's desire to upset Pruitt, who never appears in the text and yet retains the distinction of an actual proper name, clearly reveals a more complicated relationship than that of boss and employee. In fact, the woman desires to do more than impede Pruitt's acquisition of a commodity that will reflect his wealth; she appears to formulate her escape as a way to punish the "pendejo" (133) emotionally. The text, however, never allows the reader an entry into the mind of the woman or her motives.

The narrator's inability to see through the woman's opacity leads him to view her escape in somewhat romantic terms. From the moment he sees her image behind the glass window of the house, the narrator begins formulating an almost fairy-tale happy ending to their encounter: "We stared at each other for a second at the most, not enough for me to notice the shape of her ears or if her lips were chapped. I've fallen in love on less" (126). His idealism becomes evident when he attempts to have a conversation with her, realizing that she speaks Spanish. Finding out that she is from Washington Heights, he immediately voices recognition of their national and cultural bond: "Dominicana, I say. Quisqueyana" (133). His enthusiasm is matched only by the woman's nod, who responds to his identification with Dominican identity by stating, "You don't look it" (133). The woman ascertains the narrator's claim on kinship via the gaze, evaluating his physique as one that is not expressive of Dominicanness and fails to meet the stereotyped parameters of Dominican racial identity. Despite this challenge to his identity, the narrator insists on pursuing the possibility of a connection with her, asking what street she lives on in Washington Heights. When the woman confesses her desire to escape from the house and asks him for a ride to New York, the narrator initially resists the request. In the dialogue that follows, it appears that the woman has misunderstood the narrator's enthusiasm, assuming that he asked for her address because he actually lives in New York City. The failure of communication between the narrator and the woman reveals the futility of the narrator's multiple attempts at solidarity across racial, cultural, and class lines.

The point in the story where the narrator decides to help the woman escape by driving her to Washington Heights could consequently be viewed as a final attempt to engage not only in a politically committed act but also an anticolonial mode of resistance, lifting the woman up from her exploited position. Looking into the bedroom she plans to leave behind, the narrator sees that the woman does not actually have much material wealth: "Four hangers' worth of clothes in the closet and only the top dresser drawer is full" (135). Witnessing the little the woman does own, the narrator is shocked that she is unwilling to take it with her. When he asks her, "Are you going to pack?" the woman responds by "hold[ing] up her purse" and stating, "I have everything I need" (134). Given his own obsession with material goods, the narrator is unable to process the woman's willingness to abandon her possessions: "Don't be stupid, I say. I open her dresser" (134). But as he opens the dresser, he opens up another Pandora's box, and a "handful of soft bright panties fall out and roll down the front of my jeans" (134). Here is a woman with only four hangers' worth of clothes, and yet a drawer full of nothing but underwear. The narrator responds to the clothing with fear: "I try to catch them but as soon as I touch their fabric I let everything go"

(135). In leaving these pieces behind, the woman is specifically labeling them as Pruitt's property: "He can keep the rest of it" (134). Whatever secret this underwear holds is never revealed in the narrative. On the basis of this portrayal, though, it would then be a bit simplistic to label her as purely the "maid of a wealthy white man," as one critic does (Kevane 78). Exposing this private and intimate space not only complicates any understanding of the woman's position in the house, but this revelation must be contained and silenced. The woman retains her opacity, keeping "her square back" to the narrator as she places the underwear back in the drawer, and "doesn't look up" at him when he attempts to speak and connect with her (Díaz 135). It is a silence that the narrator wishes to maintain as well, in order to avoid upsetting the narrative of a romantic rescue that he hopes to construct. It is nevertheless important to state that the motives or desires of either character remain below the surface of the text, ultimately opaque to interpretation and leading the reader to put together a jigsaw puzzle of meaning that inevitably will have missing pieces. Thus, the excessive quantity of underwear serves only to hint at the type of exploitation that the woman identifies with Pruitt or the motivation behind her rash decision to flee.

During the drive to Washington Heights, the conversation between the narrator and the woman remains superficial. What is spoken has little emotional depth, and the questions that might lead to some kind of genuine interaction are left unsaid. The narrator mentions his desire "to ask her if she loves her boss," but instead asks, "How do you like the States?" (137). Since this question garners only an uninspired response, "I'm not surprised by any of it," the narrator shifts to the locale of the Dominican Republic, perhaps hoping to find a connection there. Unfortunately, the woman is not from the capital like the narrator. In an act of desperation, having exhausted the possibilities for communion through cultural affiliation, the narrator resorts to a gesture of physical intimacy: "As we cross over the bridge I drop my hand into her lap. I leave it there, palm up, fingers slightly curled. Sometimes you have to try, even if you know it won't work. She turns her head away slowly, facing out beyond the bridge cables, out to Manhattan and the Hudson" (137). The woman's interest lies elsewhere, but the rejection is formulated in silence, contributing to the same aesthetic of absence that haunts the narrator's other acts of resistance and solidarity.

The only space that appears to provide any hope for the narrator is Washington Heights itself. Similar to the way in which El Barrio functions in "El Spanglish National Anthem" and *Bodega Dreams*, the inner city appears here as a Dominican cultural paradise, a place where "you can't go a block without passing a Quisqueya Bakery or a Quisqueya Supermercado or a Hotel Quisqueya" (137). Here the narrator imagines himself achieving a state of belonging that would make his outsider status irrelevant, turn him into one of many in the neighborhood, just another Dominican: "If I were to park the truck and get out nobody would take me for a deliveryman; I could be the guy who's on the street corner selling Dominican flags. I could be on my way home to my girl" (137). Although "everybody's on the streets," the narrator does not venture out to join the community and instead stays in his truck while the woman steps out (137). This moment of return, built up in such a utopic manner, with "merengue's falling out of windows," is actually anticlimactic (137). The woman walks across the street in silence while the narrator tells her, "Cuidate" (138). Although the Washington Heights ghetto is envisioned as a positive space, the epitome of Dominican identity and culture in the United States, the narrator does not belong there. On the one hand, he does not live there and therefore he cannot come home to Washington Heights. On the other hand, as the woman's statement about his lack of Dominican appearance reveals, the narrator may never feel authentic enough to belong in this hyperauthentic space of the inner city.

If the story were to end at this point, one could at least frame the trip as a success. The narrator has saved the woman from further exploitation and returned her to her proper place with her people. A week later, curiosity gets the better of the narrator, and he calls Pruitt to see if this romance of political empowerment and independence is a reality. After a number of persistent hang-up phone calls, "she answers and the sink is running on her side of the phone and she shuts it off when I don't say anything" (139). It is apparent then that the barrio did not have a hold on her either, since she does not stay in Washington Heights but rather returns to Pruitt. Disconnected at last from the hopeful imaginary that returning to the pueblo would redeem the woman and provide her with an alternate future, the narrator is clearly transformed. Indirectly, the text informs the reader of the narrator's anger and sense of disappointment. Wayne's explanation of the woman's weakness is that "she's probably in love with the guy. You know how it is" (139). But indeed, there is another context beyond that of love that the narrator does share with the woman, and it is consumerist desire. His anger may stem from having his dream shattered, namely the hope that this woman would choose the Dominican community over the materialistic promise embodied by Pruitt. Rather, this woman, who had so little to lose and leave behind, returned to Pruitt because the value of these small things outweighed that of the solidarity offered by the ghetto. Not only is the narrator, who was born in the

Dominican Republic and "moved here when I was a little boy" (137), unable to connect with a woman who shares his immigrant status, but the utopic draw of a community that the narrator sees in Washington Heights is also an illusion. The disruption of this potential happy ending ultimately points to the dead end of solidarity in a context of materialism. This representation calls to mind our discussion of "Puerto Rican Obituary" in chapter 1. Certainly Díaz appears to be extending the Sixties critique of commercialization in "Edison, New Jersey." Yet there remains a significant difference between the critique of Pedro Pietri and that of Díaz. While "Edison, New Jersey" momentarily constructs the barrio of Washington Heights as a utopia, it proves to be an illusory site of solidarity. There is no hopeful ending in Díaz's story. There is no alternative afterlife that will engender reconnection and the overcoming of the obstacles of poverty, exploitation, and materialism.

Instead of looking forward to a future redemptive community of the sort that Pietri offers, the narrator in "Edison, New Jersey" finds himself facing a repetitive future of grim reality. The little joy left to the narrator in this life was derived from his appreciation of commerce and materialism. Now even the pleasures of consumerism have been foreclosed. The story's ending hints that the narrator cannot renew his consumerist desire after watching this romance fail. Playing the game he has played so many times before, the narrator attempts to guess what his first job will be the next day. This small act is intended to "give us something to look forward to" (139), a way to relieve the boredom of their insecure job position. Usually the narrator would "close my eyes and put my hand on the map" and "you can't imagine how many times I've been right" (139). But this time, something is not quite right: "Usually the name will come to me fast, the way the numbered balls pop out during lottery drawings, but this time nothing comes: no magic, no nothing" (140). The metaphor of the lottery indicates that this act was similar to those strategies of resistance the narrator had used before, ultimately ineffectual and fleeting in their provision of pleasure. That illusion has been broken; the woman has returned to the house she does not own and which contains an ambiguous environment of (sexual) exploitation. Tomorrow, the narrator now knows, will bring more of the same. So this time, the narrator opens his eyes, looks down on the map and chooses Edison—a place that will probably be an equally dead end.

## SINK OR DROWN: THE DOUBLE BIND OF GHETTO MASCULINITY

From the dead end of "Edison, New Jersey," the title story of Díaz's collection, "Drown," attempts to construct a way out of the ghetto only to ultimately undercut that route. Hopelessness pervades the story; the narrative posits several avenues to upward mobility, but to escape the barrio on these terms entails emasculation, which threatens the destruction of the already tenuous self constructed within that urban space. The narrator is again nameless, and the story opens with the narrator's acknowledgment that the friendship between himself and Beto lies in the past: "He's a pato now but two years ago we were friends" (91). The rupture is credited to Beto's homosexuality, yet left unexplained. Rather, the narrative proceeds as a nostalgic remembrance of those times gone by, a time when the two boys were not individuals but a collective "we" of masculine resistance: "We were raging then, crazy the way we stole, broke windows, the way we pissed on people's steps and then challenged them to come out and stop us" (91). Beto emerges as a model of masculine behavior, a courageous and unemotional trickster. His name serves to emphasize the "beast" of hypermasculinity that Beto enacts. On their regular shoplifting expeditions, the narrator is impressed with the smoothness of Beto's performance, how "he even talked to the mall security, asked them for directions, his bag loaded up, and me, standing ten feet away, shitting my pants" (97). When they do get caught, Beto wears the exemplary cara palo face that Piri Thomas exalts in his autobiography as an expression of real ghetto manhood.[2] In the glossary to *Down These Mean Streets,* Thomas defines cara palo simply as "deadpan" (Thomas, *Down* 339). In the context of Thomas's autobiography, however, cara palo is also a mode of conduct for ghetto men, one that is silent, unemotional, and loyal in the face of suffering. Beto exemplifies this code of opacity, of being unreadable, even when confronted by the police for shoplifting. Hiding underneath a jeep, the boys are discovered by the cops: "When the rent-a-cop tapped his nightstick against the fender and said, You little shits better come out here real slow, I started to cry. Beto didn't say a word, his face stretched out and gray, his hand squeezing mine, the bones in our fingers pressing together" (Díaz 99). The homosocial bond between Beto and the narrator is heightened by a common experience of truancy, adolescent resistance, and the performance of ghetto masculinity.

The bond, however, is one that is eventually broken by the blurring of the homosocial into homosexual attraction, another connecting theme with *Down These Mean Streets.*[3] This distancing is nevertheless established much earlier by Beto's desire for upward mobility. The narrator explains that Beto does not see the ghetto as a space for self-actualization;

rather, he abhors the visibility of its poverty. Beto "hated everything about the neighborhood, the break-apart buildings, the little strips of grass, the piles of garbage around the cans, and the dump, especially the dump" (91). Education is the means of Beto's abandonment of the barrio and by extension, the narrator: "Beto was leaving for college at the end of the summer and was delirious from the thought of it" (91). So passionate about his escape, Beto tries to convince the narrator to do the same: "You need to learn how to walk the world, he told me. There's a lot out there" (102). For Beto, the means do not matter as long as one gets out: "I don't know how you can do it, he said to me. I would just find me a job anywhere and go" (91).

But as the narrator states, "I wasn't like him" (92). To begin with, the future does seem as bright to him as it does to Beto, since "I had another year to go in high school, no promises elsewhere" (92). In addition, Beto's educational goals are simply not feasible for the narrator. Not only is the narrator "failing gym and screwing up math," but he also does not see education as a source of community: "I hated every single living teacher on the planet" (101). The narrator, now an adult, reviews his present life, which appears to be going nowhere. With his friendship with Beto now over, the past "we" has been supplanted by nights with his friends Alex and Danny at a "no good bar" with "just washouts and the sucias we can con into joining us" (99). The valiant resistance of the youthful past makes this adult life appear pathetic and empty. The homosocial project now consists of traveling to college bars where "none of the chicas ever dance with us" (102). The men are limited to the heterosexual gaze; they stare "at the college girls" and create fictions out of the limited attention they receive in return: "A glance or touch can keep us talking shit for hours" (103). The interaction with these women provides the illusion of connecting with an upwardly mobile college-educated population. The desperation of the men's attempt to connect with these women is further accentuated by their performances of violence against homosexual men. The friends go on ritual excursions to harass the men at gay bars: "Sometimes Alex will stop by the side of the road and say, excuse me. When somebody comes over from the bar he'll point his plastic pistol at them, just to see if they'll run or shit in their pants" (103). The threat of violence is enacted to emasculate these gay men, and yet appears already compromised by its own illusory show of power and hypermasculinity. The pistol remains a plastic one, a mere imitation. The narrator himself undercuts his friend's performance of this violent machismo, commenting: "That's original" (103). Ultimately, these rituals are inferior copies of Beto's original model of masculinity and dissent. They do not contain the same excitement, rush of fear, or bonding that the narrator experienced with Beto.

Nevertheless, the narrator eventually reveals a secret that complicates the utopic perspective through which he has thus far depicted his childhood. The motivation for the broken friendship is not so much that Beto is gay, but rather that the narrator engaged in homosexual acts with him. The crisis of masculinity that these acts create in the narrator is suggested in his perhaps neurotic assertion, "Twice. That's it," prior to actually describing these encounters (103).[4] This preface seeks to assert the singularity of these acts, already framing them as mistakes without real meaning. The fact that this description follows the dead-end social scene and performances of empty masculinist threats, however, alludes to the way in which those homosexual experiences continue to haunt the narrator with a persistent fear of the permeable boundary between the homosocial and the homosexual spheres. The first encounter takes place as the two boys are watching a porn film together:

> We were an hour into the new movie [...] when he reached into my shorts. What the fuck are you doing? I asked, but he didn't stop. His hand was dry. I kept my eyes on the television, too scared to watch. I came right away, smearing the plastic sofa covers. My legs started shaking and suddenly I wanted out. He didn't say anything to me as I left, just sat there watching the screen. (104)

Pornography as defined by heterosexual voyeurism enables homosocial bonding but at the same time facilitates the articulation of homosexual desire. Certainly, the narrator's reaction to this experience reflects a fear of contamination more than actual physical desire. He is "terrified that I would end up abnormal, a fucking pato, but he was my best friend and back then that mattered to me more than anything" (104). At this point in his youth, the narrator is not willing to compromise his bond of friendship with Beto.

And yet, the second encounter indicates that the friendship will not be strong enough to assuage the crisis of masculinity brewing within the narrator. When Beto calls the narrator after the first experience, the narrator plays it "cool" and thus imitates Beto's cara palo model of unemotional behavior (104). The strategy of coolness and silence, however, leads to a sense of complicity. Beto expresses his concern indirectly when he first sees the narrator, saying, "I was beginning to worry about you" (105). The narrator responds to this inquiry by comforting Beto: "Nothing to worry about" (105). The description of the second encounter that follows contains gaps that allude to the unspeakable desire that the narrator

remains unable to acknowledge directly. Placing his hand on the narrator's shoulder, Beto is able to read the desire that remains opaque to the
narrator and reader, "my pulse a code under his palm" (105). As opposed
to the previous seduction scene, the narrator's interest in intimacy is continually gauged by Beto. When Beto asks the narrator over to his parents'
empty apartment, he appears aware and accepting of the possibility of
rejection: "Let's go, he said. Unless of course you're not feeling good"
(105). As Beto is giving the narrator a blow job, he remarks, "I'll stop if
you want" (105). The narrator's desires are unspoken, or perhaps
expressed through silence itself: "I didn't respond" (105).

   After this intimate encounter, as Beto lays "his head in [the narrator's]
lap," the narrator reconsiders the issue of upward mobility. The narrator
realizes that "in three weeks [Beto] was leaving" for college (105). The
memory of "how beautiful the campus was" is paired with a childhood
classroom memory. In particular, the narrator recalls how a teacher
"compared us to [space] shuttles" (106). This metaphor of the space shut-
tle functions to identify which of the students will move up and out, and
which will remain to drown in the ghetto: "A few of you are going to
make it. Those are the orbiters. But the majority of you are just going
to burn out. Going nowhere. He dropped his hand on my desk. I could
already see myself losing altitude, fading, the earth spread out beneath
me, hard and bright" (106). The narrator is condemned early in his childhood by this teacher's categorization as one of the ones to be left behind,
cursed with immobility, and defined by permanent residence within the
ghetto. The narrative's conjunction of sexual intimacy with this childhood memory complicates any determination of the exact motives
behind the narrator's distance from Beto; in other words, the narrator's
sexual confusion and his lack of access to upward mobility become indistinguishable as crises. His musings are interrupted by a startling sound:
"The hallway door crashed open," prompting the narrator to almost
emasculate himself by "nearly cut[ting] my dick off struggling with my
shorts" (106). The realization that "It's just the neighbor" lends no comfort to the narrator, and Beto's laughter serves only to accentuate the narrator's confusion. Instead of interrogating this confusion, the narrator
closes off this avenue of identification and feeling: "I was saying, Fuck
this, and getting my clothes on" (106).

   The severance of the friendship and a potentially new formulation of
sexual identity is melancholic—represented in what the narrator abjects
rather than states expressly. Although he now shares Beto's desire to flee
the barrio, saying, "These days my guts feel loose and cold and I want to
be away from here" (100), upward mobility is not possible for him. The

narrator returns to his ghetto home and his last link for community and understanding via the figure of his mother. Together they sit and watch movies "dubbed into Spanish" (107) their real communion derived from their common experience of abandonment, the narrator abandoned by Beto, and his mother abandoned by his father. As his mother falls asleep, "dreaming of Boca Raton, of strolling under jacarandas with my father," the narrator remembers: "You can't be anywhere forever, was what Beto used to say, what he said the day I went to see him off" (107). The narrator realizes that his fate refutes Beto's belief, since he is condemned to the ghetto for what seems like an eternity. Consequently, the narrator throws away the book that Beto gave him as a gift, not bothering "to open it and read what he's written" inside (107). The narrator's fate is now tied to that of his mother, obsessed with "check[ing] the windows," testing the latches, because "This place just isn't safe" (96). The house of identity must be continually patrolled, policed from the inside, to make sure that the borders are intact so that nothing can contest its security. And yet, the compulsive checking and testing bespeaks insecurity about keeping the outside forces out as well as restraining the unspoken desires within.

The narratives of "Edison, New Jersey" and "Drown" reveal the limitations of the inner city as a space for progressive politics and community solidarity. Both stories allude to the literary heritage of the Sixties through a critique of materialism and the characterization of a masculine urban subject. The stories nevertheless deviate from the tracks laid down by writers like Pedro Pietri by refusing to identify a redemptive space for belonging. The absence of such a utopic elsewhere is also evident in the stylistic form of *Drown*'s narrative. The aesthetic of negation on which *Drown* is based ultimately exemplifies the constraints of realist cultural production, in effect reaching its own imaginative limitations. The narrative mode and aesthetic of the text also reveal the limits of opacity as a mode of lowercase Latino/a expression. Junot Díaz remarks in an interview with Torres-Saillant that "You know a story has to work on a bunch of levels. It can't just be political. It can't just be a good story. Does it sound real?" (Céspedes and Torres-Saillant 902). *Drown*'s narrative fractures attest to the consequences of taking this code to heart, especially the heavy creative burden imposed by the assertion that Latino/a cultural production must be political and real. The textual gaps and silences speak to the restrictions of a lowercase model of ghetto fiction in terms of heterosexuality as well as the equation of upward mobility with betrayal. *Drown* reveals cara palo opacity as a ghetto-centric writerly strategy that can ultimately lead Latino/a cultural production into a political and imaginative dead-end street.

## THE IMAGINATIVE LIMITS OF LOWERCASE REALISM

Angie Cruz's novel *Soledad* (2001) ponders the limits of the ghetto itself as a locale for the representation of the authentic Latino/a subject by also pressing the boundaries of the urban realism genre. We will read Cruz's novel as a response to the problematic outlined by Junot Díaz's *Drown* and the conflicting writerly agendas of oppositional politics versus nostalgic recuperation. *Soledad* proposes a complex and dynamic understanding of the literary traditions and genres that inform U.S. Latino/a writing, similar to the way in which Díaz describes his literary inheritances in an interview:

> I have multiple traditions, like anyone else. I'm part of the mainstream "American" literary tradition. I'm a part of the Latino/a literary tradition. I'm a part of the African Diaspora literary tradition as well as the Dominican literary tradition. But there's also the oral tradition and the rhythmic tradition of music I grew up with [...] And then there must be plenty of other traditions I'm a part of which I can't identify yet. (Céspedes and Torres-Saillant 904)

Amidst such shifting literary alliances, lowercase Latino/a literature must negotiate several binaries: the street versus the market, the resident versus the immigrant, oral versus written, resistance versus mobility. *Soledad* references these divergent literary trajectories and places them in conversation to interrogate their points of harmony and dissonance. This dialogue is initiated at the intersection of two lives: Soledad, a young Dominican-American girl trying to escape the ghetto of Washington Heights; and Caramel, a lowercase and politically conscious resident Chicana. While these two models of Latino/a identity intersect, the novel eventually moves away from this binary relationship of either/or resistance. Caramel emerges as a positive model for Latino/a activism; however, her characterization also offers a critique of realism as the ideal mode for Latino/a cultural production. The integration of magical realist tropes within the narrative serves to locate alternative sources for the Latino/a literary imagination that lie outside of the ghetto. The novel's own outward mobility via the representation of Soledad's mother, Olivia, prompts the formulation of a broader historical context for Latino/a identity beyond that of the U.S. barrio and into the Caribbean basin.

Soledad's one desire is to leave her past behind—to get out of Washington Heights and never look back: "The way I'm figuring it, my time in Washington Heights is like a prison sentence. Once I do the time, I won't have a guilt trip anymore about moving out" (Cruz, *Soledad* 3). She convinces her family to let her "go away" to college in downtown

Manhattan by telling them literal narratives of utopic upward mobility. In describing the school dorms to her family, Soledad calls them "high-rises, with a view of the East River and really great showers" (1). The reality of her situation is very different: "Every time I step into my East Village walk-up [...] the smell of piss, the halls as wide as my hips, the lightbulb in the lobby that flashes on and off like a cheap disco light, reminds me of my deception" (1). Soledad even decontextualizes the Lower East Side, absenting its Latino/a history as a Nuyorican neighborhood just a generation earlier. The desire to dissociate herself from the lowercase Latino/a ghetto moves Soledad to also fudge the details of her background when speaking with her fellow students. When asked where she is from, Soledad responds with "the Upper West Side": "I convinced myself that embroidering the truth about my living on the Upper Upper Upper West Side was my way of keeping nasty stereotypes of Washington Heights out of people's minds" (2).

But moving out doesn't just mean escaping the ghetto. For Soledad, the narrative of outward mobility has always implied disconnection from her mother. Soledad remarks, "I thought I was switched at birth, hoping my real mother would one day appear at the door and take me away. I held on to the fact that I don't look like my mother"(6). The desire to reject this matrilineal heritage is apparent from the moment that Soledad decides to leave for college and move out of her mother's apartment. Ignoring her mother's pleas for forgiveness and communication, Soledad reminds herself, "I had already found an affordable room to rent in the East Village. That I was going to a place far away from my mother, from Washington Heights" (8). With the prospect of upward mobility ahead of her, Soledad is able to remain unresponsive to her mother's screams. She then performs the final act of rejection, "tak[ing] off the gold hoops my mother gave me when I was born and plac[ing] them on the kitchen table" (8).

The character of Caramel serves as a counterpoint to Soledad while at the same time embodying the limits of a ghetto realist political vision. Caramel, Soledad's Chicana lesbian roommate, emerges as one of the central resident Latino/a voices in Cruz's novel who challenge Soledad's valuation of moving up and out. Caramel functions as a throwback to the Sixties political vision, voicing its ideological perspective to critique Soledad's assimilationist tendencies. When confronted with Soledad's narrative of Upper West Side mobility, Caramel is the first to respond negatively to this location:

When I told her I was from the Upper West Side, she cringed and looked at me pityingly. How can you stand it up there? she asked horrified. It's like gringolandia. I wasn't sure what she meant by that exactly, but I knew it was bad. It felt worse than being called a blanquita back home: a sellout, a wannabe white girl. So to calm her down I told her the truth, I'm from Washington Heights. In a loud Texan accent she boomed: Then say it like it is, mujer. Washington Heights. (3)

Caramel's reaction prompts Soledad to guiltily shift her identification from the upper-class locale of the Upper West Side to that of the Washington Heights barrio. This guilt is evoked by Caramel's signifying home in terms of community solidarity as opposed to class mobility, the barrio versus gringolandia. In addition, the guilt is also associated with a betrayal of one's cultural roots. In a move reminiscent of the anticolonial perspective, Caramel calls on Soledad to tell it like it is, to keep it real—using her "loud Texan accent" for emphasis and example. This call to tell the truth entails enunciating or publicly naming the ghetto as *the* authentic home-place.

Caramel's alternative to Soledad's ideology of upward mobility is particularly evident in their discussion of Soledad's internship in an art gallery. Soledad envisions the art gallery as another avenue for escape, one devoid of the contradictions and conflicts that plague her family. While Soledad views the gallery as a blank space in which "everything [...] has a reason and a place" (55), Caramel maintains that the organizational logic underlying this public space is not so color-blind. Looking at the white walls and ceilings that Soledad claims are "inspiring" (56), Caramel wonders aloud how she can stand working there without becoming suicidal. For Caramel, it comes down to the politics of representation; "When was the last time you saw a Latina artist in a gallery?" she asks Soledad (56). Caramel not only sees through the whitewashed artistic economy of the gallery but also presses for action. She urges Soledad to join her, to "start our own thing, make our own rules" and create a "place where our mamis can come and visit and not feel like they don't belong" (57). Soledad envies Caramel's ability to courageously embody a politics of opposition and critique, one that invokes the Civil Rights and feminist movements as antecedents. Marveling at Caramel's ability to enunciate herself, Soledad wants to "grow up to be like her. With so much strength, comfortable in her own skin, not caring what anyone thinks" (91).

This oppositionality, while enviable, has its limits as well. Caramel's authoritative voice is also didactic regarding her ability to differentiate between what's real and illusory. At times Caramel assumes she knows what's best for Soledad better than Soledad herself, and therefore speaks in "her I'm-five-years-older-than-you-and-know-so-much-more-about-the-world voice" (3). Caramel in turn defines authentic identity as something that lies within to be unearthed, a subjectivity that is pure, true, and accessible, as shown by her habit of eating "caramel-flavored things [...] to get in touch with her inner self" (67). Caramel's combination of incontestable authority and self-confidence leads her to treat Soledad as an individual devoid of context, who merely has to look inside to find her real self. In practicing her "Psych 101" on Soledad (63), Caramel's decontextualization allows her to paint a simplistic and naturalistic picture of the mother-daughter relationship, drawing clear lines of duty and responsibility that elide the complexity of the specific relationship between Soledad and her mother, Olivia. When Olivia falls into a sleeplike coma, Caramel argues that Soledad must take care of her. In response to Soledad's questions, "Why me? What has she done for me?", Caramel simply replies, "She gave you life. That's enough" (57). Because "Caramel always speaks in assertions" (57), there is no room for Soledad's "Why?" By defining Soledad's identity in terms of her innate daughterly duty and community obligations, Caramel unknowingly but effectively brands the contextual factors complicating Soledad's relationship with her mother as irrelevant. There is consequently no space in which to discuss the history of violence that came between mother and daughter or the role that a physically and sexually abusive father played in breaking the bonds of family trust. The maternal connection is a reality but is not the only context shaping Soledad. Her father's "accidental" murder cannot be narrated because Caramel has set the terms of the discussion to disallow any contestation. While Soledad clearly values Caramel as a positive model for Latina identity due to her political acuity, the framework of realism through which Caramel views the world excludes potentially significant points of experience.

One of the historical contexts that cannot be assimilated into Caramel's view of reality is referenced when Soledad is cleaning out the closets in her mother's home and comes across a metal tin inscribed with Olivia's name. Inside the box, Soledad finds "a matchbook from a restaurant called Puerto Plata Disco" and a notebook listing several men by date, nationality, and physical qualities (193). Soledad reads the list aloud, picturing each man and wondering, "Who are these men? Why would my mother describe them this way?" (194). The final entry in the list is "Junio 14 Manolo," the only man named, Soledad's father (195). Confronted by her mother's history of prostitution in the Dominican Republic, Soledad now recalls her parents' relationship from a different perspective: "I remember the way he would say to my mother [...] Not *my* daughter. *Your* Daughter. Why didn't my mother ever tell me? All these years. All these men" (195). Soledad has the opportunity to see her mother's silence physically embodied before her. In reciting the list of her mother's clients, Soledad is confronted by the very real presence of "men with big fat stomachs, nasty teeth, hairy chests, balding heads, pigeon toes, smelly armpits [and] long beards" (195). These visions act "as if they have visited this apartment in the past, they sit down on the sofa, on the windowsill, on the floor, all naked, penises exposed con mucha confianza" (195). These are the ghosts from the past that haunt Olivia, forcing her to escape into a catatonic state.

How can Soledad make sense of this bizarre experience? To whom can she turn? While Caramel has always been her confidante, Soledad knows that communication with her is impossible. On the one hand, Soledad has not "told anyone about the men, not even Caramel," because "talking about it will make them even more alive" (199). Nevertheless, Soledad comments that she "hate[s] withholding so much" from Caramel and comforts herself with the assertion that "she will know everything once this is all over" (199). It becomes evident that Soledad cannot relate this experience because it does not fit Caramel's vision of Latino/a experience. Indeed, Soledad's initial response to these ghostly figures of naked men is to follow Caramel's example and insist on keeping it real:

> Each day even when I try to psych myself out, pretending I don't care if the men are here or not, trying to make them nonexistent in my imagination as if I never read my mother's list, as if I never saw them appear, I find them hanging around in the apartment naked and sweaty. (199)

Soledad recognizes in the failure of this realist strategy that denying the men's presence in her mother's apartment entails a denial of her own and her mother's lived experience.

It is here that the narrative most forcefully questions the valuation of the resident Latino/a over the immigrant Latino/a by drawing a parallel to the ranking of ghetto realism as superior to the literary strategy of magical realism. One of Juan Flores's central criticisms of the contemporary Latino/a canon derives from the privileging of works that are "the most reminiscent of and compatible with Latin American literary models, especially those of the 'boom'" period (Flores, *From Bomba* 173), meaning those that are "in league with Latin American magical realism" (174). Flores names Ilan Stavans as "the critic who has been the most intent on configuring a Latino canon in the 1990s" (172), and therefore views Stavans as personally responsible for the emergence of this literature that is strictly shaped by market demands, including the promotion of magical realism as a genre. Stavans does indeed identify the genre of magical realism as "incredibly marketable" (Stavans, *Hispanic* 11), and even the cover of Angie Cruz's *Soledad* points to the market's valuation of this literary mode, advertising the novel as "tinted with the magical realism of Gabriel García Márquez."

The market's valuation of magical realism serves as the context for Flores's critique of the Latin American boom as a model for Latino/a literature, inflecting his designation of immigrant Latino/a literature as apolitical and "wallow[ing] in the past" (Flores, *From Bomba* 186). This reading labels references to historical contexts outside the geography of the urban United States as necessarily nostalgic, apolitical, and an ultimately empty literary move. Cruz's novel alternately allows for the possibility of reading magical realism as a potential avenue for depicting a specifically Latino/a historical baggage. We therefore propose that the narrative of *Soledad* depicts the haunting presence of transcoloniality via the transformative recontextualization provided by magical realism. These naked men who appear before Soledad are not fantastical in the sense of the UNreal, to borrow a term from Abraham Rodriguez's *The Buddha Book*.[5] Rather, they represent a historical past that is still relevant to the Latino/a present. Soledad notes, "There's a sepia cast to them all. An ancient photograph, an old memory" (Cruz, *Soledad* 195). Olivia's list describes these men as primarily European or American, marking them as embodiments of a long history of colonial exploitation in the Caribbean.[6] Olivia's victimization within the sex tourism economy provides a context for her flight to New York City and her development as an immigrant Latina.

Flores certainly does not divorce the history of neocolonization from contemporary Latino/a experience; indeed, his work seeks to highlight the role of the United States as an empire in shaping the historical development of the resident Latino/a community, the Latino/a population within U.S. borders. What the novel *Soledad* points to through the representation of Caramel and Olivia, however, is the way in which the lowercase model of U.S. Latino/a literature also privileges one form of Latino/a experience by focusing on what Flores calls the "denizens of the 'mean' but real streets" as the principal reality through which to understand Latino/a identity (Flores, *From Bomba* 185). Drawing attention solely to resident Latino/as as authentic subjects potentially excludes the "harvest of empire," to borrow Juan González's title, as a context in which to understand the multiple waves of immigration from the Caribbean and what we might call the "Other America."[7] Flores himself states that "the marking off of 'us' and 'them,' though the foundational exercise in 'imagining'

communities, has its own limits" (193). In this spirit, we wish to highlight the limits placed on imagining the Latino/a community that are
implied by the differentiation between resident and immigrant Latino/as
as responsive to wholly different histories. These communities do share a
common history of colonization, certainly not in terms of the generic
Spanish "fiesta" of 1492 that Ilan Stavans describes (Stavans, *Hispanic*
10), but a history of violence that extends into the contemporary world
order of U.S. imperialism. *Soledad* brings the voices of resident and
immigrant Latinidad together in order to draw upon this historical
context and show how the narrative strategies of ghetto realism, magical
realism, and perhaps even upward mobility are all relevant to rethinking
the progressive potential of Latino/a cultural production. *Soledad* ultimately moves away from what might become a Latino/a subject devoid of
historical and cultural specificity. Rather, the novel focuses on the narration of Soledad as specifically Dominican American, born in the United
States and therefore a resident Latina reconnecting with her Caribbean
historical context.

## OUTWARD MOBILITY INTO A CARIBBEAN CONTEXT

The ghosts of the naked men are accidentally summoned by Soledad's
reading of their notebook descriptions, but their continued presence is a
product of Soledad's desires to understand her lineage: "It's my longing
to know which one my father is that keeps them in the apartment" (Cruz,
*Soledad* 205). While her mother's catatonic state represents an attempt to
escape from this history, Soledad is wholly consumed and kept awake at
night by the possibilities of finding resemblances between herself and
these men. It is Soledad's aunt, Gorda, who determines that the only way
for these women to obtain closure and eliminate the haunting presence of
the naked men is to take a trip back to the Dominican Republic: "There's
a very special place where we can destroy this list [of men]. We can have
Olivia retrace her steps, erase her past step by step. She will start again"
(206). Gorda's understanding of what the return will do for Olivia is
decidedly anticolonial in its logic—to initiate a clean break with the past
in order to fashion a newly liberated identity sounds distinctly Fanonian.
The logic of the narrative, however, points to a different type of solution
to Olivia's trauma. By bringing Olivia back to the geographic setting of
her exploitation, she can renegotiate her relationship to that space as
someone other than a colonial victim. The return then seeks to reformulate the Caribbean as a contemporary site for recreating identity, as
opposed to a dead space of repeating history and oppression.

The novel figures the Caribbean as a space of encounter and relevance not only for Olivia but also for her daughter Soledad. Soledad is to some extent achieving her desire to get out of Washington Heights; in this case, however, moving out will not mean leaving her mother. Not only will she have to interact with her mother by accompanying her to the Dominican Republic, but the experience of travel itself also forces Soledad to confront her own relatively privileged position:

> The thought of going to DR all by myself is terrifying. With my mother, even worse. I remember the way people ask for so much. My mother's aunts, uncles, and cousins asking for mandaos [...] Because I'm a gringa, they will fill me up with refresco rojo and not let me drink the water. They will say things like, Ay Soledad, this bed is old but for a few days it should be fine, and make the kids who share that bed climb onto another crowded bed without any air-conditioning and fans, just so I, la gringa who is used to las cosas Americanas, will feel comfortable, be able to sleep alone, and hopefully grant their favors. (207)

While the return voyage seeks closure, it will not mean an engagement with a utopic homeland. Soledad must face poverty, yet not the same type of poverty that she sees on the streets of Washington Heights. Traveling to the Dominican Republic necessitates the recognition that Soledad will be viewed as an outsider, as a gringa who embodies the privilege and economic power of the United States. Soledad cannot escape her identification as a U.S. resident or the lens through which her island family will view her. The novel thus ambivalently theorizes hemispheric solidarities through Soledad's American identification.

Olivia and Soledad are led to the "very special place" in the Dominican Republic where the list will be destroyed by their Dominican family members (206). The ceremonial destruction takes place in a cavernous lagoon at night, since "the spirits don't come out in the day because of the tourists" (221). The neocolonial context of tourism continues to limit communication between these disparate communities of the island and the diaspora. Even so, the Caribbean landscape is described as hostile to the tourist presence, such that the boy navigating their raft through the waters tells of a tourist who "reached out to grab a gold necklace among the rocks in the water" (222). When the "gringo" jumps into the water to retrieve the jewelry, the boy refuses to follow and save him, explaining that "I don't mess with these waters" (222). The boy's instincts prove to be on the mark since the tourist suddenly disappears: "The necklace still there. But he evaporated. The mother said she was going to sue, but there's no one you can sue here" (222). The position of

Soledad as a gringa in the Dominican Republic is then a vulnerable one; she is in a sense trespassing in a space that is foreign to her and that may see her as a foreign presence as well.

The ceremony subsequently performed on the boat entails burning Olivia's list of men as well as constructing a family tree by placing photographs of every family member in New York City in the Caribbean waters. Cristina, Soledad's Dominican aunt, explains that the movement of the photographs, dipping beneath the water and then floating, will reflect the water's rejuvenating and cleansing effects on that particular person: "When we see them float we will know they will be OK" (223). In response to Soledad's question, "And if they don't float?" Cristina only responds, "It's not good [...] Let's just hope that doesn't happen" (223). All the pictures, including that of Soledad's father, Manolo, dip and float. When Soledad's image is placed in the water, however, it begins to sink. Soledad sees her face "bobbing underneath the water, trying to pull itself up, but it dips deeper and deeper" (224). Even as Soledad admits to herself the reality of the photograph's drowning as irrelevant to her own future, she cannot resist the temptation to jump in and retrieve it:

> I know deep down this cannot be the end-all be-all. How could this photograph tell me anything about my life, my destiny? I can't hold myself back. My mother taught me how to swim [...] I don't care about the tale of the monster. If I'm going to die, rot, who knows what terrible thing, I might as well fight. I'm not going to wait for it to happen. I'm not going to let this story haunt me for the rest of my life. (225)

Soledad refuses to play the role of a passive female victim and thereby suffer a fate similar to her mother's. By throwing herself into the water, Soledad seeks to posit the narrative force of her individual agency to contest that of the photograph as symbol of her fate.

What follows is a long narrative of Soledad's dream-like thoughts as she swims/drowns, alternating with the unspoken thoughts of Olivia, who is watching her from the boat. By detailing at length Soledad's experience of drowning, Angie Cruz composes an alternate ending to the dead-end strategy of opacity that Junot Díaz so aptly identifies in *Drown*. *Soledad*'s final narrative sequence formulates the act of drowning as a magical metaphor by which to explore the seductive limits of a lowercase realism that figures the ghetto as the only authentic location for Latino/a cultural production. Drowning as a mode of downward mobility is a fruitful image for making such a critique. Rather than the aggressive fight Soledad imagines greeting her as she enters the lagoon, she encounters instead a descent that encloses her with a seductive and comforting feeling of belonging. The immersion of the self provides Soledad with such a strong sense of entering a larger community that she actually loses her individual voice and her ability to communicate with those above the surface. Cut off from those above the water, Soledad is unperturbed by her inability to reach or communicate with them. Becoming part of "down below" is "the most wonderful thing I have ever felt," and Soledad wants her mother to join her so that "she can see I'm not drowning. That I can breathe through my pores" (226).

The metaphor of drowning indicates that the location of the subject in the ghetto entails disempowerment via opacity. The border distinguishing those outside from those inside the water slowly blurs. Soledad is unable to tell whether "they are in the ones in the water or is it me?" and she cannot determine if she is "flying in the sky or swimming in the ocean" (226). At the same time, she wonders, "Why are they looking at me that way, as if they can't see me?" (226). Her downward mobility begins to render her invisible, but Soledad still asserts that "If someone asked me what it feels like, I'd say it's more like surviving. As I swim, I'm surviving like I have never had to survive before" (226). Unseen, unheard, and literally drowning, Soledad does not realize that downward mobility is endangering her self, her ability to communicate, and her very life. What Soledad finds so seductive about the dark of the lagoon is that she is becoming marginalized. Not only is she losing contact with her relatives above the water, but she is also losing a sense of perspective. Escaping into invisibility, her loss of individuality is enabling while at the same time suicidal. As Soledad becomes one with the "riptides, spinning between the currents," she gains access to the multiple temporal moments that define identity: "When I surrender to the warmth of the water, I feel the past, present and future become one" (226–27). In this space of surrender and death, Soledad hears her mother's voice calling for forgiveness, but this moment of reconciliation brings with it a loss of direction: "I can't remember where I am or where I'm going" (227). The trans-temporal space of the lagoon is a space of reconnection, however, the narrative also configures it as an abstracted or theoretical space that cannot be a livable reality. Soledad is unable to differentiate space and time, noting that "Maybe, I'm inside a dream" (226).

Olivia, her mother, watching Soledad in the depths of the lagoon from the surface, interprets her daughter's downward mobility as suicidal:

> I want to help Soledad find a way out. I want to push Soledad back into the world, but when I look into the water the woman staring back at me can't find the strength. She doesn't know that I am here for her [...] And when I see Soledad surrender, I scream. (226)

The scream awakens Soledad from the seductive waters of the lagoon, effectively saving her from drowning: "I can hear the high pitch of my mother's scream. It makes the water lift itself into a wave. Inside this wave [...] I'm on the A train, emergency breaks [sic] go off right before I reach Washington Heights" (227). Olivia's scream stops Soledad from mentally returning to the ghetto as her place of origin, and provides Soledad with the sense of direction that the water's opacity and depth erased. Soledad swims to the surface, bringing her mother's photo with her, only to faint on the rocks beside the water. When she awakens, Olivia is holding her: "I want to ask her so any questions about my father, her past, my birth. But before I even open my mouth, she speaks" (227). It is here at the conclusion of the novel that Olivia explains the personal context of her daughter's name: "She said this name would open people's hearts to me and make them listen. She thought with a name like Soledad I would never be alone" (227). Olivia breaks the silence of her depression to provide Soledad with a community-based vision of identity, in contrast to the photograph of individual identity Soledad jumped into the water to save. While the static image of the photograph isolates Soledad's figure from what lay beyond its white borders, Olivia emphasizes Relation.[8] It is then her mother, an immigrant Latina, who reveals to Soledad the fullness of her subjectivity as a space of intersections, an expansive solidarity that connects with others through a common experience of loneliness and marginality. At the heart of this bond lies the contradiction of her name, Soledad. By signifying loneliness and marginality, Olivia hoped that Soledad would not repeat the cycle of victimization but rather form a community around shared experiences of suffering and fragmentation. This vision of community is quite different from that offered by the lagoon or by Díaz's *Drown*. The narrators in Díaz's text have their selves effaced by the narrative's opacity, similar to the way in which the lagoon erased Soledad's selfhood. Olivia's formulation of community depends on Soledad as an individual, a distinct self who connects outwards to several communities inside and outside the ghetto, crisscrossing between the United States and the Caribbean.

Angie Cruz's *Soledad* attempts to balance the double inheritances of the resident and the immigrant, the lowercase and the newcomer, and their equally powerful claims on U.S. Latino/a identity. Rather than resolving the tension or escaping it by moving up and out, *Soledad* seeks to place these two divergent Latino/a traditions in dialogue as a way of stressing the contestatory nature of Latino/a cultural production. With the characterizations of Soledad, Caramel, and Olivia, the novel imagines assimilationist tendencies alongside political resistance, ghetto realism alongside magical realism. *Soledad* ultimately broadens our vision of

Latino/a cultural production by moving toward a transformative recontextualization of the U.S. Latino/a experience within the larger framework of the hemisphere. Refuting the claim that this literature engages in the "privileging of privilege" (Flores, *From Bomba* 175), *Soledad* expands upon the definition of the lowercase Latino/a voice to include *both* resident and immigrant Latino/as by highlighting the public and personal histories of marginality and exploitation that fragment and connect Las Américas.

## THE POPULAR, THE PUBLIC, AND THE LATINO/A WRITER

The opening of this chapter reviews Juan Flores's description of Latino/a immigrant writers in general and Dominican-American authors in particular as especially fortunate in their publishing success due to the cultural capital they possess. Both Junot Díaz and Angie Cruz have enjoyed rapid recognition, however, we maintain that the effects of these *éxitos* and the authors' relationships to the market are expressed in different ways. Díaz points to the negative effects of the market on emerging Latino/a writers and Latino/a cultural production more generally, whereas Cruz represents the market as engendering an intellectual community that can positively enable the circulation and development of Latino/a writerly creativity. In this sense, the writers complicate the understanding that immigrant Latino/a narratives are easily assimilated into the market by presenting divergent perspectives on the relationship between Latino/a cultural production and the book market. For Díaz, market popularity presents serious challenges to creativity instead of easy access to a position of privilege for the Latino/a writer. Cruz also indicates that the market does not necessary entail assimilation into the mainstream but rather offers alternative networks of writerly affiliation with other U.S. minority communities and literary traditions.

Lizabeth Paravisini-Gebert notes that "the marketing of Díaz's stories reads like a cautionary tale about the commodification of Latino/a literature, its literary merit notwithstanding" (164). Díaz's inclusion in anthologies as early as 1996 and 1997 "attests to the profound impact he has made on the American literary scene" (164), but his public persona garnered him a unique level of visibility as an emerging writer. For example, Díaz was listed as one of the "new faces of 1996" by *Newsweek* in January of the same year.[9] In addition, Díaz's short stories have appeared in such magazines and journals as *African Voices, Glimmer Train,* the *New Yorker,* the *Paris Review, Story,* and *Time Out.* While providing a detailed description of how Díaz "erupted into public notice quite dramatically with a blitz of publicity" (164), Paravisini-Gebert does not provide any specific warnings about the effects of this publicity on Díaz. The most explicit suggestion offered is that market success placed Díaz "in an almost untenable situation of having to meet the highest and most overblown expectations" (165). What remains unsaid is how this success produced any negative consequences. With no explicit explanation of this danger alongside the image of what might be termed excess success, one might wonder, what's the problem?

Díaz himself appears more helpful in fleshing out the dangers of success: "Contracts, of course, create pressure [...] they entail the danger of destabilizing you to the point where you don't have your own voice anymore. Getting too much attention early on is also bad; you know, I think those are dangerous things. Especially, if you write like me" (Céspedes and Torres-Saillant 899). Despite the critics' inability to define the dangers of a quick rise to fame, Díaz directly names the consequences of such success: writer's block. Public attention appears to be something that Díaz identifies as specifically traumatic to his own writing style. While Díaz has published several stories in the *New Yorker* since *Drown* appeared in 1996, he is perhaps alluding to the conspicuous delay in the publication of his second book.[10] In the context of this chapter, it also seems plausible that this particular loss of creative voice derives from Díaz's use of opacity and its implied relationship with the reading audience as well as the actual publishing contract. As we mentioned before, Díaz's use of opacity as a protective device and political strategy within the genre of ghetto fiction leads him to also identify the creative cul-de-sac that results from such a strategy—a self-censorship that impedes communication within the Latino/a community and between the Latino/a writer and his or her reader. Díaz also points to his early literary success and acceptance by the *literati* of high society, especially represented by his publication in the *New Yorker,* as posing a serious roadblock to creativity and limiting the possibilities of a post-*Drown* imagination. Díaz's remarks on the challenges of being categorized as having literally "made it":

*Díaz:* I feel it's weird because I've been fortunate enough to be considered literary fiction. They're so happy to claim me as literature because it makes them all look better. They don't want to relegate me to areas of ethnic studies. They don't want that. The suggestion seems to be: "You are one of us now."

*Torres-Saillant:* They?

*Díaz:* The mainstream, the publishers, everybody. They want me to mainstream. (Céspedes and Torres-Sallaint 905)

Torres-Sallaint's question uncovers an anxious formulation of the pow-
ers-that-be and Díaz's desire to resist "their" mainstreaming project. At
the same time, there appears to be an inherent contradiction within this
formulation. Díaz's work seems to be already accepted as "literary" and
therefore mainstreamed; yet at the same time he indicates that this
process of acceptance is uneven and therefore incomplete. In effect, Díaz
points to the possibility that a writer can be marketed and yet not mainstreamed. The generic pronoun that Díaz uses, the mysterious "them,"
indicates the varying and often contradictory standards of authenticity to
which the Latino/a writer is expected to conform. Whether these standards are formulated by Latino/a critics or by established U.S. *literati,* the
burden remains one that censors the range of creative models available to
the Latino/a author. Therefore, Díaz highlights the difficulty of isolating
positions of oppositionality and dynamic creativity in the tenuous space
of belonging open to the Latino/a writer within the market.

Angie Cruz describes a different entrance into the publishing market
but nevertheless accords the same importance to its influence on Latino/a
cultural production. For example, Cruz pinpoints the fashion market as
the space that gave her the confidence to eventually become a writer: "I
thought artists were Picasso and Goya, all of these dead white men. I never
ever saw myself as an artist. But I could see myself as a fashion designer
because there is Oscar De La Renta. It's this simple. It was so simple in
my head" (Torres-Saillant, *Writing* 111). The circulation of de la Renta's
fashion designs and the notoriety that followed presented Cruz with a
model for her own success. Cruz emphasizes the fact that although her
thinking as a teenager was simplistic, what was of utmost importance to
her was the representation of a Dominican in the public sphere: "No one
ever told me while I was in high school that there was Frida Khalo [sic] or
Diego Rivera or Romare Bearden, anything that's connected to my life.
But I knew there was Oscar De La Renta who is Dominican. I thought,
well, maybe I can do it" (112). This early relationship to the market as a
source of artistic and intellectual models seems to inform Cruz's understanding of the dangers of literary success as well. While remarking that
she does "fear the fate of so many young writers who get fame and then
get blocked," Cruz argues that her position as a young writer has been
safeguarded by an earlier generation: "I thank God that so many young
writers have already paved the way. I don't think I have the same pressure
as they did being the first Dominican writer or the first Haitian writer"
(118). What appears to comfort Cruz is that other Latino/a and
Caribbean writers took on the arduous task of being "firsts" and bearing
the burden of establishing a market for the "new" literary category. This

first generation, according to Cruz, established a community via its entrance into the book market. Cruz explains, "I feel now that as a Dominican writer in the United States, I belong to a community" (118).

The relationship that Cruz articulates between her writing and her audience or community appears to be especially nourishing to her creativity. Cruz speaks about her cultivation as a writer within a specifically feminist and Caribbean academic network. The page of acknowledgments at the end of *Soledad* contains an impressive list of mentors, from Bill Cosby and Carole Boyce Davies, to Cristina Garcia and Edwidge Danticat, to Junot Díaz, Earl Lovelace, and Paule Marshall. Cruz explains that this community of intellectuals and writers is both a source and product of her writerly success: "I realized that it is through working that you forge relationships" (123). This belief in the importance of communal relations to the Latino/a literary imagination prompted Cruz to form an organization called Women in Literature and Letters (WILL), a group whose members exchange their writings via a "peer-like relationship" (123). In fact, Cruz mentions Junot Díaz as one of the writers who "has been really helpful" in the development of WILL (123).

Just as Díaz and Cruz are connected to a communal project through their literary activism, they also share a common understanding of their writing as a reflection of these political objectives. While Díaz uses an aesthetic of negation to point to the limits of opacity in order to critique the Latino/a community, Cruz is also wary of "writing that I don't feel has a service to render a community" (116). Similarly to Díaz, Cruz describes her writerly goals in terms of talking back to the Latino/a community: "It has to in some ways give back an idea or suggestion, something, for change" (116). For Cruz, however, the fact that writing enters the Latino/a community and circulates by means of the market is not necessarily problematic. The market then figures in her work as a potential framework for articulating a project of progressive politics. In her second novel, *Let It Rain Coffee* (2005), Cruz posits such a vision via the character of Miraluz, a factory worker in the Dominican Republic who sews underwear bearing the Victoria's Secret label. Miraluz realizes that her attempts to organize a union will not ultimately change the system of economic exploitation in the Caribbean; after all, "the reason we can't get our union is because if we all get fired, there are hundreds of women just like us willing to take this job" (Cruz, *Let* 224). Concocting an alternate plan, Miraluz decides to organize the women to start their own company, to be called El Secreto de la Victoria, by collectively pooling their money and labor, but more importantly, by creating a market for their product:

Mujeres, we must get in touch with all our family members and find out who buys Victoria's Secret and see if they will buy from us. We must involve them in this movement. If the money that our families send us makes up half our economy, then what they choose to buy can affect the conditions of the women in these factories. You'll see, a part of the money will go to building up our community. Better schools, better clinics. (229)

The character of Miraluz serves as an example of how politics can be rethought through the market, recognizing that older anticolonial models cannot be sustained in the face of the significant shifts in globalization's development. Cruz's novel constructs consumer politics as a means of renewing or recapturing the idealism of past political projects, insisting that it is possible to effect change from within the market, to create "socially responsible capitalism for the people" (278).

While the actual form of Díaz and Cruz's writing is quite distinctive, both writers have similar goals regarding the relationship they seek between their writing and the Latino/a community. By placing their narratives and interviews alongside each other, we argue that Díaz and Cruz represent opposite sides of the same coin. Whether positive or negative, the market emerges as an unavoidable space for exchange and contestation for Latino/a cultural production. These Latino/a writers' negotiation of their literary success points to the dangers and potentials inherent in entering the public sphere as well as the uneven paths through which Latino/a cultural production engages the market. In the following chapter on Cristina Garcia, we read *Dreaming in Cuban* (1992) as a Latino/a text that seeks to make sense of the market's effects on cultural production. More specifically, Garcia's novel imagines the possibilities for articulating a Latino/a public sphere and community via the market. We will compare Garcia's representation of the Latino/a public sphere with those of Ilan Stavans and Gustavo Pérez Firmat in order to show that Garcia's novel moves beyond the multiculturalists' unequivocal celebration of the marketplace. Rather, redemption through commodification comes at a price, one that the novel struggles to accept. The novel closes with a melancholic perspective on the foreclosure of the Cuban revolution as a paradigm for resistance and progressive politics.

# LATINO/A IDENTITY AND CONSUMER CITIZENSHIP IN CRISTINA GARCIA'S *DREAMING IN CUBAN*

THE GHETTO IS NOT THE ONLY SPACE IN WHICH LATINO/A THEORISTS and authors draw the parameters of Latino/a identity politics. Another popular trend within this criticism foregrounds the market as constitutive of Latino/a identity. These multiculturalist formulations of Latino/a hybridity, however, are often based on a simplistic celebration of the relationship between identity and consumption. Chapter 4 consequently begins with an analysis of two critics who have been instrumental in these market-based conceptions of Latino/a identity, Ilan Stavans and Gustavo Pérez Firmat, and the extent to which their multiculturalist theories depend on an imaginary of food as a metaphor for these interactions. Following a review of the function and shortcomings of the Latino/a food metaphor, we will turn to Néstor García Canclini and Arlene Dávila for alternative approaches to the constitution of identity through the market. This theoretical foundation provides a new entry into Cristina Garcia's now canonical novel, *Dreaming in Cuban,* as a literary intervention that imagines the market's effects on cultural production and Latino/a identity. Previous interpretations of this novel follow in the footsteps of Stavans and Pérez Firmat by depicting the main character, Pilar, as utopically recuperating a Cuban-American hybrid subjectivity. We seek to complicate these readings by highlighting how the novel defines hybridity in relation to a market-enabled Latino/a public sphere. This Latino/a consumer identity, however, also appears to entail the death of popular political movements as represented by the Cuban revolution.

## RECIPES FOR DISAPPEARING LATINO/AS

Ilan Stavans and Gustavo Pérez Firmat are central figures in the development of Latino/a studies in the United States. While emerging from different backgrounds of Mexican and Cuban culture respectively, these theorists nevertheless articulate Latino/a identity in similar ways. Published only a year apart from one another, *The Hispanic Condition* (1995) and *Life on the Hyphen: The Cuban-American Way* (1994) use the same type of gustatory terminology in order to celebrate the hybrid nature of Latino/a identity and culture. To explain what Stavans sees as a sudden popularity explosion, the "revaluation of things Latino" (Stavans, *Hispanic* 4), he pinpoints Spanglish as the major contribution of Latino/a culture to mainstream U.S. society. The Spanglish idiom is likened to "a *sopa de letras*," that contains a sabor hispano ready for consumption (10–11). Since "the Melting Pot began to boil for Latinos" (11), consumerist desire figuratively places Latino/as as the actual food being cooked in this soup to meet the larger demands of the U.S. market. Indeed, immigrant movements are also described in terms of food consumption, with Puerto Ricans and other Latino/a groups turning New York City "into a huge frying pan" (12). Gustavo Pérez Firmat also focuses on the "latinization of the United States" (Pérez Firmat 1), although specifically by Cuban Americans, and in the process articulates Latino/a culture as one that "treats consumption as a creative act" (14). Consumption turns out to be a distinctive feature of Latino/a identity as well, as evidenced by the metaphor of ajiaco soup that Pérez Firmat borrows from Fernando Ortiz, "an indefinitely renewable stew that accepts the most diverse ingredients" (15). The heterogeneity of the soup evokes Cuban culture, to the extent that Pérez Firmat employs the metaphor to equate people with food: "There are no pure people in Cuba; in Cuba even the purée is impure" (15–16).

This food metaphor poses some serious theoretical problems when it is used to express the hybridity of Latino/a identity. First, the concept of the Latino/a as *consumer* rather than *consumed* is never broached. While Latino/a culture is formulated as a transformative product of consumption in the United States, the Latino/a subject never appears as a consumer. This absence is particularly evident when Stavans articulates what he calls the "bookends of Latino culture" (Stavans, *Hispanic* 29). These bookends are represented by two figures, the Mexican painter Martín Ramírez and the pseudonymous "Latino" author Danny Santiago. Without any hint of irony, Stavans figures Martín Ramírez, "who spent most of his life in a California madhouse," as "a symbol of the Hispanic immigrant experience" (2). At first glance, Ramírez's psychological condition might seem an unappealing example of Latino/a identity, but Stavans places higher value on the circulation of this painter's creative work. The mute Ramírez began drawing while he was hospitalized and was "fortunate to be discovered" by a psychiatrist who was "so impressed by his patient's work" that he proceeded to collect Ramírez's paintings and promote exhibits of his art (2). While the popularity of Ramírez's painting may not have changed the circumstances of his mental state, it is clear that his cultural production and its consumption by the established art world are of greater importance to Stavans's formulation of U.S. Latinidad. The hyphenated existence and marginality of immigrant Latino/as can be troublesome, but their integration and consumption translates into greater cultural freedom. Because of pioneers like Ramírez, "Latinos are now leaving his frustrated silence behind" and "new generations of Spanish speakers are feeling at home in Gringolandia" (3).

The flip side of the Ramírez model is the successful cultural transition that only consumption can make possible. While "many Latinos already have a Yankee look," Stavans notes that "what is more exciting is that Anglos are beginning to look just like us" (4). To represent the double process of "the Hispanization of the United States, and the Anglocization of Hispanics" (4), Stavans turns to the example of Danny Santiago. With the appearance of *Famous All Over Town* in 1983, Santiago is greeted with positive reviews and critical accolades but is eventually exposed as a fraud in the *New York Review of Books*. It turns out that Danny Santiago is "not a young Chicano" but the pen name of Daniel Lewis James, who hails from "a well-to-do family in Kansas City, Missouri" (28). Stavans depicts James's novel as a product of his familiarity with and consumption of the Chicano community in East Los Angeles: "As a result of that relationship, James began to feel close to the Latino psyche, *digesting* its linguistic and idiosyncratic ways" (28, emphasis added). In opposition to the American literary establishment, which brands Danny Santiago as a fraud, Stavans argues that James's move towards becoming a "darling of Latino letters" makes him exemplary of a "nation consumed by wars of identities" (29). Danny Santiago is the ideal representative of Stavans's one-directional process of consumption. Although Stavans presents the Santiago case as "a paradigm" of the end product of the Latinization process (28), it is also clear that the bookends of his chronology and its movement from Ramírez to Santiago imply the erasure of the Latino/a subject as well as the Sixties. With Ramírez's death in 1960 and the publication of Santiago's novel in 1983, Stavans's historical timeline clearly omits the Sixties and the Civil Rights movements as forces shaping contemporary Latino/a identity. In addition, by opening with an acclaimed but insane Hispanic painter only to end with the assumption of a Latino/a identity by a "septuagenarian Anglo" writer (28), Stavans implies a disturbing formula for the role of Latino/as in the United States. The consumption and cannibalization of the Latino/a subject becomes constitutive of a less homogeneous mainstream American culture. At the conclusion of Stavans's cultural "*reconquista*" (5), Latino/as disappear, becoming mere disembodied abstractions, "Danny Santiago" masks that can be as easily taken off as put on.

Stavans describes this Latinization process in an overwhelmingly positive tone throughout his work, rationalizing the erasure of the Latino/a subject. The valorization of hybridity often leads Stavans to gloss over sites of struggle and violence that engender such hybridity. This attitude is particularly evident in Stavans's reference to the European conquest of the Americas as a "fiesta of miscegenation" (10). Nevertheless, it is worth noting that even in the rare moments that acknowledge the actual presence and suffering of Latino/as while describing a triumphant reconquista of the United States, the equation of the Latino/a people with food is reiterated: "This metamorphosis includes many losses, of course [...] the loss of identity; the loss of self-esteem; and more important, the loss of tradition. Some are left behind en route, whereas others forget the flavor of home. But less is more, and confusion is being turned into enlightenment" (15). If Latino/a culture is consumed in its encounter with mainstream U.S. society, then it is also an exhaustible supply. After creating a new hybrid mainstream identity, the Hispanic flavor will no longer belong to Latino/as. In effect, the loss of that special spic(e) entails "the vanishing of a collective identity" through assimilation (15): Latino/as will cease to exist.

This logical consequence leads us then to consider a second problematic involved in the theorization of the Latino/a subject within the food metaphor. Ilan Stavans does not allow for identifying the Latino/a as a consumer, but what would happen if one were to introduce the Latino/a as consumer into the metaphor? As our discussion of Gustavo Pérez Firmat will show, the terms that define consumption—eater and eaten, consumer and consumed—position the Latino/a consumer as self-cannibalizing. With the consumer and the object of consumption defined by a Latin essence, the Latino/a subject implodes, since self-cannibalization is literally self-exhaustive. Even though Pérez Firmat formulates the Latino/a as consumer, this consumption takes place within a completely self-enclosed system. Consuming the self then becomes a necessarily terminal condition, relying on a finite source and resulting in the performance of a final disappearing act. Indeed, Pérez Firmat echoes Stavans when he diverges from Ortiz's ajiaco, changing one important ingredient in the recipe for his Latino/a stew: it is not "indefinitely renewable" but in limited supply (Pérez Firmat 15). To make the case that a "well-groomed mango [...] can be just as American as apple pie," Pérez Firmat imagines consumption as an integral part of engaging with Latino/a culture (20). Narrating a typical summer afternoon of "consumerist frenzy" in Miami, Pérez Firmat reveals that his Cuban identity is intricately connected to the objects he purchases, drinking a papaya milk shake from the Love Juices Café to eating "Tropical Snow, which is Miamian for arroz con leche," at the Versailles Restaurant (21).

While this narrative asserts the existence of a Latino/a consumer, these acts of consumption producing U.S. Latinidad are not sustainable: "The Cuban-American stew can only simmer for so long" (125). The hybrid space of translation is a product of what Pérez Firmat calls the one-and-a-half generation—those who were born in Cuba and immigrated to the United States at a young age. With the passing of this in-between populace's "expiration date" (133), Latino/a hybridity comes to an end. But this "limited life expectancy" is more than just the passing of time; it also results from a process of self-consumption (17). Pérez Firmat insists that "it is not assimilation that [he] is talking about" (16), and indeed, it appears that cannibalization would be a better term for the relationship he imagines between Latino/a identity and consumption. Playing with the multiple meanings of the term "roots," Pérez Firmat makes the point that "you eat them in the knowledge that such conspicuous consumption will let you remain faithful to—what else?—your roots" (16). Consumer consciousness requires that such consumption be a public act in which culture, identity, and commodities combine to form a Latino/a subject and object of consumption. This circular logic ultimately posits the Latino/a as a "self-consuming vegetable" and therefore an endangered species responsible for its own disappearance (16).

It is no coincidence that these musings on Latino/a hybridity and its relation to market consumption lead Stavans and Pérez Firmat to also imagine the final resting places of Latino/a culture. For Pérez Firmat, the Versailles Restaurant has already become a "glistening mausoleum," compounded by its necrophilic location "only two blocks away from the Woodlawn Cemetery, which contains the remains of many Cuban notables" (135). The bizarre dream that Ilan Stavans narrates in the prologue to *The Hispanic Condition* also "witnesses the Hispanic future" in the form of a "magisterial museum" (Stavans, *Hispanic* xvi). For both critics, the end product of the food equation is the fossilization of Latino/a culture. For a more complex understanding of Latino/a culture's relationship with consumption, however, Latino/a studies must move beyond theorizations based on food as a metaphor for identity and culture. As we have shown, the metaphor is ultimately too simplistic in its formulation of the dynamics involved in the market. These recipes narrate consumption as a one-directional process, with the eater consuming a product. Consequently, these positions remain static in their relation to each other, with the active consumer subject eating a passive and exhaustible product of Latin essence. The transformative power articulated through the food metaphor operates on cannibalistic and/or assimilationist logic. Underlying this metaphor is an essentialist conceptualization of culture as static and therefore finite and exhaustible, as opposed to reproducing or shifting.

### EN GUSTOS NO HAY NADA ESCRITO: WRITING THE LATINO/A CONSUMER

We have seen how the food metaphor leads to a dead end in terms of formulating any future for Latino/a culture. We therefore now turn to Néstor García Canclini, Arlene Dávila, and Cristina Garcia to provide us with some alternative understandings of the relationship between the Latino/a subject and the processes of commodification. Both García Canclini and Dávila theorize the consumer's position along with that of the consumed product, thereby offering a view of consumption as a potential resource for the creation of a Latino/a public sphere. The principal differences between the formulation of this consumer citizenship and prior theorizations lie in the unevenness of the consumption relationships themselves, blurring the line between consumer and product, as well as in the way in which consumption prompts identification with an abstract pan-Latino/a community. Cristina Garcia's novel, *Dreaming in Cuban* (1992), is contemporary with the writings of Stavans and Pérez Firmat and it also serves to think through the possibilities of a Latino/a consumer citizen; equally important, it identifies the limits of such an imaginary.

In *Consumers and Citizens: Globalization and Multicultural Conflicts* (1995), Néstor García Canclini acknowledges the existence of theoretical gaps: "We have provided scant theoretical frameworks for understanding these popular circuits [of communication] as forums where there emerge networks for the exchange of information and citizen apprenticeship" (García Canclini, *Consumers* 23). This conceptual problem relates specifically to the power relations evident in consumer practices. In the chapter titled "Consumption is Good for Thinking," García Canclini argues that "nowadays we see consumption as more complex than the simple relation between manipulative media and docile audiences" (37). The analysis offered "does not posit the relation between senders and receivers as one of domination," as the food metaphor's duality between subject and object implies. Rather, the relationship is articulated between producer and consumer, *both* positioned as *subjects,* and the dynamic between these two agents includes "collaboration and transaction" (38). By locating agency in the acts of production and consumption, García Canclini frames the market as a much more complicated site of social interaction.

By viewing consumption as a mode of active interpretation, García Canclini's equation opens up the possibility for consumers to play a larger role in market relations. When applied to the Latino/a subject, consumption can then be a means for formulating a Latino/a public sphere through the market. García Canclini seeks to highlight the dynamic nature of consumption, asking that "we recognize that when we consume we also think, select, and elaborate social meaning" (26). The power of the consumer is framed by demand, for "to consume is to participate in an arena of competing claims for what society produces and the ways of using it" (39). Hence the relationship between producer and consumer is two-directional, in contrast to the one-directional flow of the food metaphor. Consumption becomes a "space of interaction where producers and senders no longer simply seduce their audiences; they also have to justify themselves rationally" (39). The consumer plays a significant role in shaping market production and circulation, but García Canclini also argues that consumption can be a mode of defense and protection against the dangers of the market. To consume in excess may signal an attempt to deal with the "unstable social order and uncertain interactions with others," and "make more sense of a world where all that is solid melts into air" (42).

It is important then to note that consumption as an uneven process opens certain avenues for empowerment; yet these very modes of agency remain quite tenuous. García Canclini uses two examples to show how a cultural object entering the market can take on many meanings. The first example is that of indigenous masks and their travel through the market: "Masks made by indigenous peoples for ceremonies are sold to a modern consumer and ultimately put on display in urban apartments or museums, where their economic value is forgotten" (46–47). On the other hand, García Canclini gives the example of a "song produced for exclusively aesthetic reasons, which, once recorded, attains mass appeal and profits. Then it is appropriated and modified by a political movement and becomes a resource of identification and collective mobilization" (47). These examples demonstrate the way products take on different meanings and functions—political or economic, transformative or passive—in different contexts, but ultimately the process is neither predictable nor chronological. The sense of openness and perhaps even randomness that characterizes the market may be potentially liberating or exploitative: "These changing biographies of objects and messages suggest the commercial aspect of commodities is their opportunity and their risk" (47).

The fluidity and uncertainty involved in commodification and consumption lead to a reconceptualization of culture itself. Since objects "lose any necessary tie to territories of origin" (17), culture cannot remain bound to the static terms of the food metaphor. Rather, García Canclini describes culture as "a process of multinational assemblage, a flexible articulation of parts, a montage of features that any citizen in any country, of whatever religion or ideology, can read and use" (17–18). With such a formulation of culture, it is possible to conceive of a vibrant Latino/a culture that is dynamic and responsive to contacts with other cultures, whether they be dominant or marginal. The disappearing of a Latin essence that the food metaphor's logic necessitates contrasts with this alternate Latino/a culture that is always in process of becoming. A new role arises for the Latino/a consumer, one of creation rather than self-cannibalization. Consumption offers an alternative means of belonging: "The questions specific to our citizenship, such as how we inform ourselves and who represents our interests, are answered more often than not through private consumption of commodities and media offerings" (5). Consequently, consumption carries with it the potential for creating different modes of citizenship. As García Canclini notes, the shared codes that denote belonging "refer ever less to ethnicity, class, and nation," but rather are being "reformulated as *mobile pacts for the interpretation* of commodities and messages" (43, emphasis in original). Naming these groups "interpretive communities of consumers," García Canclini conceives of the market as more than just a space for economic exchange but also "as part of more complex sociocultural interactions" (46).

García Canclini's theorizations are particularly relevant to understanding the creation of a Latino/a public sphere by means of the market. If "collective appropriation" becomes the means by which "relations of solidarity" are understood (46), then consumption may solicit identification with an abstract Latino/a community and cultural politics. Arlene Dávila's *Latinos, Inc.: The Marketing and Making of a People* (2001) indicates that the emergence of Hispanic marketing, inspired by and yet diverging from the Civil Rights movement, has played a significant role in the development of such a public sphere. The evolution of a pan-Latino/a category is one such development:

> Although Latino social movements in the 1960s defined themselves
> against anything Spanish, such distinctions have since been countered by
> the growing consolidation of a common Latino/Hispanic identity that
> encompasses anyone from a Spanish/Latin American background in the
> United States. (Dávila, *Latinos* 1)

To explain the parameters and influence of this Latino/a category, Dávila
echoes García Canclini's mapping of the relationship between consumption and citizenship. Focusing on the role Hispanic marketing plays in
the development of Latino/a identity, Dávila argues that such an analysis
reveals the double function of consumption. On the one hand, marketing trends are "particularly revealing of the relationship between culture,
corporate sponsorship, and politics" (2). In addition to this broad context of relations, Dávila points out that Hispanic marketing can "illumi-
nate how commercial representations may shape people's cultural
identities as well as notions of belonging and cultural citizenship in public life" (2). For the Latino/a community, this observation means that
such marketing has been and remains foundational in the development
of its imaginary.

It is important to note that Dávila expresses an ambivalence that is
similar to if not more accentuated than that of García Canclini regarding
the potential embodied by consumption. Dávila neither celebrates nor
condemns the consumption of Latino/a culture. Rather, she seeks to
understand the way in which marketing is "central to the constitution
and imagining of contemporary identities" in a specifically U.S. Latino/a
context (4–5). The main challenge faced by such a project is to balance
two opposed perspectives on consumption, to "recognize the blurred
nature of mass mediated culture's genres," while also acknowledging
"that in a context where nothing escapes commodification, commercial
culture cannot be easily reduced to sheer pleasure or commercial manipulation" (10). Dávila consequently calls attention to the complex layers of
interaction involved in consumption by noting that agency or power is
present on both sides of the equation even though it is distributed
unevenly. To begin with, marketing is limited by the social imaginary
that produces it: "Advertising does not invent meaning for a commodity,
but works by transferring to it meaning from the social world" (14). It
also becomes evident on both the macro and micro levels of market
economics that consumption is a powerful but not necessarily a one-
directional process. The consumer also shapes market forces; advertise-
ments "are always entangled with the interests, desires, or imaginations of
those whom they seek to entice as consumers, and are always the result of
negotiations in the process of depicting the consumer" (14–15). Thus,

Dávila concludes that the market category and the public identity of U.S. Latinidad emerge from a complex process of negotiation; to say that this consumer citizenship is a foreign concept imposed on the community would be an oversimplification. The processes that form a public Latino/a identity "are not seen as top-down development, resulting from the commodification and appropriation of Latino culture or from self-agency; rather, they stem from the contrary involvement of and negotiations between dominant, imposed, and self-generated interests" (16–17).

In addition to García Canclini and Dávila's definition of consumption as a multifaceted and uneven process that may contribute to the creation of a Latino/a public sphere, the two critics also focus on the city as the quintessential site for observing this process. In conceiving consumer citizenship, García Canclini seeks "to think of the contemporary citizen as the inhabitant of the city more than the nation" (García Canclini, *Consumers* 29). The city supersedes national identification not only because of the primacy of local culture but also because of the transnational composition of the city, which is a product of various migrant cultures. These national traditions "are reorganized by the transnational flow of commodities and messages" (29). It is probably no coincidence then that Dávila limits her research of the Hispanic marketing industry to New York City even though "Los Angeles is the largest market in terms of the number of Latinos, and San Antonio and Miami are currently sites for some of the largest and most important Hispanic agencies" (Dávila, *Latinos* 19). The reasons she gives include New York City's early role in the development of Hispanic marketing and its position as the "second largest Hispanic/Latino market in the United States" (19). The most significant factor in the selection of New York turns out to be the transnationalism of the actual Latino/a base within this area, "one of the most heterogenous, thereby functioning as an important 'homogenizing pot' of Latinidad" (19). Located at the intersection of market and migrant, global and local, the New York metropolis is an ideal site for understanding the relationship between Latino/a identity and consumption practices.

### PURCHASING MEMORIES IN THE MARKETPLACE

New York City is the backdrop for half of Cristina Garcia's novel, *Dreaming in Cuban*, a post-Sixties text that imagines the potential and limits of a Latino/a consumer identity.[1] Since its publication and nomination for the National Book Award in 1992, *Dreaming in Cuban* has enjoyed a great deal of critical interest within and outside the academy. The novel was quickly canonized and incorporated into the fields of

Latino/a and U.S. ethnic literature, as evinced by its inclusion in numerous anthologies, such as *Masterpieces of Latino Literature* (1994), *The Brooklyn Reader: Thirty Writers Celebrate America's Favorite Borough* (1994), *Little Havana Blues: A Cuban-American Literature Anthology* (1996), and *The Latino Reader: An American Literary Tradition from 1542 to the Present* (1997). The novel was even adapted for the stage in 1999 at the American Place Theatre in New York City. Cristina Garcia's first novel has become the subject of numerous doctoral dissertations, the earliest of which were completed shortly after the book's publication by David Thomas Mitchell (1993) and Ibis del Carmen Gómez-Vega (1995), indicating its rapid acceptance by the academy. This chapter, however, takes issue with the critical reception of *Dreaming in Cuban*, in particular with celebratory readings of the text's depiction of Latino/a hybridity. By reading against the grain of this discourse, we will highlight the ambivalence in the text that has been glossed over by critics as well as the imaginative limits the novel places on Pilar's act of "dreaming in Cuban" in the post-Sixties context of globalization. Our reading will consequently focus on Pilar as the embodiment of a Latino/a consumer subject, consumption being the means by which she ultimately constructs her hybridity.

The critical discussion surrounding *Dreaming in Cuban* includes a variety of approaches; however, the dominant trend tends to be a multiculturalist approach, which argues that Garcia's novel challenges the coherence of such concepts as nation, history, and patriarchy. Multiculturalist critics specifically locate such textual challenges in the novel's representation of cultural hybridity. On the whole, these interpretations follow in the footsteps of Ilan Stavans and Gustavo Pérez Firmat, presenting hybridity in uncomplicated and positive terms as beneficial and enabling cultural reconnection. The main character, Pilar, then emerges as the embodiment of a hybrid migratory subject. Critics articulate her identity as culturally in-between and therefore capable of moving physically and psychically between Cuba and the United States. Underpinning all these readings of Garcia's novel is the interpretation of Pilar's journey to Cuba as a positive move that facilitates communication across generational and geographical lines.[2] "The loss incurred by exile" is linguistic, cultural, and historical (Alvarez-Borland 46). The return consequently provides Pilar with access to a family history as well as to a Cuban culture that she previously lacked; she "can now preserve that family history and in the process know her own identity and place in this long and fascinating saga" (Payant 174). More specifically, her return is represented as a reclamation of identity, such that when Pilar leaves Cuba at the end of the novel, she takes with her a new sense of self: "The journey home to Cuba allows her to translate and define herself" (Gómez-Vega 99).

Indeed, Pilar is described as traversing "the path from exile to ethnicity" and thereby acquiring a hybrid Latina identity via migration (Alvarez-Borland 48). While traveling to Cuba provides her with "full knowledge of her Cuban ancestry, of who she is" (Gómez-Vega 98), the criticism accepts the logic behind Pilar's decision to return to the United States. This logic takes the form of a declarative statement: "Although Cuba is home, New York is more so" (Vásquez 24). Despite Pilar's "hyphenated existence," the criticism agrees that Pilar "does not belong in the real Cuba" (Payant 173). Pilar's choice to return to the United States is deemed inevitable; she has acquired the knowledge she needed, therefore it is time to leave. Celia's death at the end of the novel is consequently depicted as necessary for Pilar to fully develop her new identity and independence from Cuba. Since Pilar has inherited the mission of recording the family history, Celia's "death represents rebirth and regeneration" rather than "an act of despair" (O'Reilly Herrera 90).

Reconsidering the final image of Celia's "slow extinguishing" (Garcia 244), the present chapter reassesses the canonical readings of Pilar's return to and departure from Cuba as enabling or expressing a hybrid Latino/a subjectivity. Within this body of criticism, Pilar's nostalgia for Cuba is depicted as the product of her family's exile and thus the sole motive for Pilar to undertake her journey, which is ultimately satisfied by her reconnection with Celia. We consequently argue that this nostalgia must be read in relation to Pilar as a consumer subject and the novel's representation of her post-Sixties context. We aim to complicate the currently established reading of *Dreaming in Cuban*, moving beyond the interpretation of the novel's ending in terms of a merely positive recuperation of hybrid identity to its implications regarding the possibilities of cultural production and creativity within a post-Sixties world dominated by the global market.

"Shit, I'm only twenty-one years old. How can I be nostalgic for my youth?" (198); Pilar's question serves as the key to understanding Cristina Garcia's *Dreaming in Cuban* and its labyrinth of journeys and migrations. At her birth, Pilar inherits a mission from her grandmother—to record a family history that will serve as an alternative to the dominant historical narrative.[3] The family's exile, however, prevents Pilar from having direct access to Cuba, the origin and subject of this alternative historical project. Nostalgia consequently serves as the route Pilar travels in order to recover her family memories as well as a sense of her own identity and space of belonging. While undertaking a journey of nostalgia leads Pilar into a more complex relationship with Cuba, her negotiation of Latina identity is nevertheless overshadowed and overdetermined by this nostalgia and its own confused origins. *Dreaming in Cuban* ambivalently positions Pilar's nostalgia as both a product of her creative imagination and a post-Sixties product of globalization.[4] This longing speaks to an unconscious recognition of the shift from nation to market as constitutive of a Latino/a consumer identity while also mourning a loss of political horizons.

Within *Dreaming in Cuban*, nostalgia emerges as a desire to reconnect with the original objects of memory's gaze or to possess an alternative history, one that is personal and familial, over national and public History.[5] This formulation of nostalgia operates similarly in Angie Cruz's novel, *Soledad*, which we discuss in chapter 3 as a strategy for historical contextualization. Born in Cuba yet raised in New York City, Pilar finds her mission to record what "really happens" as informed by nostalgia. For example, Pilar asserts:

> If it were up to me, I'd record other things. Like the time there was a freak hailstorm in the Congo and the women took it as a sign that they should rule. Or life stories of prostitutes in Bombay. Why don't I know anything about them? Who chooses what we should know or what's important? I know I have to decide these things for myself. Most of what I've learned that's important I've learned on my own or from my grandmother. (28)

Pilar realizes that history is a subjective narrative process, one she can shape to include what has not been recognized as official History.[6] She is particularly interested in recovering the events marking women as active participants in history as well as personal stories about female experience.

This desire to record marginal people and events is linked to Pilar's relationship with her grandmother, Celia. What comforts Celia at the beginning of the novel is that, "Pilar records everything" (7). When Pilar finally arrives in Cuba to meet her grandmother again, Celia greets her by saying, "I'm glad you remember, Pilar. I always knew you would" (218). The last letter Celia writes, which completes the novel, reiterates Pilar's post-Sixties inheritance: "The revolution is eleven days old. My granddaughter, Pilar Puente del Pino, was born today [...] I will no longer write to you, *mi amor*. She will remember everything" (245). But why is Pilar chosen for this mission? Since Celia's children are either dead (Felicia and Javier) or deaf to her needs (Lourdes), she tells Pilar that as her granddaughter, Pilar is her last hope for salvation: "Women who outlive their daughters are orphans, Abuela tells me. Only their granddaughters can save them, guard their knowledge like the first fire" (222).

Pilar certainly excels early at her recording task, claiming that she remembers everything that's happened to her since she was a baby—even word-for-word conversations (26). Nevertheless, as Pilar becomes older, she gradually loses her ability to contact her grandmother via her dreams, and she is disconnected from Cuba, with only her imagination left to fulfill Celia's request.

In addition to the absence of an authentic connection to Cuba that prompts Pilar to recapture an alternate history via her imagination, she must also negotiate the challenges presented by the post-Sixties moment. Pilar consequently ponders the limitations placed on art and other forms of cultural production in a globalized context. In particular, she cites the mainstreaming of music as an example of the market's workings. In a record shop, Pilar sees "a Herb Alpert record, the one with the woman in whipped cream on the cover," noting that it now looks "so tame" to her (197). The once-provocative cover of the record album is revealed to be an illusion, because "the woman who posed for it was three months pregnant at the time" and "it was shaving cream, not whipped cream, she was suggestively dipping into her mouth" (197). Pilar demystifies the role of music as countercultural, but why is it no longer invested with the same ability to challenge norms? What has changed? Pilar points to the entrance of punk music into the mainstream market as a moment of loss:

> Franco and I commiserate about how St. Mark's Place is a zoo these days with the bridge-and-tunnel crowd wearing fuchsia Mohawks and safety pins through their cheeks. Everybody wants to be part of the freak show for a day. Anything halfway interesting gets co-opted, mainstreamed. We'll all be doing car commercials soon. (198)

The markers of punk, the piercings, the hair, are no longer emblems of a fringe movement but have become mainstream fashion, worn in order to fit in. Pilar remarks on the difficulty of being oppositional without having those visual markers commodified, transformed into a market category used in car commercials, for instance, to reach a specific audience. It is not simply the visual aspects of these movements that have sold out, however; the cultural production, the music itself, loses its edge through mass marketing. Pilar laments that in the initial stages of punk music "you could see the Ramones for five bucks" but "nowadays you have to pay $12.50 to see them with five thousand bellowing skinheads who won't even let you hear the music" (199). Resistance is projected into the past, no longer accessible even to Pilar, who realizes that she too has lost her rebellious edge: "How many lifetimes ago was that? I think about all that great early punk and the raucous paintings I *used* to do" (198, emphasis added). Indeed, Pilar now regularly joins jam sessions at Columbia University to play "this punky fake jazz everyone's into" (198). The punk culture's opposition to the mainstream is now a sad imitation of an original resistance movement; what is left is an illusion.

The challenge of the post-Sixties period would then appear to be the far-reaching influence of the market as well as a concurrent growing dependence on commodities to fill the void of memory. Although Pilar states that she wants to be "counted out" of the process of commercialization that tames punk music's rebellion (199), she is also affected by market trends; she depends on the flow of the marginal into the mainstream to find alternative modes of reconnecting with her Cuban past. In the very same record store where she speaks of her disillusion with punk music, Pilar buys an old Beny Moré album. By taking the role of consumer, she simultaneously engages in the commodification of Cuban culture and bonds with a member of the Latino/a population—Franco, the record store cashier. Thus the mainstreamed market category of Latin music provides Pilar with access to Cuban cultural productions and to a Latino/a community.[7] Pilar specifically connects with a Latino/a community that shares her interest in these objects of Hispanic culture as well as her experience of exile. With Franco, Pilar discusses "Celia Cruz and how she hasn't changed a hair or a vocal note in forty years. She's been fiftyish, it seems, since the Spanish-American War" (197–98). Interestingly, the figure of Celia Cruz, like Cuba itself in the novel, retains a certain timelessness and authenticity that punk music loses after its entrance into the mass market. The purity of Celia Cruz's selfhood appears to defy any and all historical changes brought about by struggles for independence, including the Cuban revolution. Stuck at "fiftyish," Cruz seems enviable and anomalous in her ability to remain unaffected by time. The representation of Celia Cruz then appears in stark contrast to that of Pilar's aging grandmother of the same name, and therefore serves to join the two veins of cultural inheritance Pilar can potentially trace, through the market or blood relation.[8]

During Pilar's visit to a botánica, Cuban culture continues to be associated with an immunity to the market's workings, or located outside of them altogether. In contrast to the theorizations of either Stavans or Pérez Firmat, Garcia's novel appears to locate static culture as resource *outside* the marketplace. Inside the botánica on Park Avenue, Pilar finds religious objects that are obviously produced for the mass market but are also markers of Hispanic-Caribbean culture, such as "plastic plug-in Virgins" (199). Nevertheless, Pilar invests a special meaning in these objects, remarking that "the simplest rituals [...] are most profound" (199). It is of central importance then that the owner of the shop refuses payment for the objects he gives to Pilar—herbs, a white votive candle, and holy water—with the explanation that, "This is a gift from our father Changó" (200). The narrative situates Pilar's initiation into the rituals of Santería outside the marketplace, such that the exchange is not a business transaction, and therefore uncorrupted by commodification. Pilar appears to be following in the footsteps of her grandmother, who "visited the *botánicas* for untried potions" to deal with the melancholia incurred by the departure of her lover, Gustavo (36). The difference, however, is that the narrative highlights the botánica as a place of inter-Caribbean commerce for Celia, since she actually "*bought* tiger root from Jamaica" and other herbs (36, emphasis added). Pilar's encounter is specifically enabled by the botánica's function as a store; but because no monetary payment is made, this exchange takes place outside the market's rules. Through Pilar's botánica experience with a difference, the novel posits the marketplace as an ambiguous venue that opens possibilities for accessing commercial yet authentic Latino/a cultural productions.

## THE REVOLUTION WILL NOT BE GLOBALIZED

While positioning Pilar's relationship to Santería and Cuban culture as outside of market influences, the narrative exhibits some discomfort with locating cultural meaning within commodities available in the marketplace. The ambivalent representation of globalization continues throughout the novel, with the character of Celia linking the market to the transformation of memory into a commodity. Celia describes memory as beyond definition or boundaries, as ambiguous as "slate gray, the color of undeveloped film" (47–48). Commodification, by contrast, seeks to concretize. Celia asserts: "It was an atrocity to sell cameras at El Encanto department store, to imprison emotions on squares of glossy paper" (47–48). Processing photographs eliminates the free form of memory in order to create concrete images that can be mass-produced and sold. Certainly, Celia's description of the relationship of photography to memory and emotion echoes Stavans and Pérez Firmat's formulation of the static culture to which commerce provides access. Photography desires to transform elusive memories into certainty, and yet the objects of memory will always escape its grasp. The photograph is a poor substitute since it must limit the range of creative possibilities that engender nostalgic desire and the search for cultural roots. For Celia, the market cannot reflect or engender a dynamic conceptualization of culture; it is not a space that allows for reconnection.

Even while Celia laments the negative effects of the market, Pilar's mother, Lourdes, views capitalism as a site of empowerment. As the proprietor of her own bakery, "Lourdes felt a spiritual link to American moguls, to the immortality of men like Irénée du Pont" (171). The immortality that the market confers on Lourdes is envisioned through the mass consumption of food: "She envisioned a chain of Yankee Doodle bakeries stretching across America to St. Louis, Dallas, Los Angeles, her apple pies and cupcakes on main streets and in suburban shopping malls everywhere" (171). Lourdes's association of capitalist success with immortality echoes Celia Cruz's representation in the novel as a mass-marketed figure whose timelessness is assured by her commodification within the music market. While Lourdes and her mother Celia are at opposite ends of the spectrum in terms of their perceptions of the market's effects as either negative or positive, both concur that the market is a space in which to gain access to a static culture. Not only is Lourdes "convinced she can fight Communism from behind her bakery counter" (136), but mass production also allows her to identify herself with an alternative community that is not Cuban. Lourdes becomes part of a nation-building project, the United States' bicentennial celebration, engaging in the marketing of American patriotism through products such as "tricolor cupcakes and Uncle Sam marzipan" (136).

Pilar stands somewhere between these two extremes, namely Lourdes's celebration of capitalism and Celia's rejection of commodification. Commodities offer Pilar possibilities for reconnection to Cuba via the Beny Moré album or the Santería herbs, yet she remains ambivalent regarding the access these products supposedly provide. Pilar alludes to this conflict when she describes the streets of Miami:

> All the streets in Coral Gables have Spanish names […] as if they'd been expecting all the Cubans who would eventually live there. I read somewhere that the area started off as just another Florida land scheme. Now it's one of the ritzy neighborhoods of Miami […] I suppose if enough people believe in the hype, anything is possible. (60)

The problem and the potential of the global market lie in its ability to create meaning out of fiction. It is here that the novel most clearly fleshes out Néstor García Canclini's definition of consumption as interpretive practice in order to clarify the implications and challenges involved in the positioning of a Latino/a subject as consumer. Pilar asserts the uneven and unpredictable nature of consumption as a process that can confuse origins or lead to an inability to isolate local positions of resistance. Pilar mentions her frustration with the system of co-optation and her inability to define herself as a result: "I guess I'm not so sure what I should be fight-ing for anymore. Without confines, I'm damn near reasonable. That's something I never wanted to become" (198).

Pilar feels she is almost complicit with the market's mainstreaming, yet she also sees potential in its commodities. Feeling that "something's dried up" in her, Pilar seeks fulfillment through the botánica and its wares, reconnecting to Cuba by means of its cultural representations. These objects, although mass-produced, make "more sense" to Pilar than "abstract forms of worship" (199). In spite of Pilar's valuation of the mar-ket's ability to provide access to Cuban culture, there remains a tension over whether the access offered is to an authentic version or merely another illusion. There is something impossible and unreal about Celia Cruz's timeless voice and face that extends itself to all commodified ver-sions of Cuban culture. Their position within the market is always tenu-ous and fraught with ambivalence. A questionable mode of access to authentic Cuban origins through commodities appears to accentuate Pilar's longing. Not coincidentally, after Pilar uses the goods from the botánica, she decides to return to Cuba and to the "real" Celia, her grand-mother: "On the ninth day of my baths, I call my mother and tell her we're going to Cuba" (203). Pilar then travels to Cuba in hopes of resolv-ing the nostalgia that the Cuban cultural products available in the United States cannot ultimately satiate.

At the age of thirteen, Pilar already felt the desire to journey to Cuba: "Our house is on a cement plot near the East River. At night [...] I hear the low whistles of the ships as they leave New York harbor [...] They travel south [...] and head out to the Atlantic [...] When I hear the whis-tles, I want to go with them" (30–31). Pilar's return to the island of Cuba within the novel carries with it the baggage of her nostalgia and her mis-sion as the family's historical recorder. The United States "doesn't feel like home to" Pilar (58), and as a result, she nostalgically identifies Cuba as the space that will localize her and give her the definition she is lacking, the definition of home. Will travel then enable Pilar to also record an alternative version of history by providing her with access to her family and their Cuban memories? Certainly, Pilar begins to collect the stories of her family members as soon as she arrives on the island, interviewing her cousin Ivanito, her aunt Felicia's friend Herminia, and her grandmother Celia (231). In fact, this activity may explain why some of the critics of *Dreaming in Cuban* insist that Pilar is also the fictional author of the novel.[9] Nevertheless, there are voices Pilar does not have access to, like those of Luz and Milagro, Felicia's daughters, whose stories Cristina Garcia does include in her novel. The narrative thus emphasizes Pilar's inability to complete the mission Celia assigns to her.

While Pilar is unable to fulfill her role as recorder, she is transformed by her trip to Cuba: "I wake up feeling different, like something inside of me is changing, something chemical and irreversible. There's a magic here working its way through my veins" (236). The mysterious changes at work within Pilar cause her to recognize the obstacles in the way of her recording task: "Until I returned to Cuba, I never realized how many blues exist" (233). The multiplicity of blues mirrors that of the various and often contradictory memories related to Pilar by her family. A new-found awareness of the competing histories and memories complicates Pilar's attempt to formulate an alternate family history that has the coherence of the family tree diagram at the opening of the novel. Pilar's reaction to the mob scene at the Peruvian embassy, the beginning of the Mariel boatlift, challenges her ability to fulfill her grandmother's imperative: "Nothing can record this, I think. Not words, not paintings, not photographs" (241). What is it about Cuba that remains unrecordable? Is Cuba's inability to be transcribed into cultural production related to Pilar's final exile from, and thus rejection of, the island?

It is precisely the narrative of Cuba's public history and position outside the post-Sixties global market that repeatedly prevents Pilar from gaining direct access to the family memory, such that the relationship between the revolution, time, and history drives Pilar's nostalgia for and rejection of Cuba. The narrative associates Cuba as object of Pilar's nostalgia with isolation: "Cuba is a peculiar exile, I think, an island-colony. We can reach it by a thirty-minute charter flight from Miami, yet never reach it at all" (219). Cuba's exile is derived from its geographic isolation; yet the novel hints that there is a further peculiarity regarding Cuba's position. Celia similarly depicts Cuba in terms of exile:

> What was it he read to her once? About how, long ago, the New World was attached to Europe and Africa? Yes, and the continents pulled away slowly, painfully after millions of years. The Americas were still inching westward and will eventually collide with Japan. Celia wonders if Cuba will be left behind, alone in the Caribbean sea with its faulted and folded mountains, its conquests, its memories. (48)

The world moves westward in a geographic flow while Cuba is left alone, apparently the only island in the Caribbean. This image evokes the concerns that Garcia mentions in an interview regarding the "U.S. policy of continuing to isolate Cuba in a world where everybody else has been accepted and dealt with" (López 105). Cuba is marked by a singularity—its inability to enter into this transcontinental movement.

In effect, the novel's Cuba is isolated because it is not part of the post-Sixties global marketplace. The revolution severed ties to the world market, and therefore it is not involved in this westward progress, a globalism reconnecting the world's continents and nations. Celia's description of Cuba's exile is preceded by her hopes for Cuba's reintegration into a global market via the processing of sugarcane: "She pictures three-hundred-pound sacks of refined sugar deep in the hulls of ships. People in Mexico and Russia and Poland will spoon out her sugar for coffee, or to bake in their birthday cakes. And Cuba will grow prosperous" (Garcia 45). This dream is not a reality, however, because the narrative emphasizes that Cuba's connections to the global marketplace belong to the past. Within the novel, the 1959 revolution not only resulted in the painful separation of families but also removed Cuba from the influence of the United States and the sea of global capitalism.

The novel's post-Sixties nostalgia for Cuba, the Cuba that Pilar can never reach, is for a pre-Sixties time period, when Cuba was a virtual colony of the United States. Celia's letters are all written before the Cuban revolution, and serve as the underlying structure and voice of the novel. In these letters, Celia describes Cuba as "a place where everything and everyone is for sale" (164). The narrative's nostalgic look into the past is particularly obsessed with the seductive presence of U.S. commerce on the island.[10] Interwoven with Celia's narrative are reminders of the already globalizing influence of American culture. The American motion picture industry promotes the dispersion of U.S. products and fashions. Celia notes that although her "Tía Alicia considered the American films naïve and overly optimistic," they were "too much fun to resist" (94). Consequently, Tía Alicia "named her two canaries Clara and Lillian after Clara Bow and Lillian Gish" (94). Celia also recalls how, "My girlfriends and I used to paint our mouths like American starlets, ruby red and heart-shaped. We bobbed our hair and [...] tried to sound like Gloria Swanson. We used to go to Cinelandia every Friday after work. I remember seeing *Mujeres de Fuego* with Bette Davis" (100). Not only is pre-revolutionary Cuba marked by the globalization of American culture, but it is also a site of American tourism and commerce. For example, during Celia's days working at the major department store, el Encanto, her biggest camera sales were to Americans (38).

Upon her arrival in Cuba, Pilar is fascinated by the remains of this influence, seeing the evidence left of this connection between the United States and Cuba:

The women on Calle Madrid are bare-armed in tight, sleeveless blouses. They wear stretch pants and pañuelos [...] A pair of frayed trousers stick out from beneath a '55 Plymouth. Magnificent finned automobiles cruise grandly down the street like parade floats. I feel like we're all back in time, in a kind of Cuban version of an earlier America. (220)

Not only does it appear that the clothing and automobiles are all that remains of Cuba's connection to American capitalism, but Cuba also appears to be stuck in time, as if history had ceased its progress. The character of Felicia in particular embodies what the novel imagines as the destructive effects of the revolution upon the Cuban people. There is a recurrent memory of Felicia as a child in the novel, playing at the beach before the arrival of a tidal wave, which appears in both Felicia and Celia's narratives. Felicia remembers "the sea's languid retreat into the horizon and the terrible silence of its absence" (11), which leaves the sand exposed for her to read the "archeology of the ocean floor" (213). The sea floor serves as a metaphor for the narrative record of history, while the catastrophic and unpredictable events within history reshape or erase what is written on the sand. The tidal wave symbolizing the revolution breaks with this historical record and blurs the boundaries between the public sand-history and the private homes of the families. Celia's insistence on not bringing the shells into her home is futile—Felicia laughs at the extent to which, "after the tidal wave, the house was full of them" (11).

Throughout the novel, Felicia functions as a representative subject of Cuba and its relationship to time and history. Felicia's deterioration from late-stage syphilis is linked to a loss of memory framed and contextualized by the Cuban revolution. Recovering from an episode of amnesia, Felicia finds herself in a room she had apparently decorated with history, with outdated calendars, "each month taped neatly to the ceiling" and "in the center of the ceiling, affixed with yellow tape, is January 1959, the first month of the revolution" (151). Felicia's amnesia mirrors a national loss of memory, identifying the revolution as a break within Cuban time. After Felicia's initiation as a santera, she "lost consciousness, falling into an emptiness without history or future" (187). She wastes away and dies, having fallen into the time(lessness) of the Cuban revolution, a space devoid of historical progress and memory. Due to Cuba's isolation from the post-Sixties global market and the progress of capitalism, the island figures as a space of unproductiveness, sickness, and death.[11] Garcia's novel thus revises Walter Benjamin's formulation of revolutionary time from his "Theses on the Philosophy of History." According to Benjamin, the moment of revolution is meant to halt or break progress and time in a positive way. If time is structured by class struggle, and a revolution creates a classless society, it can by extension create a timeless society or a shift in the conception of time, investing it with true meaning. By contrast, *Dreaming in Cuban* negatively depicts the revolutionary break in time as a trauma that puts Cuba in limbo, erasing the possibility for remembrance through cultural production. It is curious to note that the novel represents the timelessness of the Cuban revolution as stasis or death, while it associates the timelessness of the market, as evinced by Celia Cruz and Lourdes, with immortality.

The novel suggests that the revolution's effect upon Cuban time, history, and progress also influences the role of art in Cuban society. Pilar repeatedly classifies art as a space for recording, contestation, and translation. The narrative nevertheless implies that art cannot perform these functions within the context of the Cuban revolution. Celia's last case as a judge in the People's Court concerns "Simón Córdoba, a boy of fifteen, [who] has written a number of short stories considered to be antirevolutionary. His characters escape from Cuba on rafts of sticks and tires, refuse to harvest grapefruit, dream of singing in a rock and roll band in California" (158). In her sentencing, Celia aims to "reorient [his creativity] toward the revolution," stating that "Later, when the system has matured, more liberal policies may be permitted" (158). Since the aim of all art and imagination is focused towards the revolution, there can be no post-Sixties moment. There is no "later, after the revolution," because the revolution is always present. Indeed, if a revolution halts time, then there can be no past to interpret either. The revolution is infinitely present: "Within the revolution, everything; against the revolution, nothing" (235). If the role of the artist or writer is to make sense of the past, as Pilar suggests, then the artist has no role, no relevance, in Communist Cuba. By rejecting the role of art as both criticism and record, Cuba represents a space of stagnation and death for artistic creativity. According to Pilar, "Art [...] is the ultimate revolution" and if art cannot exist within Castro's revolution, then Cuba will not survive (235). It follows then that the major characters who remain in Cuba die: Celia, Felicia, and Javier. The characters who survive—Rufino, Pilar, Lourdes, and Felicia's son, Ivanito—are exiles in the United States.[12] Only the dead, like Celia's husband, Jorge, return to Cuba to stay.

In *Dreaming in Cuban*, Cuba is ultimately a dead space due to the island's severed relationship to consumption and globalization because of the 1959 revolution. Art, defined as critique and memory, cannot exist in this space. Even more importantly, art as a commodity will find no market in the novel's Communist Cuba. Although the text exhibits an anxiety regarding commodities, it is evident that within the narrative, the value of art lies in its mass marketing. As a result, the novel appears to echo Stavans's and Pérez Firmat's valorization of the market. In particular, Ivanito's dreams of being a radio personality reinforce the importance of access to an audience via the market. Ivanito walks along the beach with his radio,

> until I pick up radio stations in Key West. I'm learning more English this way but it's a lot different from Abuelo Jorge's grammar books. If I'm lucky, I can tune in the Wolfman Jack show on Sunday nights. Sometimes I want to be like the Wolfman and talk to a million people at once. (191)

The Wolfman can speak to a large audience because his show is widely distributed through the medium of radio. In addition, Ivanito pairs the Wolfman's success as a radio host with the acquisition of English, despite the proliferation of Spanish-language radio stations in the United States and especially in South Florida. It is at the Peruvian embassy, en route to beginning his new life in exile, that Ivanito exclaims, "Crraaaazzzzy!" and finds himself "talking to a million people at once" (241).

The novel identifies the post-Sixties market as a space dominated by English as the global language; success therefore entails learning English and leaving Cuba behind. It is no accident that when Celia drowns herself at the end of *Dreaming in Cuban*, she recites a poem by Federico García Lorca *in English* for the first time in the novel (243).[13] This literary translation at the moment of Celia's death signifies the novel's pessimistic prediction of Cuba's future in a global world.[14] Within the novel, translation means death; by extension, if Cuba is translated, it will die. The novel's Cuba, however, is also doomed by the language it speaks—Spanish—because it is not perceived as a global language, the language in which one can speak to a million people at once. While art is eventually co-opted by the mass market in the United States, there nevertheless remains the potential of reaching a global community or creating a community through art, as happens with Pilar and Franco in the record store.

In the end, Pilar cannot stay in Cuba or she will be restricted to being Cuban, which the novel continually associates with stagnation and death. On the other hand, the United States offers Pilar access to a commodified version of Cuban culture (represented by Beny Moré and Santería) and also to a marginalized American identity (via Lou Reed and punk music). In New York City, Pilar can take on a hybrid Latino/a identity via consumption; she can be both Cuban *and* American. The novel then makes an important break from the formulations of Latino/a identity offered by Stavans and Pérez Firmat. While the narrative's logic necessitates the death of the anticolonial hopes of the Sixties in terms of the Cuban revolution, it does not foresee the same future for U.S. Latino/a identity. Pilar's formulation of her in-between identity via globalization prompts her to help Ivanito escape Cuba on the Mariel boatlift. By telling Celia that she was unable to find Ivanito at the Peruvian embassy, Pilar accepts Lourdes's decision to initiate him into exile and nostalgia. Ultimately, the novel suggests that Ivanito is better off being Cuban somewhere other than in Cuba. In turn, Pilar accepts her own conflicted identity and the intrusion of both history and distance within the family: "I'm afraid to lose all this, to lose Abuela Celia again. But sooner or later I'd have to return to New York. I know now it's where I belong—not *instead* of here, but *more* than here" (236). Through Pilar's final betrayal of Celia and Celia's subsequent drowning, *Dreaming in Cuban* melancholically posits nostalgia as a product and point of entrance to the post-Sixties world, a better fate than never being part of the global marketplace.

Returning to New York City, the urban site that García Canclini and Dávila describe as the ideal space of transnational exchange and consumption, Pilar rejects Cuba as a site for her creative and personal growth. One might argue that New York City has something that Cuba lacks, but the logic of the text seems to imply that it is not a question of imbalance. Rather, it appears that Cuba is not chosen because it ceases to exist as a viable alternative. If Cuba equals the Cuban revolution and the possibility for a space outside the global market, then Celia's death and the concurrent imaginative death of Cuba represent a cynical commentary on the contemporary possibilities for alternative systems of exchange. The conclusion of *Dreaming in Cuban*, with the inevitability of Celia/Cuba's death, suggests that it is no longer possible to imagine a world outside the marketplace, nor for that matter a resistant Latino/a subject who is not part of the marketplace. By returning to the New York metropolis, Pilar ambivalently accepts her consumer Latino/a identity and thereby situates market consumption as the only source of future imaginings. The dreaming continues but cannot be embodied by Cuba or the 1959 revolution. The melancholic tone accompanying Celia's death hints that perhaps the nostalgia in the novel is similar to that described in *Bodega Dreams*, namely mourning the Sixties and the death of that type of progressive possibility. Nevertheless, *Dreaming in Cuban* clearly situates the future of the Latino/a subject in a U.S. urban setting, imagining a transnational botánica as the site for cultural exchange and the formation of community bonds.

In imagining a future for Latino/a identity, *Dreaming in Cuban* moves away from the simplistic terms that such critics as Ilan Stavans and Gustavo Pérez Firmat postulate between consumption and U.S.

Latinidad. The novel echoes both Néstor García Canclini's and Arlene Dávila's concerns regarding the problems and potentials of market-based citizenship, remaining ambivalent about Pilar's ability to formulate a hybrid oppositional Latino/a subjectivity. The harsh pessimism and melancholic overtones of the narrative are by-products of the novel's attempt to theorize consumer citizenship. The novel's complex picture of globalization's workings hints at the various challenges faced by the Latino/a artist in particular and Latino/a cultural production in general. In the end, *Dreaming in Cuban* does not offer a sense of celebration or closure but allows for the imagining of a post-Sixties future for Latino/a identity.

Chapter 5 turns from this discussion of consumer citizenship to the literary trajectory of one of Cristina Garcia's most accomplished contemporaries, Julia Alvarez. Alvarez also identifies the post-Sixties context as containing many of the same obstacles confronting Garcia. Reading her novels thus allows us to trace the ways in which she conceptualizes the shifting role of the writer within the U.S. public sphere. Her earliest novels highlight the loss of political certainty and the incursion of the market into artistic production as definite threats to the contemporary Latino/a writer's voice. We suggest that while what we call Alvarez's personal novels establish this context, her historical fiction turns to epic anticolonial social struggles as a potential source for a voice of authority. In the process, the more recent *In the Name of Salomé* (2000) becomes an extended meditation on the role of the writer and the possibilities of committed literature in a postcolonial, post-Civil Rights world.

## CHAPTER 5

# WRITING IN A MINOR KEY

## POSTCOLONIAL AND POST-CIVIL RIGHTS HISTORIES IN THE NOVELS OF JULIA ALVAREZ

LIKE CRISTINA GARCIA, JULIA ALVAREZ BELONGS TO THE GENERATION of Latina writers who achieved remarkable critical and popular success during the 1990s. Alvarez is perhaps the most prolific of this group, publishing five novels, a book of essays, four collections of poetry, four children's books, and two works of adolescent fiction between 1991 and 2006. While writers from this generation—especially women whose work is not obviously ghetto-centric—have been criticized for achieving their market success at the expense of the political ideals of the Sixties generation, Alvarez engages that past directly, returning throughout her writing to the legacy of anticolonialism in order to thematize and think through the role of the contemporary writer in relation to politics and the market. Far from withdrawing from the messy world of politics, Alvarez's writing has progressively ventured further and further into that field. In this chapter, we will argue that Alvarez's work has evolved from an early desire for an autonomous art free of external demands to a richer conception of the author as a kind of public intellectual, positioning writing as a process intimately connected with history and social struggles. Beginning from Alvarez's hyper-personal first novel, *How the García Girls Lost Their Accents* (1991), to the later *In the Name of Salomé* (2000) and its exploration of the writer's ability to speak in the public sphere, we can see the novelist's growing awareness of her own position within the literary marketplace.[1] This trajectory develops from her first novel's depiction of the challenges the writer faces telling her personal story to the apparent exhaustion of that project in the face of the demands of the market that we see in ¡Yo! (1997), to a consideration of political commit-ment as a new source of content and authority in *In the Time of the Butterflies* (1994) and *In the Name of Salomé*.

In the process of making that argument, we return to one of this book's premises: that post-Sixties Latino/a literature occupies overlapping territory between postcolonial and post-Civil Rights literatures, charac-terized as they are by entry into the culture industry and the crisis of the master narrative of liberation. Since postcolonial literature has essentially come to mean works written in English by writers born neither in Britain nor the United States, postcolonial studies is by definition distinct from U.S. ethnic studies, which takes as its subject groups within the United States that are not of white Anglo-Saxon Protestant descent. At the same time, the two fields share many overlaps and continuities. For example, some of the conceptual tools of postcolonial studies have been both inspired and appropriated by ethnic studies in the United States. The most noticeable efforts to connect those traditions have been to adapt some of the strategies and concepts of postcolonial studies to examining U.S. ethnic literatures, in such collections as *Beyond the Borders: American Literature and Post-colonial Theory* (Madsen) or *Postcolonial Theory and the United States* (Singh and Schmidt). The impulse exhibited in these cases is toward showing how postcolonial theorizing—for example, of the mutual implication of margin and center or of culture as a site of domi-nation and resistance—can be imported into American studies.

In addition to this tendency to apply postcolonial theory to U.S. ethnic literatures, another more historically-minded trend has been to discuss the ways in which social movements in the United States cleared space for the ascendance of postcolonial studies in the academy. Fredric Jameson and John Carlos Rowe among others in American studies have written about this history, as well as Robert Young and Gayatri Spivak from postcolonial studies. That history forms an important backdrop to our argument. At the same time, our project positions the post-Civil Rights and postcolonial era as primarily a post-Sixties period, a simulta-neous critique of and nostalgia for the politics made possible by that decade's struggles within and outside the United States. Rather than applying postcolonial concepts to a U.S. context, we will argue that look-ing at the transnational connections between the United States and the postcolonial world—in this case, examining a Latino/a-Caribbean litera-ture that shows the interdependence of these spaces—we can see parallels or points of contact and overlap between the literary and cultural history of the United States and the rest of the Americas. In so doing, we can see that contemporary Latino/a literature is one of the postcolonial and U.S.

ethnic literatures responding to a change from a modernist, anticolonial
form of literature to a postmodern, postcolonial one.

## POSTCOLONIALISM, U.S. ETHNIC STUDIES, AND THE POST-SIXTIES

Looking at Julia Alvarez's career as a whole, rather than focusing on an
individual novel as representing either ethnic or postcolonial experience,
allows us to see how her work continues to migrate between the categories
of "ethnic" and "postcolonial." Because of this complex positioning, the
novels become an especially productive occasion for placing these two
approaches in dialogue in order to see the related contexts that have energized both intellectual fields. Born in New York City to Dominican
parents and writing in English, Alvarez clearly fits the profile of a U.S.
ethnic writer. Her novels trace the transnational route between Latin
America and the United States, with her first novel, *How the García Girls
Lost Their Accents*, focusing on the immigrant experience in the United
States and the young girls' ambivalent acceptance of their acculturation.
With this perspective in mind, critics have emphasized Alvarez's resem-
blance to such U.S. ethnic writers as Sandra Cisneros, Esmeralda
Santiago, and Edwidge Danticat.[2] In the essay "On Finding a Latino
Voice," Alvarez herself credits Maxine Hong Kingston's *Woman Warrior*
as an inspiration (132). Moreover, essays about Alvarez have appeared in
such anthologies of U.S. ethnic literature as *Beyond the Binary:
Reconstructing Cultural Identity in a Multicultural Context* (Powell) or
*Evolving Origins, Transplanting Cultures: Literary Legacies of the New
Americans* (Alonso Gallo and Dominguez Miguela).

At the same time, Alvarez does not fit perfectly into the U.S. ethnic
mold. Although she was born in the United States, she spent most of her
early life in the Dominican Republic. Rather than this motherland
becoming an idealized memory—as it does, for example, in Cristina
Garcia's *Dreaming in Cuban*— the Dominican Republic remains a historically real and contested locale in Alvarez's work. In fact, while many
of Alvarez's novels, beginning with *How the García Girls Lost Their
Accents*, have been set primarily in the United States and focused on a
U.S. ethnic experience, others have moved away from this setting. For
example, *In the Time of the Butterflies* takes place entirely in the
Dominican Republic. Alvarez consequently appears to be a prime candi-
date for a postcolonial approach; she is an English-language writer working
through the inheritance of colonialism in the nations created by the end
of the modern colonial era. Certain critics thus dub Alvarez a postcolonial
writer and analyze her work as diasporic or Caribbean.[3] By downplaying

her location in the United States, these approaches tend to frame Alvarez as a native informant or translator of her Third World history.

We argue that by casting her novels as neither purely American nor Other, Alvarez positions herself at the intersection of U.S. and Caribbean history, part of what we reference in chapter 3 as an "Other American" literature. Attending to Alvarez's hemispheric perspective emphasizes her most significant contributions to rethinking the relationships within the Americas. Many readings of Alvarez's fiction focus on the way in which she "write[s] making bridges that link margin and center" and "deftly connects two different cultures" (Bados Ciria 406). In emphasizing the "difference" between the United States of America and the rest of the Americas, this celebratory multiculturalist reading—of the way in which "straddling two worlds" gives Alvarez a privileged vantage point (Jacques 22)— tends to obscure the historical inextricability of those "two different cultures." We suggest that Alvarez's novels return again and again to hemispheric history to undercut this understanding of the United States as separable from Latin America and the Caribbean. To highlight this context, Alvarez's early novels depict the effects of U.S. foreign policy and the ways in which decisions made in Washington are felt throughout the region. One recurring example of this connection appears in both *In the Time of the Butterflies* and *How the García Girls Lost Their Accents,* as the United States first supports and then cuts loose an anti-Trujillo underground movement, resulting in the massacre that the oldest Mirabal sister witnesses and that causes the García family to flee the island.

While this example still tends to figure the United States as an agent of history whose actions ripple throughout the Americas, an even more fundamental shift in the rethinking of hemispheric history appears in *In the Name of Salomé* through its contextualization of events in U.S. history as part of larger world-historical processes. Early in the novel, for example, Salomé positions the U.S. Civil War as part of the dismantling of the plantation system throughout the hemisphere, mentioning "Cuba and Puerto Rico about to fight for their independence, and [...] the United States just beginning to fight for the independence of its black people" (25). Placing U.S. history into this broader context contests the tendency toward American exceptionalism. A number of times, the novel's main characters, in looking at the United States with the eyes of outsiders, see resemblances to the so-called banana republics to the south. Camila notes that "in Washington, Senator McCarthy is launching a purge not unlike those of Batista's secret police" (69), while Salomé mentions an episode in which "American president Garfield was shot by a man who had been caught stealing stationery inside the White House. Mr. Garfield had been trying to reform his government, and this petty thief had been refused a job earlier" (184). In this way, the United States becomes a part of New World history, not only as its main protagonist but also as just another player with a history of corruption and turmoil not so different from those of its neighbors.

Because Alvarez's work calls attention to these contexts, it cannot be characterized as an uncritical celebration of a dehistoricized concept of cultural hybridity. At the same time, however, her writing cannot be identified with the opposite pole, because it refuses to reduce all cultural exchanges within the hemisphere to a totalizing cultural imperialism. The complex maneuvering of Alvarez's fiction speaks to Jean Franco's reservations about theories of cultural imperialism. These theories, as Franco notes, tend toward "considering media as uncontradictory expressions of the dominant ideology" (175), part and parcel of the "assumption that the effect of mass culture on the public is that which is intended by the emitter of the message" (176). Even though Franco urges the overcoming of this reductive assumption, she hesitates to entirely abandon the attention to hierarchies of production and reception enabled by the concept of cultural imperialism. She thus expresses some distrust of the critical movement in which "what was once designated 'cultural imperialism'— according to which Latin America was the passive recipient of Hollywood movies, Disney cartoons, and television serials—is now considered inventive cultural bricolage, whereby imported technologies and fashions are used to create new cultures" (199). She challenges us to construct an oppositional political project able to navigate between these two imperatives— to keep in mind the critique of unequal power positions undergirding the concept of cultural imperialism, while acknowledging the lesson of postcolonialism's deconstruction of margin and center, namely that hegemony is never total.

Alvarez's work is located precisely at the intersection of these demands. Just as *In the Name of Salomé* insists that the relationship between the United States and the Caribbean cannot be reduced to actions and reactions, the novel also represents how even those reactions remain unpredictable:

> Meanwhile, the present is being reported in dozens of recaps of the year's small and big news on television. Alaska and Hawaii have become states. The Barbie doll has been invented in imitation of dolls handed out to patrons of a West Berlin Brothel. Panty hose will now liberate women from girdles. In Cuba, the peasants are singing, "With Fidel, with Fidel, always with Fidel," to the tune of "Jingle Bells." (Alvarez, *Salomé* 38)

In this case, the same U.S. foreign policy that supports Rafael Trujillo in the Dominican Republic and Fulgencio Batista in Cuba is connected to territorial expansion in the Pacific and the cultural imperialism of Barbie. The popularity of the song "Jingle Bells" in countries where snow and Santa Claus remain outside people's everyday experience appears to be a perfect illustration of the way in which the spread of U.S. culture colonizes Caribbean consciousness.[4] But in this case, the consequences of the spread of U.S. culture exceed the intentionality of its producers: while North American culture, represented by the song "Jingle Bells," may permeate the hemisphere, the purposes to which that song is put remain difficult to control and may even be deployed in the name of revolution.

Alvarez depicts the complicated relationship between the United States and the rest of the Americas from this hemispheric perspective. In addition, Alvarez's novels also call attention to the ways in which U.S. and Caribbean *literary* history overlap. The scope of her work points to the connections and fissures between the fields of U.S. ethnic and postcolonial studies, particularly the extent to which the experience of the Sixties has shaped both fields. What we have been abbreviating as the Sixties represents the height of an anticolonial struggle throughout the hemisphere, undertaken not only by the conscripts of modern colonialism in Latin America and the Caribbean but also by internally colonized populations within the United States. Furthermore, as our first chapter indicates, the movements both within and outside the United States were integrally connected with the anticolonial ideal of the intellectual as leader of the people, embodied in the United States by poet-warriors like Malcolm X, Amiri Baraka, Angela Davis, the Puerto Rican Young Lords, and the Nuyorican Poets, and internationally by intellectuals like Frantz Fanon, C. L. R. James, and Che Guevara. The social movements of decolonization gave these writers an instant source of authority to speak for their people and to wield literature as a weapon against injustice and oppression.

Alvarez's novels come from a post-Sixties historical period; she writes in an era where the anticolonial literature of action is in crisis. Her work displays ambivalence toward this loss of literary authority typical of what has come to be called both postmodern and postcolonial literatures. Postcolonial and U.S. ethnic literatures have been described as literatures of mourning, in particular mourning for the motherland or the mother tongue; the title of Alvarez's *How the García Girls Lost Their Accents* reflects this sense of loss.[5] Yet we contend that being positioned in a post-Sixties moment leads both postcolonial and post-Civil Rights writers to mourn something else—a particular kind of literary vocation, a literary field in which the role of the writer is clearly defined and the writer's place assured. Alvarez offers a critique of this anticolonial ideal of the writer as spokesman and man of action; at the same time, however, she remains nostalgic for these social projects and the public voice that they offered the writer. In the rest of this chapter, we will look at the precise way in which that ambivalence is played out in her novels, and how her more recent work offers a measure of hope for a new role for the committed writer.

### SELLING FAMILY SECRETS

As we have suggested, Alvarez's fiction can be grouped into two categories: the personal novels (*How the García Girls Lost Their Accents* and *¡Yo!*), which are transparently autobiographical works about the writer and her family; and the historical novels (*In the Time of the Butterflies* and *In the Name of Salomé*), which center on heroic figures from Dominican history. Alvarez's first novel reflects her pursuit of the personal; *How the García Girls Lost Their Accents* is an overtly autobiographical account of the private tribulations of an immigrant family in the United States.[6] With a large and mobile family as its collective protagonist, the novel includes multiple points of view and changing narrators to allow everyone's story to be told. What emerges as the novel's central interest is the tension between the stories of the ensemble and the individual figure of Yolanda García. As we learn that she is the sister who loves to tell stories and aspires to be a poet, we begin to see her as the author's double. The novel begins and ends with her perspective, and her struggles to establish and maintain her voice take center stage throughout. At the same time, Alvarez expresses anxiety within these personal novels that autobiographical fiction involves selling herself and her family—that the entry of these stories into the market involves an unacceptable commodification of the private sphere.

While the *bildungsroman* is often read as an allegory of the writer's struggle to establish his or her own voice, *How the García Girls Lost Their Accents* appears to depict a loss of voice for Yolanda or at least a submerging of her individual voice as we move forward in time.[7] It is a paradoxical loss because the plot's reverse chronology means that the novel begins with Yolanda's story being told in the third person and ends with her speaking directly to us in the first. Reading forward in time, however, the chapters from the young Yolanda's life are narrated in the first person, while the chapters from her adult life are told in the third person. The crucial moment for this loss of voice, the chapter in which Yolanda's narrative switches from first person to third, occurs when she suffers a

nervous breakdown and has to be institutionalized. The breakdown man-
ifests itself in Yolanda's losing her ability to communicate. Her collapse
begins as a primarily verbal problem, with Yo hearing her husband speaking "babble babble" to her and being able to respond to him only with
"babble babble babble babble" (Alvarez, *García Girls* 78). In trying to
write a one-line note telling him she is leaving, she finds that the problem
has seeped into her writing:

> *I'm going to my folks till my head-slash-heart clear.* She revised the note: *I'm
> needing some space, some time, until my head-slash-heart-slash-soul*—No, no,
> no, she didn't want to divide herself anymore, three persons in one Yo.
> *John,* she began, then she jotted a little triangle before *John. Dear,* she
> wrote on a slant. She had read in a handwriting analysis that this was not
> the style of the self-assured. *Dear John, listen, we both know it's not work-
> ing.* "*It's?*" he would ask. "It's, meaning what?" Yo crossed the vague pro-
> noun out. (78)

After this failed attempt at authorship, Yo returns to her parents but finds
herself repeating what people around her say, as well as "quot[ing] famous
lines of poetry and the opening sentences of the classics" (79). This lack
of creativity and control clearly poses a problem for a writer. The chapter
identifies the beginning of Yolanda's recovery as the moment when she
comes up with something original to say. The recovery, we would like to
suggest, is only partial: from the chapter describing this breakdown, set in
1972, to the novel's final sequential chapter, set in 1989, Yolanda's narrative never again appears in the first person, as though something has per-
manently stifled the author's creative voice.

The novel's final line, where Yo admits to a "violation that lies at the
center of my art" (290), is a good place to begin to determine what stands
in the way of her authorial voice. Coming in the novel's first sequential
chapter, titled "The Drum," this admission points to her own discomfort
with the competing responsibilities she feels to both her family and her
craft. Within that chapter, her identification of what she terms this "violation" comes after a story involving a young cat and its family. In this
story, Yo takes a newborn kitten away from its mother to make it into a
pet, naming the black kitten Schwartz. Although Yo soon releases the kitten, the mother cat returns to haunt her dreams. In the mind of the older
Yolanda remembering this episode, the cat is clearly associated with her
writing life:

> The cat came back, on and off, for years [...] I began to write, the story of
> Pila, the story of my grandmother. I never saw Schwartz again [...] I grew

up, a curious woman, a woman of story ghosts and story devils, a woman prone to bad dreams and bad insomnia. There are still times I wake up at three o'clock in the morning and peer into the darkness. At that hour and in that loneliness, I hear her, a black furred thing lurking in the corners of my life. (290)

Two anxieties appear very clearly in this dream. Most obviously, the emphasis on the cat's blackness via its name and physical nature fore-grounds the author's working through her conflicted relationship with the Dominican pueblo; from the first pages of the novel to the last, the interactions between the young García girls and the mostly black maids, cooks, and other servants of the household remain strained.[8] The story about the kitten also fits the novel's pattern of Yo's curiosity getting the best of her; she seems never to respect the boundaries of others and repeatedly underestimates the dangers of crossing them. Especially in the context of the surrounding chapters, then, we can also see how Yo's remorse for taking the kitten away from its mother stands in for the author's fear that she has transgressed something sacred in stealing her family's private stories and making them public. Yo is not the only one to violate this family privacy; it happens throughout the novel as other family members participate in gossip and storytelling about one another's secrets. What makes Yolanda's violation appear more serious and far-reaching is the entry of her stories into the marketplace via publication.

In the stories immediately preceding "The Drum," the effect of publicity on art appears as an explicit subject. The chapter "Still Lives," also from the section "1960–1956," allows one of Yolanda's sisters, Sandi, to recount her own tentative entry into the world of cultural production as she takes painting lessons at the house of Doña Charito and Don José, a neighborhood couple who met while studying art in Europe. Sandi's access to those lessons is enabled by money in two distinct ways. First, Don José cannot make a living as an artist, meaning that "his wife was having to take in students in order to pay the bills" (243). But rather than a story of a starving artist unable to sell his work, Don José's problem comes from his *success:* "Several years back, he had been commissioned to sculpt the statues for the new National Cathedral, but the dedication had taken place in an empty church. There were rumors. Don José had gone crazy and been unable to finish this colossal project" (243). With patronage having thus corrupted Don José's creativity, the couple is left in the paradoxical position of having to further prostrate themselves before the forces of the market when Sandi's parents are seeking a teacher for her: "As I understand it, at first Doña Charito was insulted at the de la Torre request: she was an *artiste*; she took on apprentices, not children. But

paid in advance in American dollars, she made an exception in our case"
(243). In this story—which ends with the surprisingly talented Sandi
breaking her arm and, in a parallel to Yo's loss of voice, having to give up
becoming a painter herself—we see the various ways in which money and
the market are both necessary to the artist yet crippling to creativity at the
same time.

Alvarez's third novel, ¡Yo!, returns to the same set of characters and
begins with the premise of the writer's silence. As the title suggests, ¡Yo!
moves away from telling the story of the family and focuses entirely on
Yolanda. Yet despite becoming the novel's center, Yolanda's voice is completely absent from ¡Yo! Each chapter is told from the point of view of
someone around Yo, but we see nothing from Yo's own perspective.
Various family members, friends, and acquaintances attest to the ways in
which Yolanda's stories have affected them. The first and last chapters are
narrated by Yo's mother and father respectively, each talking about the
ways that Yo's stories have gotten them into nearly life-threatening trouble. Her mother tells of a visit by a social worker just after the family
arrives in the United States, a visit occasioned by Yo's telling stories at
school about her family life; the mother fears throughout the interview
that the family will be deported. Yo's father recounts that Yo found his
gun hidden beneath the floorboards of his closet while he was part of the
anti-Trujillo underground and later mentioned her findings to a general,
nearly forcing the family to flee the Dominican Republic. In each case,
the parent implores Yolanda not to tell stories to outsiders because of the
potential dangers involved.

In addition to this parental imperative, the novel identifies other
sources of Yo's loss of voice. The first of these appears in the novel's preface, which begins with one of the sisters returning to the violation at the
heart of *How the García Girls Lost Their Accents*—Yo's failure to keep
family matters private: "Suddenly her face is all over the place in a promo
picture that makes her look prettier than she is. I'm driving downtown
for groceries with the kids in the back seat and there she is on *Fresh Air*
talking about our family like everyone is some made-up character she can
do with as she wants" (Alvarez, ¡Yo! 3). The promotional picture and
appearance on *Fresh Air* symbolize not only Yolanda's betrayal of her
family's privacy but also the literary celebrity that this violation has
allowed her to achieve. In Yolanda's conversations with her sister, we see
her fears that as a crossover star, she is betraying her own community and
becoming a sellout.

The entry into the market represented by the appearance on National
Public Radio, along with the publication demands imposed by her new

tenure-track job, combine with Yolanda's family's disapproval as the primary pressures on the writer's voice. The dangers of this authorial positioning become most palpable in the novel's penultimate chapter, narrated by a stalker who embodies the threatening and menacing side effects of mainstream success. The stalker initially appears as a parody of an overzealous literary critic. He works at the University of Chicago (although not as a faculty member, but in a "shelving job") and collects her books "which I have dismembered and reassembled so that not one page is the way you wrote it, sentences spliced into different stories [...] every word tampered with" (280). He is able to rearrange her words to suit his purpose—in this case, to make her "sound like the babelite you are, writing your gibberish and pretending there is any word of truth to it" (280)—because once her books have entered the market, their meaning is thrown open to a wide audience unknown to the author. This market success places the author in this story in literal peril as this stranger develops an obsession with her. Later, the publicity machine that requires the author to promote her book puts her life in danger, as the stalker finds that she will be reading at a bookstore nearby. He even takes advantage of these market forces to get her alone, posing as an interviewer and playing on her sense of obligation to promote the book in order to arrange a meeting with her: "sorry to bother you, ms. garcía, but my secretary set this up with your publisher so I'm sorry to hear you didn't get word and I sure do hope you can squeeze me in as we've planned a big feature article for sunday with color photos and we think this will sell lots and lots of your wonderful books" (281). The commodification of the personal is thus illustrated not merely as an abstract threat to creativity and artistic integrity, but in this case a very real danger to the writer's own physical safety.

## CONJURING THE ANTICOLONIAL

Without an obvious source of literary authority—like the anticolonial master narrative of liberation—these powerful and contradictory external demands on the writer drown out her voice. Yolanda finds her private self already penetrated by the public world. The personal strand of Alvarez's fiction thus depicts the postmodern author running up against the exhaustion—or at least the extreme self-referentiality—of the writer's private struggles as a source of content. Almost as an antidote to this narrowing scope, Alvarez has repeatedly returned to grand historical themes in *In the Time of the Butterflies* and *In the Name of Salomé*. In these novels, confrontations with the difficult inheritance of the past become sources of new material for the storyteller. At the same time that the history of anticolonial struggle nourishes the writer, the novels also dramatize how these near-mythical figures cast daunting shadows over their potential heirs, demanding a heroism that seems only to reinforce the hopelessness of the postcolonial, post-Civil Rights present. Both *In the Time of the Butterflies* and *In the Name of Salomé* interpolate the stories of heroic women—the Butterflies in the first case and Salomé Ureña in the second—with the narratives of those who have inherited their stories— Dedé, the Mirabal sister who survives by declining to participate in her sisters' revolutionary activities, and Camila, Salomé's daughter, who moves to the United States and becomes a professor. Dedé and Camila, left behind to make sense of the legacies of the past and to tell these stories, regard the Butterflies and Salomé Ureña as pointed challenges. If the hopes and possibilities of epic social struggles for freedom and justice have been replaced by the commercial concerns of the literary marketplace, how can the contemporary writer live up to the standard set by these women? After anticolonial modernism's heroic roar, the decentered post-Sixties writer is hard-pressed to speak in that voice of authority. Yet what if that writer refuses to give up the grand social projects of earlier generations—for example, the project that the modernist José Martí called "Nuestra América," the progress toward freedom for the America of the oppressed and disenfranchised?

The concerns of U.S. ethnic and postcolonial literatures intersect at these questions of the writer's relationship to the collective and to the public sphere. *In the Time of the Butterflies* and *In the Name of Salomé* feature a number of characters expressing the modernist anticolonial ideology of the writer as cultural combatant in the struggle to create more just social structures. In *In the Time of the Butterflies,* that identity coheres primarily in Minerva Mirabal, the original Butterfly who gets her sisters involved in the movement to overthrow the dictator, Rafael Trujillo. Her anticolonialism is readily identifiable in both her notion of what a better world will look like, and her idea of the intellectual's role in bringing about that world. Minerva has a vision of liberation: before the underground has even gotten underway, she "suggested we just take off into the mountains like the *gavilleros* had done [a generation before] to fight off the Yanqui invaders" (Alvarez, *Butterflies* 56). From a young age, she instinctively imagines a society in which the realm of power is open to all; one of Dedé's first memories of Minerva is her proclaiming, "It's about time we women had a voice in running our country" (10). And finally, she firmly opposes political or economic privileges based on birth or social connections: even in prison, she refuses to be pardoned while other political prisoners remain incarcerated, and she equally distributes the care packages that she and her sisters receive, because "she says we don't want to create a class system in our cell, the haves and have nots" (234).

Minerva articulates a set of beliefs clearly identifiable as the anticolonialism we describe in our first chapter as expressed by the program of the Young Lords, the early poetry of Pedro Pietri, and other works of their contemporaries. Minerva finds inspiration in some of the same symbols deployed by these groups. She recites the poetry of Martí, who has served as a model of the poet-warrior for anticolonial movements throughout the Americas over the course of the twentieth century. According to her sister's diary, Minerva moves rapidly from Martí's poetry, recorded in an entry dated December 31, 1954, to even more politically charged material on January 14, 1955: "There was a broadcast of a speech by this man Fidel, who is trying to overturn their dictator over in Cuba. Minerva has big parts memorized. Now, instead of her poetry, she's always reciting, *Condemn me, it does not matter. History will absolve me!*" (123). The early Castro here appears as another incarnation of the anticolonial intellectual whose words and deeds awaken his people, and who serves as a model for Minerva's own political and intellectual projects.

As an anticolonial intellectual, Minerva attends to both the political and aesthetic dimensions of her project. Her earliest foray into political protest is a theater piece that she and her friend Sinita compose and enact in front of Trujillo, a play "about a time when we were free" (26). Acting out this drama of bondage and freedom for the country's centennial clearly evokes the island's present situation, with Minerva as "bound Fatherland" reciting, "Over a century, languishing in chains, / Dare I now hope for freedom from my woes? / Oh, Liberty, unfold your brilliant bow" (28). The play nearly becomes more than just a rehearsal for political action when Sinita breaks from the script. Instead of unchaining Minerva, she points her bow and arrow at Trujillo, and his security forces have to intervene. The play that Minerva and Sinita craft intends to fuse art and action, calling into question the legitimacy of the dictatorship and inspiring their fellow citizens to action. As discussed in our first chapter, this kind of political art typifies the anticolonial ideology articulated by Jesús Colón in *A Puerto Rican in New York and Other Sketches* or by Pedro Pietri in "Puerto Rican Obituary."

Salomé Ureña combines her vocation as poet with commitment to her nation's independence even more explicitly, making *In the Name of Salomé* the novel in which Alvarez most fully confronts the legacy of anticolonial opposition in the postcolonial, post-Civil Rights era. Salomé, the nineteenth-century heroine of the Dominican Republic's struggle for independence from Spain, learns her role as anticolonial poet from her father, a less successful writer and political figure who instructs her in "what a poet is supposed to do" (Alvarez, *Salomé* 53). He gives her two pithy and memorable definitions of poetry: first, not to waste her tears, as "tears are the ink of the poet" (24); and second, that the poet "merely put[s] into words what everyone else in the whole capital [is] thinking" (53). These two maxims frame poetry as an activity with a strong ethical imperative, most importantly a responsibility to the collective. Salomé takes up the pen to fulfill her father's political and artistic dreams, to write lines like "*wake up from your sleep, my Patria, throw off your shroud*" (63) or "*your patria still in chains* [...] *The tears you shed for her have never dried*" (62).

As Salomé develops her poetic gifts, she takes her responsibility to the patria very seriously. Reading Josefa Perdomo, a popular Dominican poet who writes "lovely verses" (56), Salomé determines that "I would never write verses out of politeness. Rather than write something pretty and useless, I would not write at all" (57). Josefa thus becomes a negative model of poetry that is too frilly, too uncommitted, and too womanly. Soon afterward, Salomé sees her poetry published in the newspaper under the pseudonym Herminia, and proudly thinks of her verses in such resonantly anticolonial terms as "waking up the body politic" and "bring[ing] down the regime with pen and paper" (62). Salomé's success is assured when she overhears her aunt comparing Herminia favorably to Josefa's "more sentimental, ingratiating style." "'This Herminia is a warrior,' my aunt said proudly. 'In fact, my theory is that Herminia is really a man, hiding behind a woman's skirt'" (63). This evaluation shows how successfully Salomé manages to live up to the anticolonial ideal of the masculine poet-warrior, an achievement that turns her into a Dominican hero in her own lifetime and beyond. Yet at the same time, the act of inhabiting this persona—a performance so successful that one of the reviewers of Alvarez's novel describes Salomé without any irony as "a sort of José Martí in skirts" (Ruta 24)—takes its toll on Salomé and eventually becomes more of a burden than inspiration for those who come after her.

### POSTCOLONIAL MELANCHOLIA

While these novels thus illustrate the ways in which Minerva and Salomé embody the ideals of anticolonialism, the most compelling aspect of both *In the Name of Salomé* and *In the Time of the Butterflies* is the movement between those larger-than-life women and the chroniclers who are left behind to tell their stories. Through these figures, Alvarez's novels become not so much stories about the past but narratives about rethinking our relationship in the present to the ambiguous demands of that past. The questions of authorial voice in Alvarez's personal novels resurface here as the historical novels also experiment with different points of view. While Minerva and Salomé speak in the first person, both Dedé and Camila narrate in the third person, even though as the ones left behind, they are ostensibly also the ones telling the story. Dedé and Camila find themselves like Yolanda, unable to find their own voices, overshadowed and silenced by the enormous demands placed upon them. In *In the Time of the Butterflies* it is Dedé, the one Mirabal sister who didn't participate in the underground and didn't die with the others, speaking in 1994; in *In the Name of Salomé* it is Camila, the daughter who can never live up to her mythical mother, looking back on Salomé's legacy from 1973.

Both Camila and Dedé are thus located in a distinctly post-Sixties present. Curiously, both novels skip ahead from 1960, the year of Camila's return to Cuba and the Butterflies' death, to their respective presents of 1973 and 1994. The years between 1960 and 1973—years that in shorthand we might call the Sixties—are thus absent from both novels.[9] This absence is especially pronounced in *In the Name of Salomé*. The novel covers many of the major events of U.S. and Dominican history from Salomé's birth in 1850 to Camila's death in 1973, yet has no scenes set in revolutionary Cuba or the United States in the Civil Rights era; its timeline jumps from Camila in Vermont in 1950 to her decision to leave the United States for Cuba in 1960 to her final arrival in the Dominican Republic to prepare for her death in 1973. While other events from U.S. history feature prominently in Camila's narrative—the renaming of the hamburger as the "liberty sandwich" and the dachshund as the "liberty pup" during World War I (238) or the segregated jazz clubs that Camila visits during the 1920s (201)—no event from the Civil Rights movement in the United States is mentioned. Furthermore, since none of the action in the novel actually takes place in revolutionary Cuba—events from that period appear only as flashbacks in the 1973 epilogue—the 1960s are narrated only as the past, an experience that Camila is still working through when the novel ends.

To add to this peculiarity of periodization, it is a remarkable historical coincidence that Camila Henríquez Ureña dies the day after the Pinochet coup in Chile, which overthrew Salvador Allende's socialist government with the aid of the U.S. Central Intelligence Agency (CIA). Allende had represented the possibility of a new kind of Latin American progressivism, steering away from the model offered by a Cuban revolution that had already become increasingly centralized and dictatorial by the early 1970s. September 11, 1973, the day of Pinochet's coup, thus marks a threshold in Our America, the moment when it becomes clear that the United States will not allow a socialist government to exist in the Americas—even one that is democratically elected and not aligned with the Soviet Union. Camila's last days coincide with the end of one of the great eras of hope for the Americas, the period set in motion by decolonization in the Caribbean and the Civil Rights movement in the United States. Her reflections on Cuba from this vantage point become an important voice for the post-colonial, post-Civil Rights era, which in many ways begins in 1973. When Camila's niece wonders, "'What would Salomé say if she could see the place now,'" Camila speaks almost directly to us today: "What would she have said, except what she must have said to herself, time after time, when her dreams came tumbling down? Start over, start over, start over" (342).

Dedé also returns to narrate the Sixties from the perspective of memory in a brief epilogue that covers the actual events of the decade in one sentence: "The coup, the president thrown out before the year was over, the rebels up in the mountains, the civil war, the landing of the marines" (Alvarez, *Butterflies* 310). Rather than recounting these events, then, the epilogue rehearses the ways in which the period continues to reverberate for Dedé even after many years. She describes the decade with a wistful, melancholic nostalgia, located much further into our postcolonial present than Camila; Dedé speaks from 1994, the year when Trujillo's own puppet president, Joaquín Balaguer, won his sixth term as president of the Dominican Republic in elections so rife with fraud that he was forced to resign before completing his term. The history of the post-Trujillo Dominican Republic is enough to depress anyone; Dedé has watched an idealistic young poet named Juan Bosch overwhelmingly win a democratic election in 1962, only to have his presidency cut short. Dedé remembers meeting Bosch and the hope he represented:

The president dropped in for a visit. He sat right there in Papá's old rocker, drinking a frozen *limonada,* telling me his story. He was going to do all sorts of things, he told me. He was going to get rid of the old generals with their hands still dirty with Mirabal blood. All those properties they had stolen he was going to distribute among the poor. He was going to make us a nation proud of ourselves, not run by the Yanqui imperialists [...] At the end, as he was leaving, the president recited a poem he'd composed on the ride up from the capital. It was something patriotic about how when you die for your country, you do not die in vain. He was a poet president, and from time to time, Manolo would say, "Ay, if Minerva had lived to see this." And I started to think, maybe it was for something that the girls had died. (310)

Dedé understands how Bosch, as a "poet president," means to establish himself as the inheritor of Martí, Minerva and Salomé, both in terms of his commitment to social justice and his aesthetic sensibility. His presence in office makes it "a manageable grief" for Dedé, allowing her to begin "hoping and planning," secure in the knowledge that the death of her sisters is something she can "make sense of" because their ideals are still alive (310). Within the year, though, a coup d'état deposes Bosch, leading Dedé to question whether her sisters' struggles will ever truly bear fruit.

Just as Bosch positions himself as heir to the legacy of the Butterflies, Minerva's husband Manolo becomes another proprietor of their memories and the anticolonial hope they represent. After he is released from prison, he becomes "our Fidel" and "drew adoring crowds" wherever he went (309). But that era of anticolonial possibility comes to a close after the overthrow of Bosch's government. Manolo attempts to rise up against the new military government, and Dedé's description emphasizes the delusion and hopelessness of Manolo's rebellion:

> "Fellow Dominicans!" he declaims in a grainy voice. "We must not let another dictatorship rule us [...] Rise up, take to the streets! Join my comrades and me in the mountains! When you die for your country, you do not die in vain!" But no one joined them. After forty days of bombing, they accepted the broadcast amnesty. They came down from the mountains with their hands up, and the generals gunned them down, every one. (311)

Manolo fails to recognize the futility of his form of anticolonial resistance against the post-Trujillo government. Dedé calls her brother-in-law's attempted uprising a "disgrace" (311) and loses faith entirely in the myth of the heroic individual leading the people to freedom.

The novel ends with Dedé wallowing in the depths of postcolonial despair. The failures of Bosch and Manolo as well as the release of her sisters' killers shortly after the beginning of their prison sentence lead Dedé to seriously doubt the possibility of any sort of social justice. The final chapter makes clear how heavily the past weighs upon her. She has become the official keeper of the story of the Butterflies, a story she obsessively tells others despite her friend imploring her to move beyond it. She recounts the tale of the Butterflies because, as she tells this friend, "after the fighting was over and we were a broken people [...] we had lost hope, and we needed a story to understand what had happened to us" (313). Yet the friend's criticism—that she is "still living in the past [...] in the same old house, surrounded by the same old things" (312)—makes Dedé question the usefulness of her coping strategy. Is she fulfilling the demands of the Butterflies by keeping their story alive, or would it be more in keeping with their legacy to bury the past and work to transform the present? How can Dedé honor that past without obsessively reliving it?

The present that Dedé inhabits has clearly not lived up to her expectations of what the anticolonial social movements would accomplish, yet she finds she has no way of critiquing that present or imagining an alternative to it. She describes her situation as "living to see the end of so many things, including her own ideas" (316). Attending a ceremony in honor of her sisters, Dedé sees another painful reminder of the past; President Joaquín Balaguer, Trujillo's old ally, is also in attendance. When her old friend, Lío, tries to comfort her by reassuring her that "the nightmare is over, Dedé. Look at what the girls have done," Dedé begins to voice her dissatisfaction with the post-Trujillo world that her sisters helped to inaugurate:

> He means the free elections, bad presidents now put in power properly, not by army tanks. He means our country beginning to prosper, Free Zones going up everywhere, the coast a clutter of clubs and resorts. We are now the playground of the Caribbean, who were once its killing fields [...] The nightmare is over, we are free at last. But the one thing that is making me tremble, that I do not want to say out loud—I'll say it once only and it's done. Was it for this, the sacrifice of the butterflies? (318)

Dedé looks at her world and sees only the failure of anticolonial modernism to produce the utopias it promised: she even remembers with bitter irony Martin Luther King, Jr.'s promise of a world that would be "free at last." Instead of social justice, she sees the spread of unfettered capitalism in the form of trade agreements and the explosion of the tourist industry, the post-Sixties economic phenomenon we refer to in chapter 4 as globalization. In Dedé's refusal to read the newspapers, she disengages from that present as an historical moment. Instead of learning from the past or using its lessons to critique the present, she becomes completely paralyzed by retelling her sisters' stories. Dedé's melancholia arises not only from her disillusionment with the modernist anticolonial struggle but also from her inability to move beyond it to formulate any other source of hope.

### REVITALIZING THE POST-SIXTIES PUBLIC SPHERE

While *In the Time of the Butterflies* ultimately ends with Dedé floundering in a postcolonial melancholia that cannot move beyond the past to engage the present, *In the Name of Salomé* offers a slightly more hopeful vision of the future by taking some distance from the past. While Camila finds the present nearly as depressing and overwhelming as Dedé does, she appears to develop more effective coping mechanisms.

The epilogue of *In the Name of Salomé* hints at a tentative closure to her mourning process as she briefly escapes the pull of the past to point towards the future. Camila appears throughout the novel as a potential critic of the strand of anticolonial modernism that magnifies the role of the heroic man of action as leader of the people. In particular, the novel allows Camila to develop a critique of the anticolonial vision of the intellectual as spokesperson for the people, and the forms of hegemony that this move may reproduce. Instead of the Salomé that her sons and husband want to preserve, Salomé as the national poet and hero of the independence struggle, Camila points to another side of her mother's legacy.

As the novel develops, Camila and her brother Pedro provide competing visions of preserving and honoring Salomé's legacy. The different ways in which these siblings remember Salomé and imagine themselves as writers and intellectuals shed light on their different relationships to anticolonial modernism. The Pedro of the novel is, as scholars of Latin American literature know, one of the great critics of modernismo, Pedro Henríquez Ureña. In the novel, it is Pedro who as a child reads Martí's *La Edad de Oro* (226) and as an adult frequently references Martí, as when he opens a meeting of his friends by reciting Martí's poetry. Pedro's conception of his role as writer and intellectual is perhaps best expressed when he tells Camila:

> I am continuing the fight. I am defending the last outpost. [...] Poetry. [...] I am defending it with my pen. It is a small thing, I know, but those are the arms I was given. Defending it because it encodes our purest soul, the blueprint for the new man, the new woman. Defending it against the bought pens, the dictators, the impersonators, the well-meaning but lacking in talent. (Alvarez, *Salomé* 125)

In explicitly equating his vocation as intellectual with the armed decolonization struggles taking place around the world, Pedro expresses the anticolonial ideal of the writer's heroic role in the social movements of the twentieth century. By emphasizing the public and action-oriented potential of poetry, Pedro positions himself as Salomé's heir and casts as illegitimate Camila's poetry, which he labels as solely for private reflection.

Although the above passage comes from a private conversation with his sister, Camila notices that everything Pedro says or writes is marked by an awareness of its potential circulation as a public document. His preferred mode appears to be the essay, a genre well suited for turning personal reflections or observations into public proclamations. Camila notes that "in one of his essays that she found in a recent journal, she was surprised to read about 'the terrible moral disinheritance of exile'" (112).

Her surprise comes from the fact that she had "to learn so impersonally of her brother's sadness" (112), which he has apparently not discussed with her privately. In addition to the essay, Pedro favors lectures and speeches as other genres that lend themselves especially well to acts of heroic enunciation. He addresses one crowd by imploring them that "we must pledge ourselves to *our* America [...] the America our poor, little countries are struggling to create," while betraying his insecurity in insisting that "we cannot be mere bookworm redeemers" (121). Even his letters are written "as if he already knows that in the future his correspondence will be published (he *is* that famous)" (109).

As a counterpoint to Pedro's very public conception of writing, Camila emerges as a different kind of writer. Unlike Pedro's energizing speeches, calling his people to arms for their patria, Camila uses more personal forms of writing. After reading her poetry, Pedro advises Camila that she "should keep writing for her own pleasure" (124). This advice assumes that Camila's poems, written in what she calls a "minor key" (177), are not suited for circulation in the same way as Salomé's or Pedro's heroic proclamations. Even Camila's letters, although addressed to her closest friend, Marion, remain unsent and thus never find an audience or a public. These letters offer Camila a chance to "try out a new life by writing to Marion about it," so that "if nothing else, perhaps the story of what is happening will begin to make sense to her" (189). Writing as a way of making sense of the personal appears to be Camila's conception at this point in the novel of the role that writing can play in her life—a form detached from all external demands.

Pedro deliberately invokes Martí and Salomé in order to align himself with the specific notion of the anticolonial writer that they represent. Camila initially agrees with Pedro's interpretation of Salomé, calling Pedro "the one who received their mother's legacy" (122). As the novel develops, however, Camila's own voice emerges through her growing realization that Pedro's reading of Salomé, defining her accomplishments according to a particularly masculinist, anticolonial model, attends to only one portion of her legacy, and perhaps not the most useful one in a post-Sixties world. Like many of the events in Camila's story, her letters contain direct echoes in Salomé's story. Camila's resolution that writing can serve personal and private needs comes in a chapter directly following Salomé's loss of faith in public poetry as corruptible and unfaithful to her true voice. As early as the chapter "La fe en el porvenir," Salomé begins to wonder how the poet can balance politics with personal thoughts and feelings. Her first love poem is rejected by her father as apolitical, and derided by her sister as "the worst poem you ever wrote" for its "silly language"

(95). In the fourth chapter, Salomé begins to express her sexuality in "Quejas," a poem that will become a source of controversy. Her sister recognizes right away that "you can't publish this. You're la musa de la patria, for heaven's sake [...] Nobody thinks you have a real body" (143–4).

Salomé comes to the conclusion that she is submerging her own voice in sounding the epic calls for the nation to throw off the shackles of Spanish rule. By allowing the nation to speak through her, her own self disappears. When her husband, Pancho, dismisses her poem "Vespertina" as "personal" and "tender" (176), she insists to him, "I am a woman as well as a poet" (177). She realizes that in these newer poems, "I had begun writing in a voice that came from deep inside me. It was not a public voice" (177). Because Salomé accepts the separation of poet from woman and public from private, she is never fully comfortable with expressing that inner voice in her poetry. In absorbing these absolute oppositions, she has trouble imagining a form of writing that would allow her to represent both at once. She finally agrees that the voice that comes from "deep inside" should not be made public and cannot be the source of poetry. As a result, she gradually shifts her energy away from poetic creation into raising her children and teaching at her school. When Pancho laments the erosion of her gift, she explicitly calls her children "the only immortality I want" (268).

Dissatisfied with her public role and discouraged by her husband from writing in her private voice, Salomé begins to withdraw from poetry. This dissatisfaction derives in large part from watching everyone around her appropriate her poetry and assign her a meaning that suits their ideological frameworks. "Vespertina" becomes the impetus for a real struggle between Salomé and Pancho over her poetic vocation. He tells her:

> You must not squander away your talent by singing in a minor key, Salomé. You must think of your future as bard of our nation. We want the songs of la patria, we need anthems to lead us out of the morass of our past and into our glorious destiny as the Athens of the Americas. (177)

In figuring the past as a "morass" to escape from, Pancho demands that Salomé fulfill her role as inspiration for and even leader of her people in overcoming that past. Pancho becomes something like Salomé's press agent, reminding her that "duty is the highest virtue" (176) and not to "shirk your duties" (177), as well as urging her to produce poems for national events. He commissions a painting of her that depicts her as "prettier, whiter" and closer to "the legend *he* was creating" (44). Pancho goes so far as to revise her older poems, to mold them to his image of a national poet. Suggesting changes to some of her early poems, he tells her,

"'Trust me, Salomé, I have your future in mind'" (170). Her son Pedro later joins Pancho's effort to remake Salomé to conform to their idea of the anticolonial writer as asexual and specifically not feminine. When publishing a posthumous edition of Salomé's collected works, Pedro omits entirely some of what he calls her "intimate verses" (161), including "Quejas."

Just as Pancho is pushing Salomé into this role, however, other forces are leading her to doubt the efficacy of poetry as a weapon in the anticolonial struggle and her own ability to control the use of her poems. Her darkest moments come when she realizes that the dictator Lilís deploys her poetry to drum up nationalist sentiment for his regime: "Hadn't I heard that Lilís himself liked to recite passages of my patriotic poems to his troops before battle [...] The last thing our country needed was more poems" (187). Seeing the martial and epic poetry she had written in the spirit of anticolonial opposition claimed by diametrically opposed ideologies, Salomé witnesses within her lifetime what happened in death to Martí, who has become a symbol employed by both Havana and Miami since the Cuban revolution. Public poetry, by definition available to all, defies the poet's intentions once it begins to circulate and become a signifier anyone can use.

Camila comes to the same realization in her visit to the national cemetery in Santo Domingo, as she sees that in death the heroes of the nation become symbols available to anyone with the power to appropriate them. Reflecting on the cemetery where her parents and brother rest, Camila realizes that "depending on the president, the pantheon of heroes changes, one regime's villain is the next one's hero, until the word *hero,* like the word *patria,* begins to mean nothing. That is another reason why I do not want to be buried here among the great dead" (338). As Camila reaches the end of her life, she decides to be buried not in the cemetery reserved for national heroes where her mother, father, and brother lie, but in a private plot with her half-brother and "those of us in the family who aren't famous" (333). In choosing the resting place of her body, she is literally deciding the part of the ancestral legacy that she will affirm.

In choosing to define her relationship to her mother's inheritance—a choice deliberately opposed to Pedro's "dying wish" to lie next to Salomé (338)—Camila resolves to be, as she puts it, not the "clarion call," but the "chorus": "She, too, wants to be part of that national self-creation. Her mother's poems inspired a generation. Her own, she knows, are not clarion calls, but subdued oboes, background piano music, a groundswell of cellos bearing the burden of a melody. Every revolution surely needs a chorus" (121). Joining the chorus rather than the actors occupying center stage appears to be the reason that Camila tells her own story in the third person, while Salomé's story is told in the first person. Camila has decided that "there are other women she can be besides the heroine of a story" (126). Yet in the novel's epilogue, Camila's narration switches from third person to first, just as Dedé speaks in the first person for the first time in the epilogue to *In the Time of the Butterflies*. In these final chapters, narrating the stories of anticolonial struggles appears to give Dedé and Camila their own voices in a way that Yolanda García's personal stories can never sustain.

Camila chooses teaching, rather than Pedro's lecturing, as the activity best suited to fulfilling her mother's legacy. Camila becomes an educator not to lead the people forward but rather to participate in the everyday struggle to build a patria. As a teacher, Camila can keep the dreams of Salomé and Martí alive, and she does maintain a religious devotion to the cult of anticolonial modernism, praying to her own holy trinity "in the name of Hostos, Salomé, José Martí" (339). In this spirit, Camila initially perceives the Cuban revolution as the fulfillment of Salomé's dreams, noting that "at last I found her the only place we ever find the dead: among the living. Mamá was alive and well in Cuba, where I struggled with others to build the kind of country she had dreamed of" (335). It is tempting for Alvarez as a U.S. ethnic writer to flee from the bleak post-Civil Rights United States to redemption in the Third World. But as the epilogue unfolds, that optimism is gradually refined. By 1973 Castro's government had already lost the support of most Latin American intellectuals after Heberto Padilla was jailed for writing poems deemed counter-revolutionary. Yet Camila sides neither with Castro's regime nor with the critics of the revolution. When her half-brother bitterly calls Cuba "the experiment that has failed," Camila argues against giving up on the dream: "That is not the point [...] We have to keep trying to create a patria out of the land where we were born. Even when the experiment fails, especially when the experiment fails" (342). The revolution is not the final product, according to Camila, but the struggle to get there.

The novel ends with this lesson—that not only can Camila live in a minor key and still move our Americas closer to liberation, but in fact it may be only such mundane acts that can bring about the desired outcome. Unlike Dedé, trapped in telling and retelling her sisters' story, teaching offers Camila a post-utopian alternative. The great actors, like Salomé and Martí, have seen their dreams of transforming the world go awry. The novel's ultimate critique of anticolonial modernism comes in Camila's response to her niece's comment, that she "[doesn't] think Castro is the answer." Camila responds: "It was wrong to think that there was an answer in the first place, dear. There are no answers [...] It's continuing to struggle to create the country we dream of that makes a patria out of the land under our feet. That much I learned from my mother" (350). Unlike the lecture format favored by Pedro, in which the lecturer processes reality for his followers and presents them with a coherent plan for action, Salomé offers the model of the teacher who values social justice and admits that the path cannot be predicted or dictated, but must be created as part of a common struggle to make meaning.[10]

At the end of her life, Camila comes to terms with the meaning of her mother's life, and decides that while she won't give up the struggle to remake the world, the struggle is also "to love the flawed thing we see" (339). While for Dedé, the flawed postcolonial world is a source of disillusionment, Camila refuses to succumb to despair. Although the revolutionary great leap forward that inspired anticolonialism no longer seems possible, Camila finally decides that it is through these fits and starts that Our America will be built, one person at a time. As she says, she "had never thought of the real revolution as the one Fidel was commanding" (347). The real revolution is not the change in leadership at the top; rather, it is found among the women sorting coffee beans who draw inspiration from Salomé's poems that Camila reads to them.

*In the Name of Salomé* ends with the hopeful scene of a blind Camila teaching a poor young Dominican boy to read her mother's name on her gravestone:

> The boy has guided my hand, and now I put my hand over his. "Your turn," I say to him. Together we trace the grooves in the stone, he repeating the name of each letter after me. "Very good," I tell him when he has done this several times. "Now you do it by yourself." He tries again and again, until he gets it right. (353)

Just as when she reads her mother's poetry to the coffee bean sorters, Camila is passing on her mother's heroic legacy to a new generation in having the boy trace Salomé's name; but just as importantly, she is passing on the quotidian triumph of literacy to the boy. The intellectual here is not the bearer of a transcendent and illuminating truth that only she can see, for the boy is leading Camila as much as she leads him, and eventually, the two will get it right together. Early in the novel, Camila mentions the "bad habit of writers, creating the world rather than inhabiting it" (113); she could be speaking to Minerva and Salomé as well as Malcolm and Che. In the end, Camila offers an alternative to the anticolonial dictum that it is the duty of the writer to show the people how to create a better world. Composing in her minor key, she is one of the people, just one of the many who will work together to form a free and just society.

This ending of *In the Name of Salomé* connects to what has become another strand in Alvarez's writing. In addition to Alvarez's personal and historical novels, she has recently begun to write books for children and adolescents. In *The Secret Footprints* (2000), *A Cafecito Story* (2001), *How Tía Lola Came to Stay* (2001), *Before We Were Free* (2002), and *Finding Miracles* (2004), Alvarez is engaged in writing as an explicitly pedagogical vocation. The novels of the 1990s lamented the irrevocable loss of the utopian horizon—progressive hope offers no sustenance in either *How the García Girls Lost Their Accents* or *¡Yo!*, and it appears only as something to be mourned in *In the Time of the Butterflies*. But Alvarez's new movement into children's literature resonates with Camila's final insight—that politics is a "minor," everyday, and collective activity. These latest works point toward Alvarez's contribution to the literature of the postcolonial, post-Civil Rights Americas, a literature in which politics takes place not only on the level of contests for national sovereignty but also in everyday struggles to build a better world.

# CONCLUSION
## NEW DIRECTIONS: THE POST-SIXTIES MIAMI IMAGINARY

AFTER DISCUSSING THE POST-SIXTIES RETHINKING OF POLITICS and the market coming out of a New York-based Latino/a tradition, we now turn to an analysis of the way in which a different Latino/a community deals with the accusation of selling out. Our goal is to show how the post-Sixties methodology we have developed in looking at New York-based Latino/a writers can also be applied to other Latino/a populations. For Miami-based Cuban-American writers, the sellout label is related to a betrayal of what is deemed appropriate politics for and by their community. Entering into the larger market of Latino/a literature while ambivalently engaging with a Sixties literary tradition, these writers run the risk of alienating their home communities, which expect Cuban-American cultural production to reflect conservative political values. By looking at the millennial generation of Miami-based Cuban-American writers, we aim to point to some of the new directions in Latino/a literature while expanding our geographic scope. Miami as a site for Latino/a cultural production might appear to be similar to New York metropolis in terms of its internationalism and diversity; however, its proximity to the Caribbean and the prominent role of the Cuban exile community present a very different public sphere for Latino/a writers. We will consequently conclude by discussing the challenges facing the post-Sixties generation of Cuban-American writers in Miami as a way of understanding the veiled politics within this writing. In particular, we will focus on the writings of Nilo Cruz, Chantel Acevedo, and Ana Menéndez as influenced by Latino/a New York literary legacies and seeking to reformulate Cuban-American identity while wrestling with the legacy of the Sixties as embodied in the Cuban revolution.

Cuban-American cultural production enters a public sphere defined by a double-bind dynamic. This double bind results from the very different definitions of authentic cultural production of the two main canons in which Cuban-American writing seeks membership: the Latino/a tradition and that of the Miami political establishment. Facing competing definitions of politics and culture, Cuban-American authors take on the challenges of speaking to two audiences without alienating either, and consequently run the risk of being labeled sellouts by both. Cuban-American writers are often counted out of the Civil Rights legacy by progressive Latino/a theorists for what appear to be their demographic characteristics but are in actuality politicized notions of authentic Latino/a production. As we note in earlier chapters, oppositionality and political resistance are often cited as defining facets of authentic Latino/a writing by anticolonial critics. The stereotype of the Cuban-American community in the United States as fleeing the 1959 revolution, predominantly white, politically conservative, and solidly middle-class is often invoked as the rationale for *not* categorizing Cuban Americans as U.S. Latino/as. Eliana Rivero's "Hispanic Literature in the United States: Self-Image and Conflict" is explicit about why Cuban Americans cannot fit : "If we define ethnic minority art and literature in the United States as a form of cultural resistance and/or protest, then the works by Cuban immigrants can never be considered" (187).[1] Cuban-American writers are accordingly not political in the "right way." The objection that Rivero has to Cuban-American writing being classified as U.S. ethnic literature is not simply a matter of pure politics, namely that Cuban exiles "oppose the socialist revolutionary process taking place in their homeland" (183). She also criticizes the community specifically for its embrace of "selfish, materialistic middle-class values" (187). Cuban Americans as a group are depicted as too open to the market, too accepting of the values of capitalist materialism, and it is their middle-class economic status that enables them to participate too fully in the market. Our project has sought to complicate such notions of the "correct" method for Latino/a expression or the political stance it should embody, including any terms of exclusion predicated on the relationship between the Cuban-American community's politics and the influence of the U.S. market.

While anticolonial Latino/a criticism maligns the Cuban-American community in terms of its relation to politics and the market, the Cuban-American writer must also face accusations of treason from the Miami exile establishment as well.[1] These Miami-based critiques similarly question the authenticity of Latino/a cultural production; these notions of authentic cultural expression are based in both geography and political ideology. As Lori Ween so adeptly depicts the situation in "Translational Backformations: Authenticity and Language in Cuban American Literature," such Cuban-American writers as Cristina Garcia and Oscar Hijuelos are delegitimized as representatives of Cuban-American culture because of their distance from Miami as the capital par excellence of exiled Cuba. Garcia and Hijuelos were "not raised in Miami" and therefore their works are described as lacking "the smell" of Cuba; rather, they "smelled of other shores, certainly not Cuba's" (131–32). Proximity to Miami functions as a litmus test for determining the writer's representative status, and this geographical proximity is defined specifically in terms of political affiliation. Being a true Cuban means being from Miami, which in turn means being on the political right. This very equation is cited by what one might call the guardian of Cuban-American culture in Miami, the *Nuevo Herald*. During the late 1990s, when Garcia and Hijuelos achieved national fame, the *Nuevo Herald* writer Soren Triff stated that it was "inconcebible" for a writer to be categorized as Cuban American if they espouse "ideas liberales" (12A). Politics is then a very specific ground for exclusion from the Cuban-American canon. According to Triff, there is no such thing as a progressive Cuban. Identification with political liberalism or the left would invalidate a writer's standing as a true Cuban American.

The Cuban-American writer then enters a public sphere comprising a Latino/a national and Cuban local market, both of which define authentic Cuban-American cultural production as Miami-centered and conservative. These notions of authenticity lead to the formation of a highly oppositional political binary within Latino/a and Miami public discourse, a binary that pushes the writer to take sides. Ambrosio Fornet remarks on this development in "The Cuban Literary Diaspora and Its Contexts: A Glossary":

> Since the advent of the Revolution in 1959, taking into account the political positions of both sides—those in favor of and those against the Revolution, those outside as well as those within Cuba—it is clear that we are confronted with a serious paradox of an ideological and semantic nature. (94)

Fornet is critical of what he calls the "Miami mafia" establishment's denial of the 1959 Cuban revolution. His formulation of the binary within the Cuban community, in the United States and on the island, is useful for understanding the divisive public sphere the Cuban-American

writer enters (95). Indeed, Fornet's political paradox highlights the
either/or relationship with the Sixties to which the writer must pledge
allegiance. In this chapter we will discuss the way in which Cuban-
American authors negotiate a path through the political division within
the Latino/a and Miami public discourse in order to imagine a third space
beyond an ideological binary that seeks to distinguish between authentic
and inauthentic cultural production.

Cuban-American writers in Miami consequently find themselves
caught between the canons of the Latino/a and Miami literary establish-
ments. Their position is therefore a tenuous balancing act between two ideological poles, with the potential hazard of alienation from the two public
spheres in which they can articulate their voices. Oddly enough, these
ideologically opposed canons appear to agree on politics as a defining
characteristic of Latino/a writing, although their definitions challenge
any Cuban-American writer seeking membership in both communities.
On the one hand, the anticolonial Latino/a critics who define left politics
as central to Latino/a production explicitly exclude the Cuban-American
community from being potential producers of such literature. On the
other hand, the Miami establishment identifies the true Cuban writer as
politically conservative. As a result, neither side leaves a space for a progressive Cuban-American writerly voice. If you are a progressive writer,
then the Miami establishment will designate you as non-Cuban; and if
you are Cuban, the anticolonial critics will define you as intrinsically
non-progressive. This catch-22 situation is a dilemma that the new generation of Cuban-American writers must navigate carefully in order to
"make it" in the publishing market. Writers who fail to obtain the stamp
of authenticity from either community may find themselves in trouble.

In view of the strict political dichotomy facing this new generation of
Cuban-American writing, we turn to the work of Nilo Cruz, Chantel
Acevedo, and Ana Menéndez as seeking alternative modes of political
affiliation that are not simply reducible to either pro- or anti-Castro ideologies. The space provided by the genre of historical fiction offers
Cuban-American writers a safe haven in which to challenge the definition
of Cuban-American identity as Miami-centered and politically conservative. These authors offer alternate versions of Cuban-American communities in the United States, communities that are located outside Miami
or the United States, and/or are part of pre-1959 migrations. By calling
attention to the historical development of these communities, Cuban-
American writers seek to complicate the terms of cultural authenticity
and to question the notion that cultural authenticity can be claimed only
by ideological opponents of Fidel Castro's regime. These writers also

propose a formulation of third-space politics through oblique references to the current political division within the Miami and Latino/a public sphere, and this indirect commentary forestalls any superficial attempts to align the text with specific political position. The layer of opacity that veils such social commentary often appears in the setting of the text itself, which in the case of Cruz and Acevedo is in pre-revolution Cuba and therefore able to avoid the post-revolutionary political divide. Menéndez sets her novel, *Loving Che*, during the Cuban revolution but uses a romantic plot in order to disrupt unequivocal political analyses of the novel. By reading beneath this surface layer of textual opacity, however, we will argue that Cruz, Acevedo, and Menéndez use the genre of historical fiction in order to directly negotiate the legacy of the 1959 revolution in ways that challenge the current for-or-against political dichotomy.

## THE LECTOR INTELLECTUAL

Nilo Cruz describes the challenges of writing directly to a Cuban-American audience in an interview with Emily Mann. In discussing the ideological fervor of the Miami establishment, Cruz acknowledges the real fear that emerged at the beginning of his playwriting career regarding his personal safety, admitting that it initially led to self-censorship:

> When I started writing, I was terrified about writing about Cuba, because the subject matter was so controversial in this country. I was in Miami doing the International Hispanic Theater Festival, and one play got bomb threats. The Cuban community in Miami thought that this particular writer was leftist, pro-Castro. The play that I had written had to do with Italian immigration wave, but basically I was writing about the Cuban exodus. Much later, when I actually embraced my culture and had the courage to write directly about it, I went back to that play and changed it all. Now they're Cuban exiles. (Mann 73)

Cruz depicts the violent reaction of the Miami establishment as one of the factors that prevented him from overtly claiming Cuban-American identity as a writing subject, choosing instead to use a different ethnic community as a substitute. While Cruz ultimately found his voice as a Cuban-American writer, his work is clearly sensitive to the problems that may arise from direct engagement with the contemporary population of Miami exiles. One of the ways that Cruz contests the influence of the establishment and yet safely communicates with the Cuban-American community is through pre–Cuban revolution settings for his drama. Cruz's Pulitzer Prize-winning play, *Anna in the Tropics* (2003), is set in

Ybor City, a company town near present-day Tampa, and chronicles the lives of the Cuban cigar rollers in the factories there. Cruz recuperates the history of what Juan González calls the "nearly forgotten" first Cuban immigration wave to the United States in the late 1800s via this play (110). According to González, about "10 percent of Cuba's population fled abroad to escape the upheavals of the independence wars"; the "majority were unemployed tobacco workers who sought jobs in the new cigar factories" in places like Tampa, New York City, and New Orleans (110).

On the one hand, this historical setting directly contests stereotypes of Cuban-American identity by highlighting the existence of a pre-revolution community in the United States. The formulation of an alternative historical lineage for Cuban Americans in the United States is particularly significant in that it decentralizes Miami as the authentic home-space for Cuban-American identity. This reconfiguration is most clearly accomplished through the setting of the play, which takes place in Tampa rather than Miami. Cruz describes Tampa as "the capital of the North American Clear Havana cigar industry" which "even rivaled Havana itself" (Mann 72). The characters in the play contest Miami's ownership of the "Little Havana" title by remarking that in Ybor City they are "trying to create a little city that resembles the ones we left back on the island" (Cruz, *Anna* 22). On the other hand, this historical setting serves as a metaphoric safe space for formulating such a contestation without incurring the harsh criticism of the Miami exile establishment. Cruz originally planned to set the action of the play in the 1800s, focusing on José Martí's involvement as a lector in the Tampa cigar factories and the way in which he "created a brigade to go fight for Cuba's independence" (Mann 71). The setting and historical baggage of Cuba's independence struggles proved too restrictive, however: "I thought, it's too much—it was so much information. I didn't know how to sculpt that kind of play [...] it would become too much of a historical play" (71). As a result, Cruz chose instead to represent the "brink of change" that emerged from the Great Depression and industrialization, in particular how "lectores were the first ones to be fired from the cigar factories" (71).

While this detail regarding the play's inspiration indicates the level of self-censorship still present, it also reveals Cruz's desire to bypass the ideological split produced by the Cuban revolution in order to reiterate a Caribbean-centered political legacy through the figure of José Martí.[2] Martí is absent as a character from *Anna in the Tropics,* but the role of the lector as intellectual remains in the narrative. In addition, by focusing on the lector's position within cigar factory society, the play initiates a dialogue with a New York-based Civil Rights literary lineage, including one of the examples from this tradition that we discuss in chapter 1, Jesús Colón's *A Puerto Rican in New York and Other Sketches,* which begins by identifying the lector with the politically progressive author. Cruz's play focuses on the changes that a lector brings about by conveying the imaginative world of *Anna Karenina* to the cigar workers, and in so doing Cruz evokes Colón's image of the lector-intellectual who awakens the body politic. The lector is accorded the privileged position of facilitating the psychological and economic liberation of the factory masses through his act of reading. Cruz's play, however, makes a clear revision of this Sixties literary tradition by imagining an alternate democratic public sphere in which cultural production is not simply owned or controlled by the cultural elite represented by the lector but also consumed and engaged by members of the working class—who in the case of the cigar factory are largely illiterate. As Celia remarks, "Some of us cigar workers might not be able to read or write, but we can recite lines from *Don Quijote* and *Jane Eyre*" (Cruz, *Anna* 27). Indeed, Cruz's play implies that the masses must take ownership of the process of liberation because the role of the lector as cultural mediator is disappearing; it is no longer economically feasible because of industrialization and violent rejection by certain subgroups of factory workers.

*Anna in the Tropics* consequently locates itself between the two competing Latino/a legacies of the New York and Miami literary scenes. Inasmuch as the play revises prevailing stereotypes of Cuban-American identity, it also challenges the anticolonial notions of the lector-intellectual. Juan Julian, the lector, finds his newly acquired position threatened by proposals to industrialize the factory. He rightly considers this to be a personal affront enacted by the factory owner's half-brother, Cheché. His question regarding the reason for Cheché's intense dislike of him is answered in the following manner: "He doesn't like lectors," and, "He doesn't understand the purpose of having someone like you read stories to the workers" (21). The lector's purpose is being called into question due to the industrialization of the cigar factories, with machines being brought in to speed up the process. Cheché's critique of the lector's lack of purpose reflects the challenges of modernization to the role of the intellectual. The lector is being made irrelevant by the industrialization of factories and integration of machines into the cigar-rolling process. For Cheché, the human cigar roller is a representative of a bygone era and since the lector benefits from his position in such a society, the lector will criticize industrialization in order to avoid losing that position of privilege: "Leonardo is a lector. That's why he doesn't value machines. The lectors are being fired from all the factories, because nobody can hear them read over the sound of the machines" (52). Cruz himself emphasizes the changes wrought by industrialization in an interview: "The world was starting to change: modernity, productivity, advancement, all came with the new era. Machines were introduced into the workplace, and the intrusion of these machines destroyed the silence necessary for a lector to read from newspapers and novels to the workers" (Mann 72). With the implementation of machines, the voice of the lector would be drowned out—and besides, reading works of literature does nothing to meet Cheché's goal of speeding up factory production.

Cheché, however, represents more than simply the profit logic of capitalism that rationalizes the lector's position as irrelevant. Cheché also symbolizes a class of disaffected Cuban Americans, ignored by the anticolonial project of revolution as a potential audience for the intellectual-lector. Juan Julian's response to Cheché's criticisms is to assert his duty as lector: "Why? Because we read novels to the workers, because we educate them and inform them?" (Cruz, *Anna* 21). The condescension in this remark indicates the level of superiority Juan Julian ascribes to his lector status, as a teacher who has knowledge to pour into the factory workers as if they are empty vessels. Even more problematic is the lector's inability to grasp the real issue at stake—jealousy. According to the female factory workers, Cheché dislikes lectors for much more personal reasons: "His wife ran away with a lector" (21). The narrative thus points to the danger of communities that are alienated by this process of "enlightenment" or awakening of the proletariat. Juan Julian does not regard Cheché as an audience for his readings; rather, the lectures are intended solely for the workers. Juan Julian identifies Cheché as part of the ownership class, and therefore neither a worker in need of enlightenment nor a potential participant in a progressive political movement. This blindness to Cheché's relevance is a fatal mistake on Juan Julian's part, for at the end of the play he is shot and killed by Cheché while lecturing to the workers. Cheché's position at the factory is in fact illegitimate; being the owner's half-brother, he owns no shares himself and therefore is also a marginalized presence in the factory. Cheché's double alienation leads him to strike out against the lector, and it is this marginalized and violent character who most resembles the Cuban-American establishment in Miami as potential silencers of the voice of the writer-intellectual. The disappearance of the lectors is then brought about by both modernization processes and the violence exerted by those who feel excluded and therefore threatened by progressive projects.

*Anna in the Tropics* thus articulates a transition in the public sphere, the silencing of the lector in the 1920s as a metaphor for the similar changes occurring in the post-Sixties period. The play grieves the loss of this public voice for the intellectual, evoking our discussion in chapter 5 of Julia Alvarez's novels, which mourn the passing of an anticolonial conception of the writer's role. Within the setting of the play, a new era of industrialization initiates a crisis for the intellectual: not only is the public work s/he performs being rendered irrelevant if not illegitimate, but the lector is also the victim of violence from reactionary movements. Through this turn of the twentieth-century setting, Nilo Cruz is able to foreground similar challenges faced by the millennial generation of Cuban-American writers. The lector functions as a double for the contemporary writer—the dramatist in this case—which is even more poignant. Drama as a genre certainly can entail a more direct relationship with its audience than prose fiction. The contemporary conditions of cultural production, however, place limits on the ability of the writer-lector to awaken this mass of people. The post-Sixties period sees the delegitimization of traditional genres through the proliferation of new media, another form of technological modernization. In addition, the play alludes to the real danger presented by the community that potentially consumes this cultural product—the violence of censorship from the Cuban-American establishment.

Given the disappearance of the lector's role, past and present, the play attempts to imagine a third space of democratization through cultural production. The ending of the play reveals that "a metal blanket" of silence has fallen on the workers after the lector's murder (82). Rather than finding a replacement or giving up the project of public speaking, the workers decide to take on the lector's role themselves. In so doing, the play warns that the role of the intellectual must not be formulated in hierarchical terms: not only will it be destroyed by those like Cheché or the Cuban exile community, who are excluded from progressive movements, but it will also be unable to adapt to a new context of social relations, whether they be industrialization or globalization. Indeed, the work of the lector has transformed the factory society in the play by inspiring the creation of a new cultural product, a new cigar line called "Anna Karenina." Although the intellectual no longer has a public domain of influence because his function can no longer be maintained, the tragic story he told will be reimagined by the workers themselves into a commodity that will enter and circulate within a different public space—the market.

## GHOSTS OF CLASS CONSCIOUSNESS

Chantel Acevedo's debut novel, *Love and Ghost Letters* (2005), also reflects upon the demands of the Cuban-American establishment and the general Latino/a book market by engaging and then frustrating their expectations regarding the form of Latino/a cultural production. In a recent interview, Acevedo complains "that hardly a Latin-inspired book can be written before someone begins to yell 'magical realism' and starts discussing Marquez [sic]" (Machado Sáez, "Family's" 18). This is a complaint that, as we mention in previous chapters, is shared by such other Latino/a writers and critics. In *Love and Ghost Letters*, Acevedo appears to intentionally undercut this stereotype about Latino/a literature in the United States by presenting the reader with the delivery of ghost letters but refusing to provide us with an actual ghost. The letters in question are missives sent by an exiled father to his daughter living in Cuba. The daughter, Josefina, believes her sergeant father was killed in the recent uprisings against the Cuban government and therefore assumes these letters to be literally heaven-sent. Magical realism tends to present magic as an everyday occurrence, with the presence of the otherworldly providing an escape from or panacea for suffering. By contrast, Acevedo's novel continually frustrates the desire for miraculous interventions, focusing instead on a personal narrative of family conflict and struggle that mirrors the upheavals in pre-Castro Cuba.

In addition to undercutting the genre expectations of the Latino/a book market, Acevedo's novel also engages the Cuban-American market's claims of cultural authenticity. Set in pre-revolutionary Cuba, the novel certainly caters to the nostalgia of the Miami exile establishment for the time before Castro.[3] While the narrative draws in the audience with this nostalgic entry, it refuses to idealize the Cuban past. Rather, *Love and Ghost Letters* historicizes this pre-revolutionary past by pointing to the social contradictions that made possible the Cuban revolution. The novel opens with Regla, an Afro-Cuban house servant, reading the fortune of the child in her care, Josefina, the main character. Regla's prediction of Josefina's future personal unhappiness links with the larger context of Cuban history: "The reason she saw such a future was the time itself, the past century still a part of the island's memory, a place where the poor were fearsomely poor and the rich awesomely rich" (3). Through Regla, who is described as "trapped by both conditions," the novel foregrounds the marginalized Afro-Cuban and working class populations early on in the narrative (3). In so doing, Acevedo's text refuses to reproduce a nostalgic and idyllic picture of social stability in pre-1959 Cuba.

Accommodation and contestation of exile nostalgia is also accomplished by means of a romantic plot that alludes to class conflicts already simmering in Cuban society of the 1930s. Beginning with a simple love story between a rich girl and a poor boy, the narrative reflects on the way in which a family is torn apart by the youthful romance between Josefina and Lorenzo. On the level of the plot, Josefina's fall into poverty results from her father's disapproval of their marriage. Nevertheless, Josefina's relationship with Lorenzo is also condemned to failure because her attraction to him is based on exoticism. What is so appealing to Josefina about Lorenzo is that he embodies the contradictions of the racial and economic strata in Cuban society. The first time she sees Lorenzo, he is standing outside her house watching the upper-class dance taking place inside. Lorenzo is not part of the island's aristocracy, a fact he highlights when he tells Josefina: "I have no money, and I drink rum and whiskey" (6). Yet it is precisely his marginality that is so alluring, the fact that he "dissolv[es] into the humid darkness" and is "dark and long, like an afternoon shadow" (7). Lorenzo's combination of whiteness and blackness, his "visage made whiter by the harvest of black hair on his head" (5), also leads Josefina to remark that he is "handsome" (7). It is then the exoticism of the Other that is responsible for the rupture within Josefina's family. The separation of daughter and father is heightened by the sergeant's publicly announced death, and while in mourning Josefina begins receiving letters from her father, presumably written from the grave. Since the letters the sergeant writes are in reality mailed from Florida, the narrative depicts revolts and exile as a pattern of social disruption that defines Cuban society well before the 1959 revolution. Furthermore, the novel here questions the exceptionalism of the Cuban exile establishment and its anti-Castro identity by identifying Cuban-American communities in the United States from prior migration waves.

Pre-revolutionary Cuba is not represented as a Garden of Eden, a product of Cuban-American nostalgia, but rather as a society fractured by class conflict. The class wars are evident not only in the political instability that forces the sergeant to leave the island but also in the family saga that evolves as a commentary on materialist desires. Josefina's love for Lorenzo is tied to her fascination with lower-class customs and culture, especially the rites of Santería. And yet, when Josefina must live in poverty due to her marriage and estrangement from her father, she begins to long for the comfort that her father's presence brought her as well as the financial benefits of his membership in the upper class. The family's personal sphere thus functions as a microcosm of Cuban society. Attending church, Josefina and her daughter Soledad are entranced by the unspoken rules that the religious community observes, with the rich seated on the right side of the aisle and the poor on the left. Josefina's sadness in the novel is as much about her loss of privilege as about the loss of her father. Looking at the well-dressed church members, Josefina remembers her girlhood in Vedado, the elite neighborhood of Havana, "when she was one of those on the right, unaware of those that sat just a few feet away, shuffling and daydreaming about the things they couldn't own" (126).

The class segregation in the church not only emphasizes a class consciousness that an exile nostalgia would abject, but also references in a veiled manner the political divide between left and right that still haunts the Cuban and Cuban-American communities. Downward mobility produces in Josefina a complex identification with both the pueblo and the wealthy elite that informs the double vision of Acevedo's text. In so doing, Acevedo explores the knot of community and economics from a specifically Cuban-American viewpoint, referencing the role that political corruption and the gap between the rich and poor played in the various insurrections throughout Cuban history. Vedado is the site where this knot is untied, as it ambivalently embodies both classism and familial affection. Josefina revisits Vedado, recognizing it as a forbidden place that "kept out those who could not afford its soaring rents," and yet also as a welcoming home, "like returning to her mother after so many years" (310). Nostalgia here produces an ambivalent identification with a past and a home that was predicated on exclusion. Here, the challenge facing the post-Sixties Cuban-American writer is clear: how to reconcile the competing contexts of a history of social inequality with the comforting familiarity of personal memory? *Love and Ghost Letters* draws on a romantic narrative as a metaphor that allows safe exploration of the social fractures that led to the Cuban revolution. A critique of Miami exile nostalgia alongside demands of the Latino/a market for magical realism is accomplished by offering a personal narrative of the trials of a Cuban family in order to also comment on the contradictions informing the Cuban-American public sphere.

## A CUBAN REVOLUTION ROMANCE

While the authors we've discussed so far must veil their discussions of the Cuban revolution and its legacy through metaphor or displaced time settings, Ana Menéndez emerges as one of the few Cuban-American writers who seek to directly represent this highly contested, mythologized, and divisive historical event through her novel, *Loving Che* (2003). By reimagining the larger-than-life historical persona of Che Guevara,

Menéndez claims the anticolonial Civil Rights Sixties as the common inheritance of Cuban Americans as a Latino/a community. The novel itself references the dangers of claiming such a legacy via the narrator's search for the Cuban mother she never met, a search that serves as the frame of the novel. The narrator's search is predicated on an obsession with a very specific mode of cultural production—photographs. At the opening of the novel, the narrator describes her hobby of collecting photographs as a source of comfort, a way of dealing with her personal loss: "The photographs of strangers, especially, have always brought me a gentle peace" (1). By collecting these photographs and imagining spheres of relation—for example, "that the stranger caught there is a half-forgotten old aunt"—the narrator is inspired to play "a game of history" (1). While the possibilities for relationship and community are acts of the imagination ultimately "silenced by the years between us" (1), the narrator embarks on an archival cultural project that attempts to make these imaginative strands a reality. Interested specifically in photographs of Cuban exiles, she decides to "construct a traveling exhibition of these photographs, and was even able to secure funding for the project" (2). Despite this financial support, the narrator is ultimately unable to complete her project due to the reticence of the Cuban-American community to participate in such an exhibition. On the one hand, potential donors are unwilling to lend their personal property for such a public and collective project: "Many families, I was dismayed to learn, would not give up their photographs, not even for a few days" (2). More disturbing to the narrator, however, are the criticisms she receives about her desire to include exiles from the pre-revolutionary period: "And when in a purely innocent gesture, I agreed to accept the photographs of exiles who had fled Batista, my political motivations were put in question and my entire project fell apart" (2). The cultural project is then silenced by the Cuban-American establishment's strict definition of the exile community in terms of anti-Castro politics, such that the narrator's broadened definition of Cuban exile is considered a threat and a sign of community betrayal.

This silencing of cultural production in the public sphere is connected to the gaps in the narrator's own personal life, who states that "of my own origins, I know little" (3). The narrator's struggle to recover her familial history, in particular that of her missing mother, Teresa, consequently mirrors the narrative's move to recover another more publicly silenced inheritance. Although the traveling exhibition the narrator planned never takes place, photographs are integral to the development of Menéndez's own novel which includes pictures of Che Guevara intertwined with a package of letters that the narrator receives from her mother, forming the bulk of the text. It appears that this search for and desire to uncover a lost past is itself a cultural project: "I wonder now if this backward looking of the exile—the Cuban one in particular, so hysterical and easy to carica-ture—could be an antidote to a new and more terrible kind of madness" (2). The narrator locates the root of this madness in a "trauma of separa-tion" as a global condition (2–3). Consequently, the rupture caused by the Cuban revolution appears to serve as the originating trauma that must be resolved in order to allow for a new conception of community. In a sim-ilar way to Cristina Garcia's rendering, nostalgia emerges as a potential antidote to the more pervasive contemporary trauma of globalization and its discontents.

The dangers implicit in attempting to formulate such a public project as the photography exhibit serve to explain the novel's consequent with-drawal into a personal narrative of family reunification. This private realm, however, functions not only as a response to the censorship of the Miami establishment but also speaks to the nostalgia evident in Latino/a studies in general. In the package of letters that the absent mother, Teresa, sends to the narrator, the mother alludes to the blurred line between public history and private life: "I wonder now if our recorded history isn't like this, if our idea of history isn't another way of saying an idea of ourselves" (17). The romance that these letters narrate between Teresa and Che Guevara is itself a reflection of a larger historical conver-sation about the romance of revolution and progressive resistance. Teresa expresses the very same nostalgia for the Sixties articulated by Latino/a criticism: "How much lovelier to think on the past when we were young and untested and our beginning lay behind us like a forgotten dream" (18). Teresa appears to indicate that already in the time of youthful ide-alism the beginning lay behind, not ahead. This forgotten beginning indicates that the potential for creating anew is frustrated, a dream possi-ble only if one turns a blind eye to originating events. Indeed, Latino/a critics also exhibit a nostalgic fixation on the Sixties as a moment that broke with the past, yet they look backward in order to idealize a time that rejected the definition of the present through the past. *Loving Che* speaks to the extent to which this progressive romance implies a tragedy of memory, one that cannot recognize the trauma of revolution—the trauma inflicted by a break in time that violently abjects the past.

Teresa's letters challenge the narrator's sense of history and Cuban-American identity to the extent that she even feels compelled to destroy them, to "throw the entire contents of the package away": "I was not so removed from exile chatter that I didn't understand the implications of her story. Miami was not a city for romantic heroes; here an association with the revolution was something to be hidden, denied, and ultimately forgotten" (158). Although the narrator finally resists this temptation and does not destroy the letters, her encounters with members of the Cuban exile establishment reveal the danger of exposing such a narrative to a Miami audience. The professor who reads the packet of letters is critical of the story they tell, explaining that she "cannot agree with your Teresa when she likens history to personal events" (172). The professor implies that connecting the public and the personal leads to false ties of relation, defining the letters as "an impossible reinvention of history, a beautiful fraud" (174). At the heart of this critique is a discomfort with the roman- tic qualities of the narrative: "There are some errors in the dates, she said. Omissions. Maybe this isn't important to a love story. I don't know. Myself, she said smiling, I would have liked to have seen something about how we have Mr. Guevara to thank for introducing Soviet-style prisons in Cuba" (175). The professor assumes that the narrator has "written Teresa's account [her]self" and expresses disappointment that the letters are not political indictments of El Che (175). The professor's critique also hints that the genre of romance is not the correct mode for narrating history—it is too personal and therefore cannot accommodate historical facts that complicate an idealization of Che Guevara. The narrator iden- tifies this response as something she encounters "so often in Miami," a "sense that the person chatting so pleasantly with me was only waiting to be offended, to detect in some innocent or ignorant statement a secret adherence to repellent beliefs" (175).

The novel does not simply identify the difficulties in making sense of the past in a context of censorship as endemic to politically conservative Miami but finds them in Cuba as well. In her final visit to the island, the narrator is told that the history of Havana "could be seen as a collec- tive interest in outrunning the past" (198). Indeed, denying or avoid- ing the subject of the Cuban revolution is also evident: "The tendency of the Cuban to talk about everything except the subject at hand had worn me down to the size of a pencil stub. I'd come to see it as a kind of aggres- sion, a particular type of aggression perhaps indigenous to people who felt they had no other weapon at their disposal but the power to drive some- one slowly mad through endless soliloquies" (203). The aggression lies in the opacity of the speaker, preventing the listener or reader from being able to discern any sort of meaning in the speaker's words. The narrator identifies the excessive orality of island Cubans as a mode of resistance modeled on Castro's own speechifying, yet emerging in defiance of that regime—to speak critically would be counterrevolutionary, so the alter- nate form of resistance is to say nothing of any consequence. This tactic of opacity, however, creates the same atmosphere of distrust that the narrator senses in Miami: "Every trip to Havana was a dance between wanting to believe in the good of people and protecting oneself from the desperation that poisons every interaction" (204). It is in Cuba that the veracity of Teresa's narrative is questioned again: "Your mother loved Che very much, yes, as we all did. But only from a distance. [...] Many people loved him, men and women. Many people. But your mother never knew him" (212). The point of contention here is not so much Teresa's relationship with Che but the individualist form it takes. Asserting that Teresa was merely one of many, this critique calls into question her individualism and thus her interpretation of history. Similarly to the Miami professor, the problem is a matter of the distance between the public and the private, in this instance between the icon of the 1959 revolution and the people. The two sides formed by the trauma of the Cuban revolution agree on one thing then: any attempt to bridge the gap between public history and personal memory is a dangerous falsification of reality.

At the close of *Loving Che*, the narrator is transformed by her mother's act of imagination, whether false or true, and ultimately lays claim to the Cuban revolution as part of her historical inheritance. Browsing for photographs in a shop, the narrator comes across a picture of Che Guevara with a camera: "There he stands for all eternity, the young soldier with a yearning to record the world that lies before him, his hands light on the camera, his eyes searching ahead" (226–27). The photographed Che models the desire to record the present and the future, but this snapshot also evokes the desire to recapture that revolutionary moment of hope, "when the future was not yet a darkened plate" (228). The photograph metaphor provides a complex and productive imagery of how the future versus the present is and was defined. The future for the narrator does not appear to hold the same possibilities as it seemed to in the Sixties. The novel ends by identifying the forward-looking perspective of revolution as well as its frustration as the central inheritance of the post-Sixties Cuban-American and by extension, Latino/a generation of writers.

The struggle for space in a Latino/a canon poses a double obstacle for Cuban-American writers because their entry into the market entails negotiation of two completely opposed political poles of canon formation. Nevertheless, as our discussion of Nilo Cruz, Chantel Acevedo, and Ana Menéndez reveals, this crossroads of institutionalization and marginalization offers dynamic possibilities for Latino/a cultural production. Contemporary Cuban-American and Latino/a literature identifies anticolonial and Civil Rights histories as a common inheritance, appropriating and revising the literary traditions of the Sixties in order to imagine their relevance to the present development of Latino/a communities. Post-Sixties Latino/a writers are indeed reinvesting hope and possibility in their work, imagining a place for a new progressive politics while remembering the Sixties as a past wherein such possibilities were both opened and closed. The Sixties signify a legacy of romance and tragedy that continues to shape the development of contemporary Latino/a cultural production.

Our own work in many ways parallels that of the post-Sixties Latino/a writers discussed in this book. We also seek to articulate a third space for literature; noting the complex theorizations of music's relation to politics and the market in Latino/a studies, we aim to position Latino/a literature in a comparable manner. We also, however, face similar challenges in terms of the dynamics that organize the field of Latino/a studies. As we mention in our introduction to this project, Latino/a literature is entering a critical phase of consolidation; as a result, this field of cultural production is encountering its own form of canon wars. In this period of exclusion and inclusion, we endeavor to connect various strands of Latino/a literature—Nuyorican, Dominican-American, and Cuban-American— in order to show the ways in which this literature wrestles with the legacy of the Sixties that also haunts Latino/a theory. Our formulation of a post-Sixties Latino/a canon is shaped by our desire to envision new directions in progressive thought, and we see ourselves in conversation with the Civil Rights and anticolonial struggles that gave birth to Latino/a studies. Nevertheless, we are also aware of the public sphere into which our project enters, wherein the relationship of Latino/a literature to politics and the market is binary in understanding. Latino/a literature, whether viewed through the lens of anticolonial or multiculturalist politics, is deemed to unequivocally reject or celebrate the market. We hope that our project articulates a third space for Latino/a literature, one that grapples with the possibilities and the limitations embodied by the market. Post-Sixties Latino/a literature remains ambivalent about its own positioning and yet embodies the productive tension that emerges from such a conflicted space of identification. At the crossroads of the millennium, looking back at the cultural inheritance of the Sixties, this literature and this project look forward to imagine the applications of such a tradition in a new context.

# NOTES

### INTRODUCTION

1. George Yúdice's definition of society as a "field of force" (*Expediency* 39) references the sociological approach to cultural texts that Pierre Bourdieu develops in *The Field of Cultural Production*. In theorizing that "the role of culture has expanded in unprecedented ways into the political and economic at the same time that conventional notions of culture largely have been emptied out" (9), Yúdice clearly belongs to the Latino/a cultural studies tradition that we discuss throughout our introduction.

2. The transition from being oppositional to entering the mainstream has been discussed more generally within the interdisciplinary field of Latino/a studies, as seen in the title of Pedro Cabán's essay, "Moving from the Margins to Where?" Appearing in the inaugural issue of the journal *Latino Studies,* an event which itself marks a panethnic consolidation of the field, Cabán's essay tells the history of how "Latino Studies has evolved from its insurrectionary and somewhat turbulent origins as Chicano and Puerto Rican Studies into its current incarnation as a multidisciplinary academic field" (6).

3. In addition to these anthologies of Latino/a creative writing, a number of anthologies of Latino/a literary criticism emerged as this book was going to press in 2007. For example, see the volume *Companion to Latina/o Studies* edited by Juan Flores and Renato Rosaldo as well as *Contemporary U.S. Latino/a Literary Criticism* edited by Richard Pérez and Lyn Di Iorio Sandín.

4. The *Norton Anthology of Latino Literature* is mentioned as a forthcoming project by Ilan Stavans in the *Chronicle of Higher Education* (9 Jan. 1998) as well as in the *Amherst College Newsletter* (19 June 2001). Copies of the table of contents were made available to reviewers in 2005.

5. An anthropologist and published poet, Ruth Behar has written reviews on Julia Alvarez (*Women's Review of Books* 1995), Cristina Garcia (*Chicago*

*Tribune* 1997), and Chicano anthologies (*Women's Review of Books* 1993), in addition to serving as editor of the *Bridges to Cuba/Puentes a Cuba* anthology and as columnist for the *Chronicle of Higher Education.* Ilan Stavans has published numerous reviews and interviews of Latino/a writers during the 1990s, including Virgil Suarez (*New York Times* 1991), Julia Alvarez (*Commonweal* 1992, *The Nation* 1994), Richard Rodriguez (*Commonweal* 1993, *The Nation* 2002), Ana Castillo (*Commonweal* 1994), Piri Thomas (*Massachusetts Review* 1996), Cristina Garcia (*The Nation* 1997), and Sandra Cisneros (*The Nation* 2003). Alan West-Durán has reviewed Cristina Garcia (*Washington Post* 1992) and Ruth Behar (*Boston Phoenix* 1993), and has edited *Latino and Latina Writers* (2003) and *African Caribbeans: A Reference Guide* (2003).

6.  Flores's writing on Puerto Rican literature and culture includes *Insular Vision* (awarded the Casa de las Américas Prize in 1980), *La Carreta Made a U-Turn: Puerto Rican Language and Culture in the United States* (1981), *Divided Borders: Essays on Puerto Rican Identity* (1993), and *From Bomba to Hip-Hop: Puerto Rican Culture and Latino Identity* (2000). Flores is also the co-founder of the Afro-Latin@ Project, which is housed in the Latin American and Latino Studies Program at Queens College.

7.  The notion of a specifically Latino-Caribbean literary tradition is developed most explicitly by William Luis in *Dance between Two Cultures* (1997).

## CHAPTER 1

1.  Lyrics and performances of both poems can be found online at 15 January 2007 <http://prdream.com/pedro_pietri/>.

2.  In *Divergent Modernities*, Julio Ramos writes about José Martí's struggle to create a heroic vocation for the writer. Ramos seeks to establish Martí as the first modern writer of the Americas, but we might also call Martí the first anticolonial writer. The anticolonial role is rearticulated in Frantz Fanon's *The Wretched of the Earth*, C. L. R. James's *Black Jacobins*, and George Lamming's *The Pleasures of Exile*.

3.  The Young Lords platform is available online at 15 January 2007 <http://palante.org/YLPProg.html>.

4.  One of the most insightful readings of "Puerto Rican Obituary" is found in Arnaldo Cruz-Malavé's essay, "Teaching Puerto Rican Authors: Identity and Modernization in Nuyorican Texts." He draws out many important elements of the poem's ideological positioning, although it is curious that he argues that the poem "perhaps [...] best exemplifies this dialectic between demythification and utopia and its vicissitudes in the present post-nationalist era of the 1980s" (47). This approach leads him to locate in the poem a critique of false consciousness "consistent with the Frankfurt School's" (48). We depart from Cruz-Malavé's identification of this critique as the project of the "postnationalist era of the 1980s"; we make the

case that "Puerto Rican Obituary" (and the Frankfurt School) belongs to the anticolonial 1960s.

5. Lisa Sánchez González's acknowledgment of the "convenience" of the term *salsa*—despite its origins in the contaminated world of marketing—suggests the meaning-making purposes that the market can serve.

6. Unless otherwise noted, all translations are our own.

7. Willie Colón and Héctor Lavoe's album covers are analyzed in Otero Garabís's *Nación y Ritmo,* Wilson Valentín Escobar's "El Hombre que Respira Debajo del Agua," and Angel Quintero Rivera's "La gran fuga, las identidades socio-culturales y la concepción del tiempo en la música 'tropical.'"

8. Juan Flores (along with George Yúdice) takes one of Blades's album titles for the title of the last chapter of *Divided Borders,* "Living Borders/*Buscando América:* Languages of Latino Self-Formation." Sánchez González criticizes Rubén Blades's 1990s album *Amor y control* in her chapter on salsa, but it is only within the context of his "characteristically progressive" politics (182) that this album "seems a large step to the right of Blades's own earlier albums" (187). For other analyses of Blades, see Jorge Duany's "Popular Music in Puerto Rico: Toward an Anthropology of *Salsa,*" Brittmarie Janson Perez's "Political Facets of *Salsa,*" Angel Quintero Rivera's "La Música Puertorriqueña y la Contra-Cultura Democrática: Espontaneidad Libertaria de la Herencia Cimarrona," or the afterword to José David Saldívar's *The Dialectics of Our America.* Frances Aparicio has an extended commentary on Blades in *Listening to Salsa,* although she interrogates his resistant persona much more critically.

9. For a more detailed reading of "Plástico" and its historical moment, see Raphael Dalleo's essay, "Readings from Aquí y Allá: Music, Commercialism, and the Latino-Caribbean Transnational Imaginary."

10. Danny Shot, a publisher who worked closely with Pietri, discussed the poet's virtual refusal to seek out large publishers and allow his books to be marketed in his presentation, "A Biographical Look at Pedro Pietri's Evolution as a Writer," on April 8th, 2005 at the MELUS Conference in Chicago, Illinois.

11. *El Puerto Rican Embassy* is available on the web at 15 January 2007 <www.elpuertoricanembassy.org>.

12. Although "El Spanglish National Anthem" does not yet appear in any collection of Pietri's work, the complete text can be found online at 15 January 2007 <www.elpuertoricanembassy.org/anthem.html>.

13. As Lowell Fiet puts it, "what is recorded here is no longer the immigrant experience. This community has arrived" (54).

## CHAPTER 2

1. Sánchez Gonzalez's other example, Pedro Pietri, is the topic of our first chapter. See footnote 10 from chapter 1 for a discussion of Pietri's relationship to the publishing industry.

2. Robin Kelley describes a very similar trajectory between the first and second halves of Malcolm X's autobiography, noting that once Malcolm turned to the Nation of Islam, he had to disavow his younger "Detroit Red" self as deluded and misled. The irony, of course, remains that the older Malcolm was still able to write about that younger self with affection and nostalgia. See chapter 7, "The Riddle of the Zoot," in *Race Rebels*.

3. As of January 2007, the MLA international bibliography lists 17 book and journal articles about Piri Thomas written over the past 30 years, all of which focus primarily on *Down These Mean Streets*. A few mention *Savior, Savior, Hold My Hand* in passing, but none go into detailed analysis of the latter book.

4. In his essay "Nihilism in Black America," Cornel West explicitly identifies the penetration of market forces as the root of "the nihilistic threat":

> None of us fully understands why the cultural structures that once sustained black life in America are no longer able to fend off the nihilistic threat. I believe that two significant reasons why the threat is more powerful now than ever before are the saturation of market forces and market moralities in black life and the present crisis in black leadership [...] Many black folk now reside in a jungle ruled by a cutthroat market morality devoid of any faith in deliverance or hope for freedom (West 15–16).

Michael Eric Dyson, on the other hand, argues that "West's theory of nihilism is driven by a nostalgic vision of black life" (Dyson 138). According to Dyson, nostalgia for the past prevents West from seeing the aspects of contemporary black popular culture that are not nihilistic or destructive:

> It may be that the belief in nihilism is too hopeless about the black future, too out of touch with the irreverent spirit of resistance that washes over black culture. A belief in nihilism is too, well, nihilistic. But nostalgia can do that. By viewing the black past as morally and spiritually distinct from the present, we lose sight of the resources for ethical engagement that are carried forward from the past into our own thinking, believing, hoping, praying and doing (139).

5. Black Artemis's *Explicit Content* bears much in common with both *Spidertown* and *Bodega Dreams,* including a charismatic character, Gregory Downs, who seeks to achieve legitimate success like Willie Bodega and help his people through illegal means. But *Explicit Content* focuses much more on the drug trade's violence and exploitation, especially of women, which is glossed over in Chino's idealization of Bodega.

6. For an example of the way in which one progressive political thinker has apparently taken Bodega's project seriously, see Arlene Dávila's *Barrio Dreams,* a consideration of the future of El Barrio. Her title appears to reference Quiñonez's, and her first chapter begins by citing Quiñonez's novel (27).

7. Again, the fathers come in for the most severe criticism in *Spidertown,* in the case of Miguel (10), Firebug (23), Spider (69), and even Amelia (27). In this context, the nastiest insult Miguel can come up with on the street is not "your mother," but "your father" (48).

8. In "Life Off the Hyphen," Flores seems to agree with Rodriguez's idea that part of *Spidertown*'s project is feminist because "it is the young women who serve as catalysts of challenge and change and stand up to that stubbornly sexist environment by word and example" (Flores, *From Bomba* 181). Despite the suggestion towards the end of the novel that Miguel is "throwing it all away, the ghosts of a hundred million Latin machistas" (Rodriguez, *Spidertown* 308), we maintain that the novel's aggressively sexualized gaze toward its female characters as well as the repeated return to male fantasies (as when Miguel ends up with both Amelia and Cristalena) is inconsistent with the author's apparently antisexist intentions.

9. June Dwyer's argument, that Quiñonez's appropriation of *The Great Gatsby* is part of his project to "assure the validity of [his] own vernacular literature by imitating classical models" (Dwyer 169) ignores these very obvious ways in which *Bodega Dreams* foregrounds an already existing *Nuyorican* tradition into which the writer can enter.

10. Associating the movement from New York to Miami with a transition from political commitment to selling out suggests the political implications of each metropolis as a center of Latino/a culture that we return to in our conclusion. For discussions of the effects of moving the salsa industry's center from New York to Miami after the 1970s, see Frances Aparicio's *Listening to Salsa* and María Elena Cepeda's "Mucho Loco for Ricky Martin."

11. Scott cites the following passage from historiographer Hayden White to define tragedy:

> There are no festive occasions, except false or illusory ones; rather, there are intimations of states of division among men more terrible than that which incited the tragic agon at the beginning of the drama. Still, the fall of the protagonist and the shaking of the world he inhabits which occur at the end of the Tragic play are not regarded as totally threatening to those who survive the agonic test. There has been a gain in consciousness for the spectators of the contest. And this gain is thought to consist in the epiphany of the law governing human existence which the protagonist's exertions against the world have brought to pass (qtd. in Scott 47).

## CHAPTER 3

1. This narrative opacity may explain the surprisingly small body of criticism written since 1996 on such a well-received work as *Drown,* at least in comparison to the number of essays and books dedicated to such a comparable contemporary text as *Dreaming in Cuban* (1992).

2. For more extensive analyses of masks in Piri Thomas's and Junot Díaz's work, see Lyn Di Iorio Sandín's "Melancholic Allegorists of the Street: Piri Thomas, Junot Díaz, and Yxta Maya Murray" as well as Anne Connor's "Desenmascarando a Ysrael: The Disfigured Face as Symbol of Identity in Three Latino Texts."

3. In *Down These Mean Streets,* Piri puts on his "cara palo" when entering an apartment of homosexual men, noting that the reason why they were "making it up to the *maricones'* pad" was because "belonging meant doing whatever has to be done" (55). For a more detailed analysis of the homoerotic in *Down These Mean Streets,* see Arnaldo Cruz-Malavé's "What a Tangled Web!: Masculinity, Abjection and the Foundation of Puerto Rican Literature in the United States" (1996) and Robert F. Reid-Pharr's "Tearing the Goat's Flesh: Homosexuality, Abjection and the Production of a Late Twentieth-century Black Masculinity" (1996).

4. Some of the criticism appears to share this anesthetizing impulse. The compulsive tendency of critics to gloss over this scene reflects their difficulty in interpreting such ambivalent spaces of desire and consent. For example, Bridget Kevane remarks that, "The narrator is not gay but allows one moment to transpire. In the end, he does not forgive Beto's transgression, though he still yearns for his friendship" (77). Such a reading overlooks the fact that *two* sexual encounters take place between Beto and the narrator.

5. In *The Buddha Book* (2001), "UN" is capitalized and emphasizes the "not being" or lack in a specific identity. For example, "UNreal" (90), "UNspick" (21), "UNposse" (78).

6. We are reminded here of Ian Strachan's description in *Plantation and Paradise* (2002) of the tourist industry as an extension of the plantation system that continues to shape Caribbean reality.

7. Michael Dash adapts this idea from Édouard Glissant in his *The Other America: Caribbean Literature in a New World Context.*

8. We are referring to Édouard Glissant's formulation of the term: "Directed by Relation, errantry follows neither an arrowlike trajectory nor one that is circular and repetitive, nor is it mere wandering [...] in errantry one knows at every moment where one is—at every moment in relation to the other" (xvi).

9. Díaz was also awarded the Pushcart Prize in 1997 and received a Eugene McDermott Award in 1998.

10. What Junot Díaz is perhaps also referring to is the contract he received from Riverhead Books for his second novel, called *The Cheater's Guide to Love,* which was scheduled to come out in 1997 but has not been published as of early 2007. This particular detail is included in the author description of Díaz available via the Penguin Putnam website: 15 January 2007 <www.penguinputnam.com/nf/Author/AuthorPage/0,,0_1000039301,00.html>. Several of Díaz's short stories have appeared in the *New Yorker* and been included in anthologies. Some of those published in the *New Yorker* are: "Homecoming with Turtle" (June 14 and 21, 2004), "The Brief Wondrous

Life of Oscar Wao" (December 25, 2000 and January 1, 2001), "Nilda" (October 4, 1999), and "The Sun, the Moon and the Stars" (February 2, 1998), which was the first story to be published after *Drown*'s success. In the December 2005 issue of *The Writer's Chronicle,* Díaz explains that he has just finished writing one novel and has an unfinished science fiction manuscript. As our book goes to press, *The Brief Wondrous Life of Oscar Wao* is slated for publication in the fall of 2007.

## CHAPTER 4

1. Much of the material that follows appears in the essay, "The Global Baggage of Nostalgia in Cristina Garcia's *Dreaming in Cuban*," by Elena Machado Sáez.
2. Such critics as Josefina Acosta Hess, Josefa Lago-Graña, David Thomas Mitchell, Ivelisse Santiago-Stommes, Joseph Viera, and Maite Zubiaurre read Pilar's journey as intersecting with and thereby redefining the concepts of nation, family, and exile. These critical interpretations of the novel predominantly focus on the narration of gender liberation through a "matrilineal chain" (Vásquez 22). Rocío Davis's essay, for example, centers on generational mother-daughter relationships.
3. Andrea O'Reilly Herrera argues that Pilar's family history parallels that of Cuba as a nation.
4. We define globalization here as an intensified form of capitalism that has led to an increased and uneven global flow of products and cultures through the development of new technologies. There is an enormous bibliography on globalization; our ideas, however, have been particularly influenced by Michael Hardt and Antonio Negri.
5. Maya Socolovsky figures violence as a motivating force behind Pilar's recording mission.
6. Andrea O'Reilly Herrera discusses the novel's insertion of women into the narrative of H/history as a move to "dismantle Western colonial History and its discourse" (85).
7. In the essay, "How Cristina Garcia Lost Her Accent and Other Latina Conversations," Raphael Dalleo argues for a similar process by which the circulation of Latino/a literature as a commodity gives Garcia access to Sandra Cisneros's *The House on Mango Street.* Drawing on intertextual references, Dalleo notes that the novel builds on pan-Latino/a connections by positioning itself as the heir of a U.S. Latino/a literary lineage in conversation with a canon of U.S. Latino/a writers, primarily Cisneros.
8. We are grateful to Veronica Makowsky for calling our attention to the coincidence of the two Celias. Her remark helped us further flesh out the significance of Celia Cruz within Garcia's novel.
9. See for example Isabel Alvarez-Borland, who argues that the novel is Pilar's diary.
10. In the article, "'Latino, U.S.A.': Statehooding Puerto Rico in Rosario Ferré's *The House on the Lagoon*," Elena Machado Sáez discusses a similar narrative

obsession regarding the representation of U.S. economic influence in the pre-Sixties Caribbean.

11. For another perspective on the representation of illness in Garcia's novel, see April Shemak's article, "A Wounded Discourse: The Poetics of Disease in Cristina Garcia's *Dreaming in Cuban*."

12. Luz and Milagro could be claimed as exceptions because they presumably continue to live in Cuba after Ivanito defects. Since the novel never fully develops these characters, their survival in Cuba does not symbolically outweigh the deaths of the more important characters, especially Celia and Felicia. Nevertheless, if one were to consider Luz and Milagro further, it is possible that they become irrelevant within the narrative's symbolic logic because of their opacity. By refusing to speak with Pilar, the sisters remain inaccessible. In addition, they do not display the same fascination with American culture as Ivanito and therefore cannot assimilate into U.S. culture or the market. Ultimately—according to the logic of the text—their fate is a dubious one if they remain in Cuba.

13. Celia recites the poetry at an earlier point in the novel in italicized Spanish without an accompanying translation. For example, see Celia's recitation upon her son Javier's return, sickness, and eventual death (Garcia 156–57).

14. Lori Ween provides an interesting analysis of the novel's critical reception as motivated by a desire to untranslate and reframe the text in its "original" language, Spanish.

## CHAPTER 5

1. Alvarez's novel *Saving the World* (2006) was published after this chapter had already been completed. It makes explicit the connections between the historical and personal strands that the earlier novels had only suggested. The latest novel uses the same alternating structure as *In the Name of Salomé*, but now the contemporary figure is a post-Sixties Dominican-American woman writer, suffering from writer's block explicitly derived from (a) a feeling of impotence about her ability to change the world; (b) the pressure put on by her agent and publisher; and (c) the attack on her authenticity at the hands of "Mario González-Echavarriga, the patrón of Latino critics," who labels her "a Machiavellian user of identity" who "undermine[s] the serious political writing by voices long kept silent" (Alvarez, *Saving* 20). This example shows Alvarez, more than perhaps any other writer we have discussed in this book, in direct conversation with her critics—in this case apparently referencing Roberto González Echevarría, whose review of *In the Time of the Butterflies* in the *New York Times Book Review* questioned Alvarez's ability as an "Americanized Dominican woman" to "really be able to understand" Dedé and the other Dominican women of the novel (28).

2. For example, see Carine Mardorossian's essay "From Literature of Exile to Migrant Literature" on Alvarez and Danticat, or Ellen Mayock's "The Bicultural Construction of Self in Cisneros, Alvarez, and Santiago."

3. For example, David Thomas Mitchell in his essay "The Accent of 'Loss': Cultural Crossings as Context in Julia Alvarez's *How the García Girls Lost Their Accents*" repeatedly refers to Alvarez as a "postcolonial writer."

4. Kamau Brathwaite is one of the Caribbean artists who talks about how his early poetry, about snow falling on cane fields, illustrates the influence of the Northern imaginary on the Caribbean mind. See *Three Caribbean Poets on Their Works: E. Kamau Brathwaite, Mervyn Morris, Lorna Goodison* (Chang).

5. The reader is again referred to "The Accent of 'Loss'" for a reading of *García Girls* as a melancholic novel.

6. We call Alvarez's first novel "overtly autobiographical" because in her personal essays, for example those collected in *Something to Declare*, Alvarez recounts many of the same anecdotes as episodes from her life that are attributed to her characters in *How the García Girls Lost Their Accents* and *¡Yo!*

7. Bakhtin discusses the *bildungsroman* in these terms in *The Dialogic Imagination*. Lisa Sánchez González invokes Bakhtin's theorization of genre in her chapter "The Boricua Novel: Civil Rights and 'New School' Nuyorican Narratives" (106).

8. Marta Caminero-Santangelo notes that "the dangers of speaking for/representing others are arguably the central theme of *¡Yo!*" (Caminero-Santangelo, "Speaking" 61), in making the broader case for Alvarez's novels as meditations on the relationship of the author to the people she represents.

9. As in Stavans's bookends or Alvarez's historical novels, the Sixties become a conspicuous absence in Cristina Garcia's *Dreaming in Cuban* as well. The main action in *Dreaming in Cuban* begins in 1972 and moves forward to 1980. Interspersed with this narrative, Celia's letters provide historical background beginning in 1935 and end at the beginning of 1959. The novel thus spans the period from 1935 to 1980, skipping only the years between 1959 and 1972.

10. One of the most famous theorists of the relationship between pedagogy and revolution, Paolo Freire, describes this form of lecturing as a two-stage process: "During the first, [the lecturer] cognizes a cognizable object while he prepares his lessons in his study or laboratory. During the second, he expounds to his students about that object" (67). As a result, the lecturer-intellectual speaks to the people with conclusions already drawn, trying only to persuade them to pursue this cause. By contrast, Camila eventually arrives at a view of pedagogy as a process of negotiation and dialogue.

## CONCLUSION

1. Marta Caminero-Santangelo discusses Rivero's construction of Cuban-American literature in "Contesting the Boundaries of Exile Latino/a Literature" and "Margarita Engle, Cuban American Conservatism, and the Construction of (Left) U.S. Latino/a Ethnicity."

2. In this conclusion we distinguish between the Cuban-American community as a racially and economically diverse population formed by different sets of

historical circumstances within the United States, and what we will call the "establishment." When we discuss the Cuban-American establishment, we refer to a group of Cuban exiles located primarily in Miami that often makes public claims on Cuban-American identity and regards itself as the arbiter of Cuban-American culture.

3.  In his essay on *Anna in the Tropics,* Rick Mitchell interprets the lack of historical context surrounding the lector as a revolutionary figure to be representative of "Cruz's depoliticization of the lector" in favor of a politics of "bodily desire" (19). In our analysis of the play, we argue that the displacement of history within the play does not translate into an apolitical rendering of the lector persona.

4.  This specific type of nostalgia could be termed the Buena Vista Social Club phenomenon in its articulation of nostalgia for a pre-revolution Cuba. The movie, *Buena Vista Social Club,* casts Afro-Cuban music as timeless or outside of time, and therefore uncontaminated by the trauma of the Cuban revolution. The movie's decontextualization of the Cuban musicians and its exoticization of Afro-Cuban music, not to mention its commercial success and popularity, present an interesting example of nostalgia's appeal as a cultural product. In chapter 4, we discuss the way in which *Dreaming in Cuban's* representation of Celia Cruz similarly uses Afro-Cuban music as symbolic of pre-revolutionary Cuba. See Román de la Campa's work for further analysis of this phenomenon.

# BIBLIOGRAPHY

Acevedo, Chantel. *Love and Ghost Letters.* New York: St. Martin's Press, 2005.

Acosta Hess, Josefina. "La emigración como factor subversivo en la experiencia femenina: *How the García Girls Lost Their Accents* y *Dreaming in Cuban.*" *Alba de América* 20.37–38 (2001): 221–228.

Alcoff, Linda Martín. "Puerto Rican Studies in a German Philosophical Context: An Interview with Juan Flores." *Nepantla: Views from South* 4.1 (2003): 139–146.

Alonso Gallo, Laura P., and Antonia Dominguez Miguela, eds. *Evolving Origins, Transplanting Cultures: Literary Legacies of the New Americans.* Huelva, Spain: University of Huelva Press, 2002.

Alvarez, Julia. *How the García Girls Lost Their Accents.* New York: Plume Books, 1991.

———. *In the Name of Salomé.* New York: Plume Books, 2000.

———. *In the Time of the Butterflies.* New York: Plume Books, 1994.

———. "On Finding a Latino Voice." *The Writing Life: Writers on How They Think and Work.* Ed. Marie Arana. New York: Public Affairs, 2003. 126–133.

———. *Something to Declare.* New York: Plume Books, 1998.

———. *¡Yo!* New York: Plume Books, 1997.

Alvarez-Borland, Isabel. "Displacements and Autobiography in Cuban-American Fiction." *World Literature Today* 68.1 (1994): 43–48.

Aparicio, Frances. "Latino Cultural Studies." Interview with Juan Zevallos Aguilar. *Critical Latin American and Latino Studies.* Ed. Juan Poblete. Minneapolis: University of Minnesota Press, 2003. 3–31.

———. *Listening to Salsa: Gender, Latin Popular Music, and Puerto Rican Cultures.* Hanover, NH: Wesleyan University Press, 1998.

Augenbraum, Harold, and Margarite Fernández Olmos, eds. *The Latino Reader: An American Literary Tradition from 1542 to the Present.* Boston: Houghton Mifflin Company, 1997.

———. *U.S. Latino Literature: A Critical Guide for Students and Teachers.* Westport, CT: Greenwood Press, 2000.

Bados Ciria, Concepción. "History, Fiction, *Testimonio* and the Dominican Republic: *In the Time of the Butterflies* by Julia Alvarez." *Monographic Review/Revista Monográfica* 13 (1997): 406–416.

Bakhtin, M. M. *Speech Genres and Other Essays*. Trans. Vern W. McGee. Ed. Caryl Emerson and Michael Holquist. Austin: University of Texas Press, 1986.

Behar, Ruth. Rev. of *The Agüero Sisters*, by Cristina Garcia. *Chicago Tribune 8* Jun. 1997: 1.

Benjamin, Walter. "Theses on the Philosophy of History." *Illuminations*. Trans. Harry Zohn. New York: Schocken Books, 1968. 253–264.

Black Artemis. *Explicit Content*. New York: New American Library, 2004.

Bourdieu, Pierre. *The Field of Cultural Production: Essays on Art and Literature*. Ed. Randal Johnson. New York: Columbia University Press, 1993.

Brameshuber-Ziegler, Irene. "Christina [sic] Garcia, *Dreaming in Cuban* (1992): Collapse of Communication and Kristeva's Semiotic as Possible Remedy." *Language and Literature* 24 (1999): 43–64.

Cabán, Pedro. "Moving from the Margins to Where? Three Decades of Latino/a Studies." *Latino Studies* 1.1 (2003): 5–35.

Caminero-Santangelo, Marta. "Contesting the Boundaries of Exile Latino/a Literature." *World Literature Today* 74.3 (2000): 507-517.

———. "Margarita Engle, Cuban American Conservatism, and the Construction of (Left) U.S. Latino/a Ethnicity." *Literature Interpretation Theory* 13.4 (2002): 249–267.

———. "Speaking for Others: Problems of Representation in the Novels of Julia Alvarez." *Antípodas: Journal of Hispanic Studies of the University of Auckland* 10 (1998): 53–66.

Cepeda, María Elena. "'Columbus Effect(s)': Chronology and Crossover in the Latin(o) Music 'Boom.'" *Discourse* 23.1 (2001): 63–81.

———. "*Mucho Loco* for Ricky Martin; or the Politics of Chronology, Crossover, and Language within the Latin(o) Music 'Boom.'" *Popular Music and Society* 24.3 (2000): 55–72.

Céspedes, Diogenes, and Silvio Torres-Saillant. "Fiction Is the Poor Man's Cinema: An Interview with Junot Díaz." *Callaloo: A Journal of African-American and African Arts and Letters* 23.3 (2000): 892–907.

Chang, Victor, ed. *Three Caribbean Poets on Their Works: E. Kamau Brathwaite, Mervyn Morris, Lorna Goodison*. Mona, Jamaica: Institute of Caribbean Studies, 1993.

Cisneros, Sandra. *The House on Mango Street*. Houston: Arte Público Press, 1984.

Colón, Jesús. *A Puerto Rican in New York and Other Sketches*. 1961. New York: International Publishers, 1982.

Colón, Willie. *The Big Break—La Gran Fuga*. Fania Records, 1976.

Colón, Willie, and Rubén Blades. *Siembra*. Fania Records, 1978.

Connor, Anne. "Desenmascarando a Ysrael: The Disfigured Face as Symbol of Identity in Three Latino Texts." *Cincinnati Romance Review* 21 (2002): 148–62.

Cruz, Angie. *Let It Rain Coffee*. New York: Simon and Schuster, 2005.

———. *Soledad*. 2001. New York: 1ˢᵗ Scribner Paperback ed., 2002.

Cruz, Nilo. *Anna in the Tropics*. New York: Theatre Communications Group, 2003.

Cruz-Malavé, Arnaldo. "Colonial Figures in Motion: Globalization and Translocality in Contemporary Puerto Rican Literature in the United States." *Centro Journal* 14.2 (2002): 5-25.

———. "Teaching Puerto Rican Authors: Identity and Modernization in Nuyorican Texts." *ADE Bulletin* 91 (1988): 45–51.

———. "What a Tangled Web!: Masculinity, Abjection and the Foundation of Puerto Rican Literature in the United States." *Differences: A Journal of Feminist Cultural Studies* 8.1 (1996): 132–151.

Dalleo, Raphael. "How Cristina Garcia Lost Her Accent and Other Latina Conversations." *Latino Studies* 3.1 (2005): 3–18.

———. "Readings from Aquí y Allá: Music, Commercialism, and the Latino-Caribbean Transnational Imaginary." *Only the Bitter Come: Constructing Vernacular Culture in the Trans-Caribbean*. Ed. Holger Henke, Karl-Heinz Magister, and Alissa Trotz. Lanham, MD: Lexington Books, [c. 2007].

Dash, Michael. *The Other America: Caribbean Literature in a New World Context*. Charlottesville: University of Virginia Press, 1998.

Dávila, Arlene. *Barrio Dreams: Puerto Ricans, Latinos, and the Neoliberal City*. Berkeley: University of California Press, 2004.

———. "Culture in the Battlefront: From Nationalist to Pan-Latino Projects." *Mambo Montage: The Latinization of New York*. Ed. Agustín Laó-Montes and Arlene Dávila. New York: Columbia University Press, 2001. 159–180.

———. *Latinos, Inc.: The Marketing and Making of a People*. Berkeley: University of California Press, 2001.

Davis, Rocío G. "Back to the Future: Mothers, Languages and Homes in Cristina Garcia's *Dreaming in Cuban*." *World Literature Today* 74.1 (2000): 60–68.

De la Campa, Román. "Postcolonial Marketing and Global Nostalgia: The Case of *Buena Vista Social Club*." Humanities Institute at Stony Brook (HISB) Faculty Colloquium Lecture. State University of New York (SUNY) Humanities Institute at Stony Brook. SUNY Stony Brook, Stony Brook, New York. 30 Oct. 2002.

Derrickson, Teresa. "'Cold/Hot, English/Spanish': The Puerto Rican American Divide in Judith Ortiz Cofer's *Silent Dancing*." *MELUS* 28.2 (2003): 121–137.

Díaz, Junot. *Drown*. New York: Riverhead Books, 1996.

Duany, Jorge. "Popular Music in Puerto Rico: Toward an Anthropology of *Salsa*." *Latin American Music Review* 5.2 (1984): 186–216.

Dwyer, June. "When Willie Met Gatsby: The Critical Implications of Ernesto Quiñonez's *Bodega Dreams*." *Literature Interpretation Theory* 14 (2003): 165–178.

Dyson, Michael Eric. "We Never Were What We Used to Be: Black Youth, Pop Culture, and the Politics of Nostalgia." *Race Rules: Navigating the Color Line*. New York: Vintage Books, 1997. 109–149.

Fiet, Lowell. "'end false illusions of the beginning of time': the poetic space of e/im/migration in the poetry of Pedro Pietri." *Caribe 2000: Definiciones, Identidades y Culturas Regionales y/o Nacionales*. Eds. Lowell Fiet and Janette Becerra. San Juan, PR: Caribe 2000, Universidad de Puerto Rico, Recinto de Río Piedras, 1997. 45–57.

Flores, Juan. *Divided Borders: Essays on Puerto Rican Identity*. Houston: Arte Público Press, 1993.

———. Foreword. *A Puerto Rican in New York and Other Sketches*. By Jesús Colón. New York: International Publishers, 1982.

———. *From Bomba to Hip-hop: Puerto Rican Culture and Latino Identity*. New York: Columbia University Press, 2000.

Flores, Juan, and Renato Rosaldo, eds. *Companion to Latina/o Studies*. Malden, MA: Blackwell Publishing, [c. 2007].

Fornet, Ambrosio. "The Cuban Literary Diaspora and its Contexts: A Glossary." *boundary2* 29:3 (2002): 91–103.

Franco, Jean. *Critical Passions: Selected Essays*. Durham, NC: Duke University Press, 1999.

Fraser, Nancy. *Justice Interruptus: Critical Reflections on the "Postsocialist" Condition*. New York: Routledge, 1997.

Freire, Paolo. *Pedagogy of the Oppressed*. Trans. Myra Bergman Ramos. New York: Herder and Herder, 1970.

Garcia, Cristina. *The Agüero Sisters*. New York: Knopf, 1997.

———. *Dreaming in Cuban*. New York: Ballantine Books, 1992.

García Canclini, Néstor. *Consumers and Citizens: Globalization and Multicultural Conflicts*. Trans. George Yúdice. Minneapolis: University of Minnesota Press, 2001.

———. *Transforming Modernity: Popular Culture in Mexico*. Trans. Lidia Lozano. Austin: University of Texas Press, 1993.

Gatto, Katherine Gyekenyesi. "Mambo, Merengue, Salsa: The Dynamics of Self-Construction in Latina Autobiographical Narrative." *Philological Papers* 46 (2000): 84–90.

Glissant, Édouard. *Poetics of Relation*. Ann Arbor: University of Michigan Press, 1997.

Gómez-Vega, Ibis del Carmen. "The Journey Home: Caribbean Women Writers Face the Wreckage of History." Diss. University of Houston, 1995.

———. "The Journey Home: Defining Identity in Cristina García's *Dreaming in Cuban*." *Voces* 1.2 (1997): 71–100.

González, Juan. *Harvest of Empire: A History of Latinos in America*. New York: Viking, 2000.

González Echevarría, Roberto. "Sisters in Death." Rev. of *In the Time of the Butterflies,* by Julia Alvarez. *New York Times Book Review* 18 Dec. 1994: 28.

Gúzman, Pablo. "*La Vida Pura:* A Lord of the Barrio." *The Puerto Rican Movement: Voices from the Diaspora.* Eds. Andrés Torres and José E. Velázquez. Philadelphia: Temple University Press, 1998. 155–172.

Habell-Pallán, Michelle, and Mary Romero, eds. *Latino/a Popular Culture.* New York: New York University Press, 2002.

Hall, Stuart, and Martin Jacques, eds. *New Times: The Changing Face of Politics in the 1990s.* New York: Verso, 1989.

Hardt, Michael, and Antonio Negri. *Empire.* Cambridge, MA: Harvard University Press, 2000.

Henríquez Ureña, Pedro. *Literary Currents in Hispanic America.* Cambridge, MA: Harvard University Press, 1946.

Hijuelos, Oscar. *The Mambo Kings Play Songs of Love.* New York: Harper Perennial, 1989.

Irizarry, Guillermo. "Travelling Textualities and Phantasmagoric Originals: A Reading of Translation in Three Recent Spanish-Caribbean Narratives." *Ciberletras* 4 (2001). 15 January 2007 <www.lehman.cuny.edu/ciberletras>.

Jacklosky, Rob. Rev. of *Drown,* by Junot Díaz. *Studies in Short Fiction* 35.1 (1998): 93–94.

Jacques, Ben. "Julia Alvarez: Real Flights of Imagination." *Americas (English Edition)* 53.1 (2001): 22.

Jameson, Fredric. "Periodizing the 60s." *The 60s without Apology.* Eds. Sohnya Sayres et al. Minneapolis: University of Minnesota Press in cooperation with Social Text, 1984. 178–209.

Janson Perez, Brittmarie. "Political Facets of *Salsa*." *Popular Music* 6.2 (1987): 149–159.

Kapschutschenko-Schmitt, Ludmila. "Julia Alvarez y Cristina García: Hibridización cultural en la novela exílica hispano-estadounidense." *Proyecciones sobre la novela; actas del XIV Congreso de Literatura Latino/a.* Eds. Linda Gould Levine and Ellen Marson. Hanover, NH: Ediciones del Norte, 1997. 115–32.

Kelley, Robin. *Race Rebels: Culture, Politics, and the Black Working Class.* New York: Free Press, 1994.

Kevane, Bridget. *Latino Literature in America.* Westport, CT: Greenwood Press, 2003.

Lago-Graña, Josefa. "Despertar de un sueño: Exilio, hogar y familia en *Soñar en Cubano* de Cristina Garcia." *MaComère* 4.1 (2001): 165–72.

Laviera, Tato. *La Carreta Made a U-Turn.* Houston: Arte Público Press, 1979.

López, Iraida H. ". . . And There Is Only My Imagination Where Our History Should Be: An Interview with Cristina Garcia." *Bridges to Cuba/Puentes a Cuba.* Ed. Ruth Behar. Ann Arbor: University of Michigan Press, 1995. 102–14.

López, Kimberle S. "Women on the Verge of a Revolution: Madness and Resistance in Cristina Garcia's *Dreaming in Cuban.*" *Letras Femininas* 22.1–2 (1996): 33–45.

Luis, William. *Dance Between Two Cultures: Latino Caribbean Literature Written in the United States.* Nashville, TN: Vanderbilt University Press, 1997.

Machado Sáez, Elena. "A Family's Bonds of Love, Money." Rev. of *Love and Ghost Letters,* by Chantel Acevedo. *South Florida Sun Sentinel* 11 Sept. 2005: A&E 18.

———. "The Global Baggage of Nostalgia in Cristina Garcia's *Dreaming in Cuban.*" *MELUS* 30.4 (2005): 129–148.

———. "'Latino, U.S.A.': Statehooding Puerto Rico in Rosario Ferré's *The House on the Lagoon.*" *Phoebe* 16.1 (2004): 23–38.

Madsen, Deborah, ed. *Beyond the Borders: American Literature and Post-Colonial Theory.* Sterling, VA: Pluto Press, 2003.

Magill, Frank, ed. *Masterpieces of Latino Literature.* New York: HarperCollins, 1994.

Mann, Emily. "Nilo Cruz." *BOMB* 86 (2003–2004): 70–75.

Mardorossian, Carine. "From Literature of Exile to Migrant Literature." *Modern Language Studies* 32.2 (2002): 15–33.

Mayock, Ellen C. "The Bicultural Construction of Self in Cisneros, Alvarez, and Santiago." *Bilingual Review/La Revista Bilingüe* 23.3 (1998): 223–229.

McAuliffe, Jody. "Interview with Nilo Cruz." *South Atlantic Quarterly* 99. 2–3 (2000): 461–470.

McLane, Maureen. "Three Hispanic Authors Explore the Displaced Lives and Fractured Identities of Their People." *Chicago Tribune* 20 Oct. 1996: 6.

Méndez Ródenas, Adriana. "En busqueda del paraíso perdido: La historia natural como imaginación diaspórica en Cristina Garcia." *MLN* 116.2 (2001): 392–418.

Menéndez, Ana. *Loving Che.* New York: Grove Press, 2003.

Mitchell, David Thomas. "The Accent of 'Loss': Cultural Crossings as Context in Julia Alvarez's *How the García Girls Lost Their Accents.*" *Beyond the Binary: Reconstructing Cultural Identity in a Multicultural Context.* Ed. Timothy B. Powell. New Brunswick, NJ: Rutgers University Press, 1999.

———. "Conjured Communities: The Multiperspectival Novels of Amy Tan, Toni Morrison, Julia Alvarez, Louise Erdrich and Cristina Garcia." Diss. University of Michigan, 1993.

———. "National Families and Familial Nations: Communista Americans in Cristina Garcia's *Dreaming in Cuban.*" *Tulsa Studies in Women's Literature* 15.1 (1996): 51–60.

Mitchell, Rick. "Up in Smoke: Cigars Hecho a Mano, Radical Storytelling in the Tabaqueria, and the Processed Drama of *Anna in the Tropics.*" *Sargasso* (2004–2005): 5–24.

Mort, Frank. "The Politics of Consumption." *New Times: The Changing Face of Politics in the 1990s.* Eds. Stuart Hall and Martin Jacques. New York: Verso, 1990. 160–172.

Nance, Kimberly. "If English is Spanish then Spanish is . . . : Literary Challenges of Representing Bilingual Speech Production and Reception in Esmeralda Santiago's *América's Dream*." *International Fiction Review* 30 (2003): 60–65.

Negrón-Muntaner, Frances. "Barbie's Hair: Selling Out Puerto Rican Identity in the Global Market." *Boricua Pop: Puerto Ricans and the Latinization of American Culture.* New York: New York University Press, 2004. 206–227.

Negrón-Muntaner, Frances, and Ramón Grosfoguel. *Puerto Rican Jam: Rethinking Colonialism and Nationalism.* Minneapolis: University of Minnesota Press, 1997.

Oboler, Suzanne. *Ethnic Labels, Latino Lives: Identity and the Politics of (Re)Presentation in the United States.* Minneapolis: University of Minnesota Press, 1995.

O'Reilly Herrera, Andrea. "Women and the Revolution in Cristina Garcia's *Dreaming in Cuban*." *Modern Language Studies* 27.3–4 (1997): 69–91.

Otero Garabís, Juan. *Nación y Ritmo: 'descargas' desde el Caribe.* San Juan, PR: Ediciones Callejón, 2000.

Paravisini-Gebert, Lizabeth. "Junot Díaz's *Drown*: Revisiting 'Those Mean Streets.'" *U.S. Latino Literature: A Critical Guide for Students and Teachers.* Eds. Harold Augenbaum and Marguerite Fernández Olmos. Westport, CT: Greenwood Press, 2000. 163–173.

Payant, Katherine. "From Alienation to Reconciliation in the Novels of Cristina Garcia." *MELUS* 26.3 (2001): 163–182.

Pérez, Richard, and Lyn Di Iorio Sandín, eds. *Contemporary U.S. Latino/a Literary Criticism.* New York: Palgrave Macmillan, [c. 2007].

Pérez-Firmat, Gustavo. *Life on the Hyphen: The Cuban-American Way.* Austin: Texas University Press, 1994.

Peterson, Nancy. "Say Make Me, Remake Me: Toni Morrison and the Reconstruction of African-American History." *Toni Morrison: Critical and Theoretical Approaches.* Ed. Nancy Peterson. Baltimore, MD: Johns Hopkins University Press, 1997. 201–221.

Pietri, Pedro. "El Spanglish National Anthem." *El Puerto Rican Embassy,* 1993. 15 January 2007 <www.elpuertoricanembassy.org/anthem.html>.

———. *Puerto Rican Obituary.* New York: Monthly Review Press, 1973.

Piñero, Miguel. *La Bodega Sold Dreams.* Houston: Arte Público Press, 1985.

Potvin, Claudine. "Dreaming in Cuban: La deconstrucción de las utopías." *Celebración de la creación literaria de escritoras hispanas en las Américas.* Ottowa, Canada: Girol Books, 2000.

Powell, Timothy B., ed. *Beyond the Binary: Reconstructing Cultural Identity in a Multicultural Context.* New Brunswick, NJ: Rutgers University Press, 1999.

Quintero Rivera, Angel. "La gran fuga, las identidades socioculturales y la concepción del tiempo en la música 'tropical.'" *Caribe 2000: Definiciones, Identidades y Culturas Regionales y/o Nacionales.* Eds. Lowell Fiet and Janette Becerra. San Juan, PR: Caribe 2000, Universidad de Puerto Rico, Recinto de Río Piedras, 1997. 24–44.

Quiñonez, Ernesto. *Bodega Dreams.* New York: Vintage Books, 2000.

———. "La Música Puertorriqueña y la Contra-Cultura Democrática: Espontaneidad Libertaria de la Herencia Cimarrona." *Folklore Americano* 49 (1990): 135–167.

Reid-Pharr, Robert F. "Tearing the Goat's Flesh: Homosexuality, Abjection and the Production of a Late Twentieth-century Black Masculinity." *Studies in the Novel* 28.3 (1996): 372–395.

Richardson, Lynda. "How to Be Both An Outsider and An Insider." *New York Times* 13 Nov. 1999: B13.

Rivero, Eliana. "Hispanic Literature in the United States: Self-Image and Conflict." *Revista Chicano-Riqueña* 13.3–4 (1985): 173–191.

Rodriguez, Abraham. *The Boy Without a Flag: Tales of the South Bronx.* Minneapolis: Milkweek Editions, 1992.

———. *The Buddha Book.* New York: Picador, 2001.

———. *Spidertown.* New York: Hyperion, 1993.

Rowe, John Carlos, ed. *post-nationalist american studies.* Berkeley: University of California Press, 2000.

Ruta, Suzanne. "Daughters of Revolution." Rev. of *In the Name of Salomé,* by Julia Alvarez. *New York Times Book Review* 16 July 2000: 24.

Saldívar, José. *The Dialectics of Our America.* Durham, NC: Duke University Press, 1991.

Sánchez González, Lisa. *Boricua Literature: A Literary History of the Puerto Rican Diaspora.* New York: New York University Press, 2001.

Sandín, Lyn Di Iorio. "Melancholic Allegorists of the Street: Piri Thomas, Junot Díaz, and Yxta Maya Murray." *Killing Spanish: Literary Essays on Ambivalent U.S. Latino/a Identity.* New York: Palgrave Macmillan, 2004. 101–133.

Santiago, Roberto. Rev. of *Drown,* by Junot Díaz. *Hispanic* 9.12 (1996): 70.

Santiago-Stommes, Ivelisse. "Nación, cultura y mujer: La identidad nacional y las relaciones entre hombres y mujeres en *Soñar en Cubano* de Cristina Garcia" *MaComère* 4.1 (2001): 101–107.

Scott, David. *Conscripts of Modernity: The Tragedy of Colonial Enlightenment.* Durham, NC: Duke University Press, 2004.

Shemak, April. "A Wounded Discourse: The Poetics of Disease in Cristina Garcia's *Dreaming in Cuban.*" *Postcolonial Text* 2.3 (2006): 1–23.

Singh, Amritjit, and Peter Schmidt, eds. *Postcolonial Theory and the United States: Race, Ethnicity and Literature.* Jackson: University of Mississippi Press, 2000.

Socolovsky, Maya. "Unnatural Violences: Counter-Memory and Preservations in Cristina Garcia's *Dreaming in Cuban* and *The Agüero Sisters.*" *Literature, Interpretation, Theory* 11.2 (2000): 143–167.

Sommer, Doris. *Foundational Fictions: The National Romance of Latin America.* Berkeley: University of California Press, 1991.

Spivak, Gayatri. *A Critique of Postcolonial Reason: Toward a History of the Vanishing Present.* Cambridge, MA: Harvard University Press, 1999.

Sprouse, Keith Alan. "Between Bilingüe and Nilingüe: Language and the Translation of Identity in Esmeralda Santiago's Memoirs." *American Studies in Scandinavia* 32.1 (2000): 107–116.

Stavans, Ilan. "Daughters of Invention." Rev. of *How the García Girls Lost Their Accents*, by Julia Alvarez. *Commonweal* 10 Apr. 1992: 23–25.

———. *The Hispanic Condition: The Power of a People*. 1995. Second Edition. New York: Rayo, 2001.

Strachan, Ian Gregory. *Paradise and Plantation: Tourism and Culture in the Anglophone Caribbean*. Charlottesville: University of Virginia Press, 2002.

Suarez, Virgil, and Delia Poey, eds. *Little Havana Blues: A Cuban-American Literature Anthology*. Houston: Arte Público Press, 1996.

Thomas, Piri. *Down These Mean Streets*. 1967. New York: Vintage Books, 1997.

———. *Savior, Savior, Hold My Hand*. Garden City, NY: Doubleday and Company, 1972.

Torres-Saillant, Silvio. "Problematic Paradigms: Racial Diversity and Corporate Identity in the Latino Community." *Latinos: Remaking America*. Eds. Marcelo M. Suárez-Orozco and Mariela M. Páez. Berkeley: University of California Press, 2002. 435–456.

———. "Writing Has to Be Generous: An Interview with Angie Cruz." *Calabash: A Journal of Caribbean Arts and Letters* 2.2 (2003): 108–127.

Triff, Soren. "El último cubanoamericano." *El Nuevo Herald* 15 May 1997: 12A.

Valentín Escobar, Wilson. "El Hombre que Respira Debajo del Agua: Trans-*Boricua* Memories, Identities, and Nationalisms Performed through the Death of Héctor Lavoe." *Situating Salsa: Global Markets and Local Meaning in Latin Popular Music*. Ed. Lise Waxer. New York: Routledge, 2002. 161–186.

Vásquez, Mary S. "Cuba as Text and Context in Cristina Garcia's *Dreaming in Cuban*." *Bilingual Review* 20.1 (1995): 22–27.

Viera, Joseph. "Matriarchy and Mayhem: Awakenings in Cristina Garcia's *Dreaming in Cuban*." *Americas Review* 24.3–4 (1996): 231–242.

Vorda, Allan. "A Fish Swims in My Lung: An Interview with Cristina Garcia." *Face to Face: Interviews with Contemporary Novelists*. Ed. Allan Vorda. Houston: Rice University Press, 1993. 61–76.

Ween, Lori. "Translational Backformations: Authenticity and Language in Cuban American Literature." *Comparative Literature Studies* 40.2 (2003): 127–141.

West, Alan. Rev. of *Dreaming in Cuban*, by Cristina Garcia. *Washington Post* 1 Mar. 1992: x9.

West, Cornel. *Race Matters*. Boston: Beacon Press, 1993.

Whalen, Carmen. "Bridging Homeland and Barrio Politics: The Young Lords in Philadelphia." *The Puerto Rican Movement: Voices from the Diaspora*. Ed. Andrés Torres and José E. Velázquez. Philadelphia: Temple University Press, 1998.

Wyatt, Andrea, and Alice Leccese Powers, eds. *The Brooklyn Reader: Thirty Writers Celebrate America's Favorite Borough*. New York: Harmony Books, 1994.

Young, Robert. *Postcolonialism: An Historical Introduction*. Oxford, UK: Blackwell Publishing, 2001.

Young Lords Party. "13 Point Platform and Program." 15 January 2007 <http://palante.org/YLPProg.html>.

Yúdice, George. *The Expediency of Culture: Uses of Culture in the Global Era*. Durham, NC: Duke University Press, 2003.

———. "From Hybridity to Policy: For a Purposeful Cultural Studies." Introduction. *Consumers and Citizens: Globalization and Multicultural Conflicts*. By Néstor García Canclini. Minneapolis: University of Minnesota Press, 2001.

Zubiaurre, Maite. "Hacia una nueva geografía feminista: nación, identidad y construcción imaginaria en *Dreaming in Cuban*." *Chasqui* 28.1 (1999): 3–15.

# INDEX

(Please note that page numbers in *italics* indicate endnotes.)

Cuban revolution and art in,
    127–28
drowning and, 118, 129, 130
globalization and, 117, 119, 120,
    122, 126, 128, 130, 131
historical focus of, *185*
nostalgia and, 118–19, 124–26,
    130, 172
*Drown* (Díaz), 13–14, 73, 77–89
    community and, 71
    consumption and, 80, 83, 84
    ghetto fiction and, 72
    narrative fractures in, 77, 89
    sexuality and, 82, 85, 86–89
    upward mobility and, 78, 79–80,
        85, 88
Dwyer, June, 69, *181*

Esteves, Sandra Maria, 24, 68
ethnic studies, U.S., 38, 102, 134,
    135–39

false consciousness
    American dream and, 46, 49
    formal education and, 23
    ghetto fiction and, 13, 51–56
    "Puerto Rican Obituary" and, 18,
        *178*
    *Spidertown* and, 45–46, 51, 53–56
Fanon, Frantz, 6, 20, 96, 138
Flores, Juan, ix, 9, 13–14, *178, 179,*
    *181*
    anticolonialism and, 6–7, 24–29,
        56, 74–76
    on Colón, 24
    on contemporary Latino/a litera-
        ture, 45, 94, 101
    on ghetto fiction, 46, 48–49
    on immigrant vs. resident
        Latino/as, 13, 74–75, 95–96
    on lowercase literature, 13, 32, 71,
        75–76
    on music, 29, 31–32, 33, *179*
    on neocolonization, 95

on Puerto Rican writing in English,
    24–25
on *Spidertown*, 45–46, 48, 54, 75,
    *181*
Sánchez González on, 25–26
See also *Divided Borders*; *From
    Bomba to Hip-Hop*
food metaphor, 14, 107, 108–12,
    113–14, 123
Fraser, Nancy, 3
*From Bomba to Hip-Hop* (Flores),
    31–33, 45, 74–75
    "Life Off the Hyphen" chapter in,
        28, 32, 48, 74, *181*

Garcia, Cristina, 4, 10, 14, 112, 124,
    131, 161, 172, *177, 178, 183*
    criticism of, 45
    on U.S. policy toward Cuba, 125
    *Soledad* and, 104, 119
    See also *Agüero Sisters, The*;
        *Dreaming in Cuban*
García Canclini, Néstor
    on consumption, 39, 112–16, 123
    on cultural codes, 40
    *Dreaming in Cuban* and, 130–31
    on identity, 10, 14, 39, 107
    on negotiation, 10
    on race, 39
    See also *Consumers and Citizens*
García Márquez, Gabriel, 95
ghetto fiction
    American dream and, 46–50
    anticolonialism and, 42, 43
    assimilation and, 13
    commercialization and, 13
    dead end of, 78–84
    false consciousness and, 13, 51–56
    lowercase model of, 89
    marketing of, 10
    opacity and, 78–84, 102
    romance of the Sixties and, 65–72
    Sixties dreams and, 56–64
    *Spidertown* and, 42, 45–46, 75

Printed in the United States
202800BV00002BC/1-30/P